ESSAYS ON CHAUCERIAN IRONY

These essays, written by Earle Birney between 1937 and 1960, have remained classics of their kind. They include important discussions on irony – its native traditions and its occurrence in early English literature, an account of critics' appreciation of Chaucerian irony prior to this century, and a detailed examination of four of the *Canterbury Tales*.

Internationally, Earle Birney is known as one of Canada's finest poets; among medievalists he is known for his essays on Chaucer and Irony. His career in medieval studies began with graduate work in medieval Indo-Germanic literatures at the University of California at Berkeley, after which he secured his doctorate at the University of Toronto in 1936 with a thesis on Chaucer's Irony. He taught Old and Middle English there and later at the University of British Columbia. In 1958/59 he undertook post doctoral research in Chaucer at the University of London, England, on a Nuffield Fellowship, later publishing numerous essays on Chaucer in European and North American journals. He has taught creative writing and served as writer-in-residence at several universities, and has twice received the Governor-General's Award for his poetry.

Beryl Rowland is currently the President of the New Chaucer Society, the sole international organization of Chaucerians, and serves on the boards of the *Chaucer Review* and *Florilegium*. She is the author of *Blind Beasts: Chaucer's Animal World (1971)*, *Animals with Human Faces: A Guide to Animal Symbolism (1973)*, *Birds with Human Souls: A Guide to Bird Symbolism (1978)*, *Medieval Woman's Guide to Health: The First Gynecological Handbook (1981)*, and numerous articles published in international journals. She is also the editor of the *Companion to Chaucer Studies (1968; revised edition, 1979)* and *Chaucer and Middle English Studies in Honour of Rossell Hope Robbins (1974)*. A professor at York University since 1963, Professor Rowland has lectured extensively at universities in Canada, the United States, Europe, and Australia. In 1983 she was given the title of Distinguished Research Professor by York University, an honour awarded for life, in recognition of her contribution to international scholarship.

EARLE BIRNEY

ESSAYS ON Chaucerian Irony

EDITED, WITH AN ESSAY ON IRONY,
BY **BERYL ROWLAND**

UNIVERSITY OF TORONTO PRESS
Toronto   Buffalo   London

© University of Toronto Press 1985
Toronto   Buffalo   London
Printed in Canada
ISBN 0-8020-5624-5 (cloth)
ISBN 0-8020-6525-2 (paper)

Canadian Cataloguing in Publication Data

Birney, Earle, 1904 –
  Essays on Chaucerian irony
  Includes bibliographies and index.
  ISBN 0-8020-5624-5 (bound). – ISBN 0-8020-6525-2 (pbk.)
  1. Chaucer, Geoffrey, d. 1400 – Criticism and interpretation.   2. Irony in
  literature.   I. Rowland, Beryl.   II. Title.
  PR1924.B57 1985   821'.1   C85-098992-2

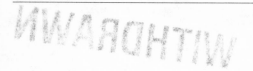
Cover illustration by permission of the British Library (Add. Ms 42120 f. 163)
PUBLISHER'S NOTE: Except for minor stylistic alterations, the texts of Earle
Birney's essays are given in this volume as originally published.

Contents

202465

78-5-20

vi Contents

Preface

CARLE BIRNEY WAS AMONG the first to consider irony extensively in Chaucer's works. Germaine Dempster's *Dramatic Irony in Chaucer* was published in 1932, and David Worcester's *The Art of Satire*, providing a systematic classification of the modes of irony in English literature generally, appeared eight years later. But Birney's doctoral dissertation, completed in 1936 at the University of Toronto, was the first testimony to the extraordinary variety in Chaucer's irony.

Recognizing that irony is basically a form of withholding, of saying one thing and meaning another, Birney defined various types of irony and showed how they functioned in Chaucer's art. He placed the greatest emphasis on two principal modes: 'dramatic irony,' which, in his words, 'characterized passages in drama or dramatic narrative where a speaker's words convey more to the alert and the informed reader or spectator than they convey either to the speaker or to some other character or characters listening to him within the world of the story itself'; and 'verbal irony,' which, superimposed on dramatic irony, is one of the most pervasive and familiar kinds. His most illuminating findings concerned these two modes and one arising from them, 'structural irony.' His approach is strikingly illustrated in his analysis of the *Miller's Tale*. He shows how Chaucer subtly prepares the reader for Alison's particular kind of playfulness, for Absolon's misdirected kiss, for Nicholas being 'scalded in the towte,' and for old John's fall from the rafters, by innumerable ironic foreshadowings throughout the work.

Birney published some of his findings in three general articles on the native traditions of irony, Chaucer's early use of irony, and the extent to which Chaucer's irony had been noted by scholars in previous centuries. He stressed in these early articles that although Chaucer learned of attitudes fundamental to irony in Latin and French literature, he had no need to be dependent on foreign sources for his knowledge. He was heir to a long tradition in English writers and he was subject to their influence from the beginning. Birney showed that despite their traditional form, irony was present even in Chaucer's earliest lyrics.

Birney's subsequent studies were on the individual tales belonging to the Miller, Friar, Summoner, and Manciple, and his essays show how well he knew what he was doing. The art of literary criticism is not fully understood, even today. It is sometimes thought to be a lowly craft, carried on by sterile, untalented individuals at the expense of creative writers whose genius they tap. The fact is that true critics, who seek to give permanence only to great works of art, are themselves creative. 'A book is a machine to think with,' said I.A. Richards, on the first page of *Principles of Literary Criticism*. It may consist of ideas devised by someone else, but when readers become involved they are the people that do the thinking. To be fully realized, the work must engage the readers' imaginations and activate their creative participation. Only when text and readers converge does the work take on its full existence. While no single reading can ever exhaust the full potential of a work, gifted critics must offer innovative interpretations and perspectives to which their own rich literary culture and experience of life have uniquely contributed. They are concerned with author-reader relationships and are engaged not only in interpreting but showing why the effects are so. This task Birney well understood. He also knew that, to be effective, the critical essay had to be a miniature work of art, paying tribute to the great master. As a creative artist himself, he was able to look at Chaucer in a fresh, original way; as a poet, he had eloquence to give shape to the experience that he had felt imaginatively. The result is that these essays are classics of their kind, to be read with enjoyment as they were when they first appeared.

My association with Earle Birney began as a graduate student at the University of British Columbia some twenty-five years ago. Since that time Chaucerian scholarship has been prolific – in the last ten years alone a thousand articles and some forty books have been published – but these essays have not dated. They are, however, not readily available today, and I hope that this collection will prove useful not only to the university student, for whom the new bibliographies are intended, but to a wider and less specialized audience. My introductory essay offers a method for distinguishing and classifying the various kinds of irony. Birney's essays reveal the nature of Chaucer's achievement and provide the perceptions that anticipate the now widely held view that Chaucer's comic tales are among the most artistic of the *Canterbury Tales*.

BR

Acknowledgments

PUBLICATION OF THIS BOOK is made possible by grants from the Canadian Federation for the Humanities, using funds provided by the Social Sciences and Humanities Research Council of Canada, and from the Publications Fund of University of Toronto Press.

'The Two Worlds of Geoffrey Chaucer' reprinted from *Manitoba Arts Review* 2 (1941) 3–16; 'English Irony before Chaucer' reprinted by permission from *University of Toronto Quarterly* 6 (1937) 538–57; 'Is Chaucer's Irony a Modern Discovery?' reprinted from the *Journal of English and Germanic Philology* 41 (1942) 303–19; 'The Beginnings of Chaucer's Irony' reprinted by permission from the *Publications of the Modern Language Association of America* 54 (1939) 637–55; 'The Inhibited and the Uninhibited: Ironic Structure in the *Miller's Tale*' reprinted by permission from *Neophilologus* 44 (1960) 333–8; 'After his Ymage': The Central Ironies of the *Friar's Tale*' reprinted from *Mediaeval Studies* 21 (1959) 17–35 by permission of the publisher, © 1959 Pontifical Institute of Mediaeval Studies, Toronto; 'Structural Irony within the *Summoner's Tale*' reprinted by permission from *Anglia* 78 (1960) 204–18; 'Chaucer's "Gentil" Manciple and his "Gentil" Tale' reprinted by permission from *Neuphilologische Mitteilungen* 61 (1960) 257–67.

The editor wishes to express her thanks to Professor George Doxey, the Master of McLaughlin College and to the Administrative Assistant, Molly Klein, for their genial moral support, and to Flo Smith for her indefatigable secretarial assistance.

Abbreviations

LITERARY WORKS CITED

AA	*Anelida and Arcite*
Boece	*Boece*
CA	*Confessio Amantis* (Gower)
CT	*Canterbury Tales*
CYT	*Canon's Yeoman's Tale*
FrankT	*Franklin's Tale*
HF	*House of Fame*
KnT	*Knight's Tale*
Lady	*A Complaint to his Lady* (also called *A Balade of Pity*)
MancT	*Manciple's Tale*
Mel	*Tale of Melibee*
MilT	*Miller's Tale*
NPT	*Nun's Priest's Tale*
PardT	*Pardoner's Tale*
PF	*Parliament of Fowls*
PhysT	*Physician's Tale*
Pity	*The Complaint unto Pity*
PriorT	*Prioress's Tale*
SqT	*Squire's Tale*
SumT	*Summoner's Tale*
T&C	*Troilus and Criseyde*
Thop	*Tale of Sir Thopas*

JOURNALS AND REFERENCE WORKS CITED

Ang	*Anglia*
AnM	*Annuale Mediaevale* (Duquesne University)
AN&Q	*American Notes and Queries*
BUSE	*Boston University Studies in English*
CE	*College English*
ChauR	*Chaucer Review*
CLAJ	*College Language Association Journal*
CritQ	*Critical Quarterly* (London)
DNB	*Dictionary of National Biography*
E&S	*Essays and Studies by Members of the English Association*
EETS	*Early English Text Society*
EIC	*Essays in Criticism*
EIE	*English Institute Essays*
ELH	*Journal of English Literary History*
ELN	*English Language Notes* (University of Colorado)
EM	*English Miscellany*
EngR	*English Record*
ES	*English Studies*
ESC	*English Studies in Canada*
Expl	*Explicator*
FMLS	*Forum for Modern Language Studies*
JEGP	*Journal of English and Germanic Philology*
JEP	*Journal of Evolutionary Psychology*
JLS	*Journal of Literary Semantics*
JMRS	*Journal of Medieval and Renaissance Studies*
JNT	*Journal of Narrative Technique*
MAE	*Medium Aevum*
MLN	*Modern Language Notes*
MLQ	*Modern Language Quarterly*
MLR	*Modern Language Review*
MLS	*Modern Language Studies*
MP	*Modern Philology*
MR	*Marche Romaine*
MS	*Mediaeval Studies* (Toronto)
N&Q	*Notes and Queries*
Neophil	*Neophilologus*

NM	*Neuphilologische Mitteilungen*
NED/OED	*Oxford English Dictionary*
OL	*Orbis Litterarum*
PBA	*Proceedings of the British Academy*
PLL	*Papers on Language and Literature*
PMLA	*Publications of the Modern Language Association of America*
PQ	*Philological Quarterly* (Iowa City)
RA-A	*Revue Anglo-Américaine*
RES	*Review of English Studies*
RR	*Romanic Review*
SAC	*Studies in the Age of Chaucer*
SAQ	*South Atlantic Quarterly*
SFQ	*Southern Folklore Quarterly*
SP	*Studies in Philology*
Spec	*Speculum*
SR	*Sewanee Review*
SSF	*Studies in Short Fiction*
TSE	*Tulane Studies in English*
TSLL	*Texas Studies in Literature and Language*
UCPES	*University of California Publications, English Studies*
UCSLL	*University of Colorado Studies in Language and Literature*
UMSE	*University of Mississippi Studies in English*
UR	*University Review*
UTQ	*University of Toronto Quarterly*
YWMLS	*Year's Work in Modern Language Studies*

Seven Kinds of Irony

BERYL ROWLAND

ANYONE WHO TRIES to define irony is asking for trouble. The subject of many excellent books and articles,[1] irony has been so variously and profusely analysed that some critics are now reluctant to consider it at all, preferring to regard it rather as a temporary literary obsession or as a modern concept almost totally irrelevant to medieval poetry. As for diehard ironymongers, they are becoming too canny to define their terms: they either force readers to sort out for themselves the various modes of irony or imply that only one type of irony existed in medieval times.[2] Yet if we wish to discuss irony in Chaucer's works we need to establish what it is and define the different kinds that Chaucer used.

The question arises: if the classical and medieval literary theory with which Chaucer was familiar posited only a limited view of irony, must we conclude that only one kind of irony exists in Chaucer's works? Birney's contemporaries of the 1930s, when he was writing his dissertation, would have said yes, and even today some critics maintain that if a response to Chaucer's poems is modern, it must be wrong. I would argue the contrary: theory, inasmuch as it is based on what has been, always lags behind practice, especially that of a truly innovative poet; the ironies discovered in Homer in the seventeenth and eighteenth centuries, in Dante in the early twentieth century, and, more recently, in Chaucer were always there and must have been perceived by the most sensitive readers in any age. Birney's approach predicates a similar point of view. While his contemporaries were concerned with sources, 'realism,' dramatic qualities, philosophical outlook, and surface characteristics of the language, he made a close textual examination, focusing on structure, patterns of imagery, and meaning, in order to articulate the various modes of irony that he found there. The early rhetoricians' pronouncements on verbal irony are undoubtedly important, but we must bear in mind that there are many other kinds of irony.

Most of the classical and early medieval rhetoricians whose precepts were familiar to Chaucer make some reference to irony. To them it was a derisive mode of speech, of saying one thing and meaning the contrary. It was a game of opposites. According to the Roman grammarian Donatus in the fourth century AD, 'ironia est tropus per contrarium quod cognatur ostendens' ('irony is a trope that shows the opposite of what one perceives')[3] It was also, less radically, a statement whose real meaning *diverged* from the ostensible one, *aliud*, a different expression, taking the place of *contrarium*, a contrary one.[4] Not surprisingly, the author of *Ad Herennium*, Quintilian, and others, classified irony under allegory[5] in that both say one thing but mean another, the distinction being that whereas allegory concentrates on the similarities in a comparison, irony tends to focus on the points of contrast. The fact that irony emphasizes incongruity, some kind of disparity or even diametrical opposition, also distinguishes it from metaphor, which is based on analogy (metaphora brevior est similitudo).[6] The essence of rhetorical irony was to blame by praise and frequently involved the use of *insinuatio* or *dissimulatio* to control the listener's response.[7] For Cicero, who was one of the earliest to give irony its status not only as a figure of speech but as a pervasive mode of discourse, the starting point was Socratic dialectic: 'Among the Greeks, history tells us, Socrates was fascinating and witty, a genial conversationalist; he was what the Greeks call *eiron* in every conversation, pretending to need information and professing admiration for the wisdom of his companion.'[8] This mode of ironic deception ultimately stemmed from Greek comedy, in which the humble but crafty dissimulator (*eiron*) triumphed over his stupid and boastful dupe (*alazon*).[9] As an orator, Cicero, in common with other rhetoricians, thought of irony in terms of public speaking. The tone of voice revealed that the meaning was opposite to what was actually said. Similarly, St Augustine emphasized the importance of *pronuntiatio* (delivery) when referring to irony of blame-by-praise: 'In irony,' he said, 'we indicate by tone of voice the meaning we wish to convey, as when we say to a man who is behaving badly: "You are doing well!"'[10]

The writers of rhetorical handbooks in the twelfth and thirteenth centuries reinforced the importance of irony and its cognate tropes.

Geoffrey of Vinsauf, Chaucer's own 'Gaufred, deere maister soverayn' (NPT 4537), while not using the word *irony*, frequently touched on it by definition or example. He described what we would call verbal irony with the traditional emphasis on an accompanying quality of urbanity: 'If you wish to inveigh fully against foolish people, attack in this way: praise, but facetiously; accuse, but bear yourself good humoredly and in all ways becomingly; let your gesture more than your words nip the ones mocked.'[11] In considering ambiguity, he offers a further example: '*that peerless man*: the word means *most excellent*; but *most vicious* glances at us obliquely; this is its meaning. The word belies its appearance or else our perception errs.'[12] Under allegory, Geoffrey of Vinsauf gives another example of irony: 'I transfer a noun for other reasons, that it may not be a true resemblance, but rather through antiphrasis, derision as it were, as when someone deformed in body is called "Paris," ... or someone of rude speech "Cicero." '[13] Many of Geoffrey of Vinsauf's 'difficult' and 'easy' ornaments of style may carry ironic implications, such as *superlatio, permutatio, adnominatio, contentio, occupatio, dubitatio*, and others.

The rhetoricians were mainly concerned with verbal irony, and it is the most common kind even today. 'They're not exactly stealing out of town,' said a television commentator on 29 July, 1981, as the glittering coach of the Royal honeymoon couple bowled along Whitehall towards Victoria Station, accompanied by deafening cheers from an ecstatic mob. All literary irony may be said to be verbal, but in a restricted sense verbal irony makes use of a particular word or phrase which has an immediate impact on the sophisticated listener. Here, a simpler and more obvious irony would have been: 'They *are* stealing out of town!' But the presence of the negative and the qualifier help to convey an appropriate lightness and an impression of detachment on the part of the ironist, contributing a tone which establishes an understanding or even an intimacy between him and the more perceptive in his audience.[14] While the uninitiated take the statement at its face value, the initiated perceive the absurdity of implying even the possibility that the behaviour of the Royal couple might have any resemblance to that of commoners. Does the statement also carry a hint of disapproval, the suggestion that a display of pomp and circumstance is at odds with the contemporary world? It is difficult to say. But we must remember that for the rhetoricians some kind of oblique judgment of social mores, individual conduct, or of life itself was implicit.

The qualities inherent in verbal irony apply to irony in general. Irony is present when a statement, action, or situation conveys a feigned meaning to the imperceptive that is incongruous, inadequate, or even directly opposed to the intended meaning apparent to the perceptive; usually the intended meaning implies criticism. 'An irony,' observed a grammarian in 1656, ... 'hath the honey of pleasantness in its mouth, and a sting of rebuke in its taile.'[15] Such irony may be the most genteel of derisions but it is still 'a child of that Roman flyting whose origins are in personal abuse, and cousin to the primitive Irish charm-chanting by which the poet-sorcerer, if he stood on one foot and pointed his finger in the right direction, could raise blisters on the face of his enemy.'[16]

If by 'genteel' we mean the urbanity extolled by Cicero, the term certainly applies not only to the precepts of the rhetoricians but to Chaucer's observance of them, especially with regard to verbal irony. Chaucer placed verbal irony within the traditional rhetorical figures, such as *diminutio* (understatement), *expolitio* (embellishment), figures of diction, the so-called 'plain colours,' *conduplicatio* (repetition of a word), *praecisio* (incomplete statement), and various other figures of 'difficult' and 'easy' ornament. A favourite device is *paranomasia* (word play), as, for example, in the *Shipman's Tale* where the association of money and sex is emphasized by the pun on *taille*,[17] meaning both a woman's 'tail' and 'tally or reckoner':

> For I wol paye yow wel and redily
> Fro day to day, and if so be I faille,
> I am youre wyf; score it upon my taille,
> And I shal paye as soone as ever I may ...
> Ye shal my joly body have to wedde;
> By God, I wol nat paye yow but a-bedde! (B 1604–14)

Verbal irony also concludes the *Reeve's Tale*:

> Thus is the proude millere wel ybete,
> And hath ylost the gryndynge of the whete, (A 4313–14)

By exploiting both the literal and the slang sexual meaning of *gryndyng*,[18] Chaucer neatly sums up the Miller's misfortunes: he has failed to cheat his customers and his womenfolk have been sexually abused.

These lines, like those from the *Shipman's Tale* cited above, are part of complex structural and dramatic ironies within the tale. But both examples possess a characteristic common to verbal irony: to the initiated, the irony in the word or phrase is usually immediately apparent. A proverbial expression can produce a similar effect. When the Wife of Bath declares 'Whoso that first to mille comth, first grynt' (D 389), she is using a common phrase meaning 'first come, first served.' She is stating that before any of her husbands could complain about his misconduct, she attacked them for theirs. The presence of the sexual metaphors *mill* (traditionally the woman or the pudenda) and *grind* also reveals that the Wife is declaring her acceptance of the promptest lover. She is proverbing simultaneously on her adroitness in argument and on the behaviour that occasioned it.

The second kind of irony is one that has received much attention from Chaucer critics in recent years. It concerns the essentially Socratic fictional character, the 'I' that is a major implement of Chaucer's narrative technique. This kind of irony arises from a discrepancy between narrator and poet. While it shows a debt to the modesty topos of the rhetorician, it is part of the strategy of a poet who, because his status is inferior to his listeners', feels the need to dissimulate, to conceal the fact that he is their mentor. Such irony of the narrator, in Green's view, only became possible when oral tradition began to give place to written composition. Face to face with the poet, listeners would have made no distinction between him and the narrator because they regarded a poet as the mouthpiece of historical fact. It was when poetry became written that the medieval poet began to develop his art beyond the limits prescribed by the rhetoricians and was able to introduce another perspective by distancing himself from his audience.[19] Muecke terms this kind of irony 'self-disparaging irony':

The sort of person the ironist presents himself as being is our guide to his real opinion. He understates or overstates himself, assuming such qualities as ignorance, deference, complaisance, cooperativeness, naivety, over-enthusiasm, eagerness to learn, and inability to understand. But his disguise is meant to be penetrated, and our judgement is directed not against the ignorance or naivety of the speaker but against the object of the irony.[20]

Worcester and Knox prefer to call this kind of irony the irony of manner. 'The character,' says Knox, 'is one of good modesty and self effacement joined to sympathetic admiration of others, and as such represents the principles of praise-by-blame and blame-by-praise projected to the whole image of a personality.'[21]

I prefer the term irony of manner with reference to Chaucer to disassociate myself from the view that Chaucer created a consistent persona in his works.[22] Despite the growth of a 'manuscript culture' that reflected rich and diverse literary traditions, despite the increase in the number of manuscripts apparently intended to be read either individually or in small groups, the poet's voice was still a speaking voice. In the context of the actual performance, with the speaker immediately and constantly visible, the narrator and poet would appear as one personality. When we read *Troilus* now, the narrator's presence may appear to be intermittent, but to that first audience it must have been continuous and compelling. However much this fictional version of the poet is a self-consciously contrived projection, we cannot assume that the listeners were aware of any dichotomy or that Chaucer would have confused them by giving his 'I' different personalities, two identities (in the opinion of one critic) out of a possible three – narrator, poet, and man. In the General Prologue to the *Canterbury Tales* the sophisticated concept of a dim-witted narrator raises other problems. We cannot with justice say that the narrator is 'an almost unfailingly simple-minded observer' when he shrewdly discloses the nature of the Pardoner's relics and the thievery of the Manciple or when he inveighs against the teaching of the Summoner or compares the practices of the Parson with those of less scrupulous clerics. The irony that a mask creates could be achieved without it. The delivery gave the interpretation.

Our third kind of irony, dramatic irony, immediately allows listeners to play a knowledgeable role, and gives them an advantage over the protagonist in that they are aware of a truth that has been withheld from the character. When used in conjunction with irony of manner, the form gives rise to a disconcertingly shifting perspective, now encouraging, now undermining the reader's confidence in his or her own assessments. Whereas in verbal irony the speaker is conscious of his irony even though its effectiveness may depend in part on a momentary unawareness in the victim, in dramatic irony the speaker is ignorant of the *double entendre*, and the irony is further intensified in the extreme case in which the victim goes to his or her death without enlightenment. Germaine Dempster, who was the first to demonstrate its importance in Chaucer's works, defined dramatic irony as 'the irony resulting from a strong contrast, unperceived by a character in a story, between the surface meaning of his words or deeds and something else in the same story.'[23] The most common form of dramatic irony occurs when someone acts or speaks in complacent ignorance of what is or is not about to happen. Troilus refers to Criseyde as his 'swete fo' (I 8714). This oxymoron is not only verbally ironic in itself but ironic dramatically. His love is indeed his foe, causing not his metaphorical death as a courtly lover but his actual death when he seeks to kill his rival in battle.

Here the irony is verbal as well as dramatic. In many instances, the dramatic irony is mainly situational. The *Legend of Good Women* provides the most obvious examples. In each of the legends of Dido, Cleopatra, Hypsipyle and Medea, Ariadne, Philomela, and Phyllis, the heroine is infatuated with a lover who we know will ultimately fail her and bring about a tragedy. More subtle dramatic irony occurs in *Troilus* when Criseyde promises to see Troilus 'tomorwe' (III 809), using a word that becomes charged with meaning as the story proceeds. 'Tomorwe? allas, that were a fair!' exclaims her importunate uncle. Criseyde's habitual procrastination is her undoing. Held in the Greek camp, she still intends to return to Troilus:

> I shal tomorwe at nyght, by est or west,
> Out of this oost stele on some manere syde,
> And gon with Troilus where as hym lest. (v 751–3)

The comment of the narrator underlines her fatal weakness:

> But God it wot, er fully monthes two,
> She was ful fer fro that entencioun!
> For bothe Troilus and Troie town
> Shal knotteles thorughout hire herte slide. (v 766–9)

When dramatic irony is extended to the dimensions of the world stage, it becomes irony of fate. This kind of irony embraces tragic irony, irony of life, of chance, of detachment, of events, philosophical and cosmic irony, all metaphysically loaded expressions, dependent for their meaning on the views of those who use them. The medieval theory that tragedy concerned

> hem that stoode in heigh degree,

> And fillen so that ther nas no remedie
> To brynge hem out of hire adversitee, (B 3182–4)

naturally involves irony of fate and tragic irony. The protagonist ex-
periences a grim reversal of circumstances that is in direct contradiction to what he has anticipated. Usually a sense of doom hangs over
the action, accompanied by the mocking laughter of the Gods. But at
the centre is the hero, perhaps aware of the vagaries of Fortune yet
blindly trusting her. Irony of chance, of life, of event intensifies the
focus on the microcosm: it may consist of no more than an unfore-
seeable turn of events, bringing about a sequel totally opposed to that
expected by the protagonist. Philosophic irony is irony of fate writ
large and, as Ramsey observes, involves two basic perspectives,

one earthly, time-bound and limited, the other celestial, timeless and limit-
less ... The earthly vision discerns such various forces as fortune and destiny
and the stars, then struggles helplessly to relate them to free will and the
'purveiaunce' of God. From the 'other worldly' perspective, the larger vision
directs the ironies down to man and his merely natural activities (e.g. Troilus'
laughter from the eighth sphere and the theme of the palinode generally). The
ironies from this perspective tend to be objective rather than self-directed and
turn on the difference between ignorance and knowledge, false love and true
love – the general conflict between the apparent and the real.[24]

Philosophic irony is compatible with medieval thought in that Christianity sought to reconcile the futility of man's endeavours with a belief
in the justice of an omniscient Deity. The perception of the discrepancy
between intention and result, aspiration and ultimate failure encour-
aged an ironic vision. In the palinode to the *Troilus*, with its overall
poignant sense of the ephemeral nature of all striving and loving and
the need to turn from 'wrecched worldes appetites' to divine love, the
Christian poet demonstrates an irony that may properly be termed
philosophical. Such irony is also often present within a smaller compass, as when the narrator comments on Troilus' sudden capitulation
to love:

> O blynde world, O blynde entencioun!
> How often falleth al the effect contraire
> Of surquidrie and foul presumpcioun;
> For kaught is proud, and kaught is debonaire,
> This Troilus is clomben on the staire,

And litel weneth that he moot descenden;
But alday faileth thing that fooles wenden.   (I 211–17)

The philosophic ironist may seem to assume an almost God-like stance,
viewing the contradictions of life impartially, distancing himself from
the fictional world that he has created, arranging human lives like
Jehovah or the Olympian Gods, and foreseeing their doom. The cosmic
ironist may adopt a similar posture, but he lacks the sense of com-
mittal, the unwavering belief that lies behind the philosophical ironist's exposure of the instability of this brittle world. Worcester sees
him striving for the unattainable: 'Cosmic irony is the satire of frustration, uttered by men who believe that however high man's aspirations and calculations may reach, there is always a still higher
unattainable level of knowledge, in the light of which those aspirations
and calculations must be stultified and aborted.'[25] Muecke regards the
cosmic ironist as one who confronts life in all its most meaningful
actions with a sense of the ultimate total purposelessness of man's
existence.[26] This kind of irony has no relevance to the peculiarly medieval way of viewing things.

A fifth category may be termed the irony of values, whereby the
writer obliquely points out contradictions and disparities between ide-
als and actualities in contemporary culture. Here the writer induces
his audience to react critically to received opinions, especially those
having to do with courtly values, conduct of individuals according to
their estate, literary conventions, or current intellectual fads. Chaucer's application of this kind of irony is characerically low key, even
in the House of Fame where figments of the imagination, the invented
wonder-world itself, derive support from factual observation, scientific
proof, and the laws of physics. He may consider modern learning, the
lore of dreams, the values of the epic, but he carefully avoids personal
pronouncements on moral, philosophical, and religious controversies
of his age. Very general social values are his customary targets and,
not surprisingly, contemporary concepts of love are a frequent subject
for irony. Indeed, the religious vocabulary customarily applied to romantic love facilitates the irony inherent in the disparity between
sacred and secular love. As Robertson observes, 'the fact that the word
love (amor) could be used for either charity or cupidity opened enor-
mous possibilities for literary word play.'[27]

The treatment of love in the Prologue to the Legend of Good Women
is deliberately ambiguous. Although the initiated realize that the object
of worship is the cult of the Margarite, not the daisy itself, the naïve

fervour of the speaker and the artificiality of the description in all matters save the daisy's smell[28] make such devotion seem ludicrously excessive. Moreover, the respectful, admiring tone of the awed narrator is undercut by chirpy pounding rhymes that mock not only the sentiments but the dream vision convention itself. In the *Parliament of Fowls*, the birds celebrate the occasion of their annual mating instead of singing praise to God as in the traditional Bird Mass. Posing *questioni d'amor*, problems of love that are interesting topics for discussion, Chaucer explores various attitudes to love, demonstrated by the individual birds as representatives of their class. Some critics would say that Chaucer's delicate irony does not permit us to draw any fundamental conclusions about distinctions between natural and courtly love. Others contend that each point of view throws ironic light on the limitations of *fin' amor*. Another view is that serious moral intent reaches beyond irony: the exponents of chivalric love 'have created momentary chaos in the society of birds, disrupting Nature's harmony and bringing into their society unnatural vices beyond the understanding or cure of Nature.'[29] In some poems the ironic portrayal of *fin' amor* is less in doubt, especially when it is conveyed through a mode of literary expression that is inappropriate in context. Church Fathers and poets employed the imagery of the Canticles for their panegyrics of the Madonna, depicting her as a young bride. In the *Merchant's Tale*, instead of the Son-Bridegroom calling Mary's soul to himself, an aging, lecherous husband calls for a sexual encounter with a young wife who is the faithless woman of the fabliau tradition:

'Rys up, my wyf, my love, my lady free!
The turtles voys is herd, my dowve sweete;
The wynter is goon with alle his reynes weete.
Come forth now, with thyne eyen columbyn!
How fairer been thy brestes than is wyn!
The gardyn is enclosed al aboute;
Com forth, my white spouse! out of doute
Thou hast me wounded in myn herte, O wyf!
No spot of thee ne knew I al my lyf.' (E 2138–46)

In many instances, irony of values is associated with modes already described and with a seventh mode, structural irony, to be discussed later. *Sir Thopas* exploits verbal, dramatic, and structural ironies as well as irony of values in order to tilt at the excesses of both the language and content of a hackneyed literary form and at the extravagance and artificiality of chivalric sentiments. The irony is also complex in the *Reeve's Tale* (4236–9), when Aleyn, who has seduced Malyne to avenge himself on the Miller, unexpectedly breaks into an *aube*, the traditional parting song of lovers, and lyrically declares that he will be Malyne's 'awen clerk':

> Aleyn wax wery in the dawenynge,
> For he had swonken al the longe nyght,
> And seyde, 'Fare weel, Malyne, sweete wight!
> The day is come, I may no lenger byde;
> But everemo, wher so I go or ryde,
> I is thyn awen clerk, swa have I seel!'
>   'Now, deere lemman,' quod she, 'go, fareweel!'   (A 4234–40)

Here the parody of sentiments of high-life romance is intensified by verbal echoes from secular lyrics concerning clerks and their mistresses. But the irony of courtly values is also allied to dramatic irony: as a suitor for Malyne, Aleyn, with his uncouth speech sprinkled with Northernisms, falls far short of 'som worthy blood of auncetrye' into which Malyne's grandfather aspires to marry her.

Another type of irony characteristic of Chaucer concerns theme. This kind of irony directs the whole action of the tale towards one central statement. In the *House of Fame*, for example, an unheroic character is caught up to heaven, like saints and heroes; then he is provided with a vision that is especially concerned with secular matters having to do mainly with earthly fame, and with the literary treatment of profane, not spiritual, love. In *Troilus*, the delights of passionate love are celebrated in a world whose instability must inevitably destroy them. In the *Canterbury Tales*, erring humanity embarks on a spiritual pilgrimage but is almost totally committed to the world of the flesh. The theme of the *Pardoner's Tale*, 'radix malorum est cupiditas,' unifies all the lesser ironies present and creates a perspective beyond that allowed to the central character. Love of money whereby the misguided hope to achieve happiness leads only to death, says the Pardoner in his exemplum, and he is describing a fate that is spiritually his own.

The seventh kind of irony, structural irony, is a mode not always recognized by critics. Yet it is, as Earle Birney demonstrates, the most innovative and striking characteristic of Chaucer's narrative style. Structural irony gives the poetry unity because it relates one part to

another and to the overall theme by pointing out contrasts and dis-
crepancies and frequently making subtle and complex use of symbol
and metaphor. Irony of this kind may exist between tales. The tales
of the Clark and the Merchant, for example, complement each other,
and they in turn relate to tales known as the Marriage Group. The
Clerk, having told a tale of a young marquis and his marriage to an
impossibly devoted wife, concludes by exhorting wives to be as gay as
a leaf on a linden tree and let their husbands 'care, and wepe, and
wrynge, and waille.' In his reply, the Merchant makes earnest of game.
He savagely applies the words to himself: 'Wepyng and waylyng, care
and oother sorwe I knowe ynogh, on even and a-morwe' (E 1213–14).
He declares that he is married to a woman who would be more than
a match for the devil and proceeds to tell a tale that inverts the plot
outline of the clerk's. His tale is sometimes said to reflect characteristics of Gothic art, to be extraordinarily un-unified, bristling with
discordant elements and chunks of disparate materials. But the total
effect is of unity. The ironic thematic statement – that an old man's
fantasy of marriage as an earthly paradise can only be retained through
blindness – is developed in a series of sharply contrasting scenes all
linked structurally by controlling symbols, having to do with blindness,
courtly romance, and earthly and spiritual gardens. The structural irony
creates an effect rather like a well-darned sock, if anyone today has
seen such a thing. With much criss-crossing and overlapping, all the
strands interrelate, some over, some under, some skipping a few stitches
here and there but finally fitting into place, and looking very neat on
the right side. It is only the critics who insist on turning the sock inside
out to demonstrate how matted threads from previous patchings, not
always of the same colour or texture, provide an untidy foundation.
The imagery through which the irony is conveyed may seem simple
– a commonplace metaphor or simile in colloquial style – but it can
have associations that reverberate through different parts of the whole
work. Some figures may have no unifying function, but many of them
set up a series of responses, related by contrast or congruity, that are
crucial to the poetic meaning of the poem. The numerous connotations
which they possess in themselves acquire a rich texture because of the
way that clusters of individual images are threaded through the tale
to form patterns.

In conclusion, how are we to explain the ironic Chaucer? To be sure,
he is not always an ironist; he is also an idealist, moralist, conventional
Christian, and, at times (as in the *Prioress's Tale*), even a sentimen-

talist. Yet irony is his most consistent position and is so unique in spirit that we refer to such irony as being distinctively Chaucerian. Urbane in the Ciceronian sense, this kind of irony totally lacks the thundering *saeva indignatio* with which the great rhetorician denounced Catiline in the Roman senate. Untouched by a reforming spirit, making no more than a furtive derisive comment on the major social conflict of his time, he produces an irony that stings like the hairs of a common nettle rather than the tail of the legendary scorpion. Unlike many ironists, he has no sense of commitment to any class or cause, and his detachment frequently creates ambiguities so pronounced that critics still argue over his intentions.

Critics are less contentious about the reason for Chaucer's irony. They agree that although Chaucer owed his living to the old establishment, his daily immersion in political and business affairs intensified his awareness of a more vital, upward-striving world. The irony was a compromise. Tolerant and genial by nature, unwilling to forgo his role as a well-established civil servant and court poet, he exhibited the same kind of discretion that must have preserved him for years in face of all the power struggles on the London docks. According to his nature, his irony is light rather than dark, but it stems from an unsparing, sympathetic yet unsentimental scrutiny of both sides, neither of which he would ever want to align himself with openly. As Earle Birney observed in his dissertation:

The well spring of his irony lay in the ambiguity of his own class-position in an epoch of transition. Not only did many of his flippancies and his unsurpassed self-ironies flow from a need to entertain, orally, an upper class audience grown bored with its own culture, but the whole startling yet deepening current received both its impetus and its direction from the fact that an entirely different society was springing up amid the decay of the old and that Chaucer himself drew physical life from the outworn, and intellectual energy from the new.[30]

Birney's essays that are published here are classics of their kind. They enable us to look at Chaucer as Birney looked at him, in a fresh way. A poet himself, Birney knew that a critical essay has to be a miniature work of art, paying tribute to 'il miglior fabbro,' for what is true of the poet transmuting experience into art – 'It is myself that I remake' – is no less true of the critic who must invert the process as he seeks to communicate the nature of the poetic achievement. His literary analysis is not of the kind known as 'New Criticism' which isolates the text. His interpretations show a comprehensive awareness of the cultural, social, literary, and historical milieu of the period. As a result, his kind of criticism cannot, in my opinion, go out of fashion until the critic runs out of ideas.

NOTES

A shortened version of this paper was given to the 16th congress of the International Federation for Modern Languages and Literatures at the Hungarian Academy of Sciences, Budapest, 25 August 1984.

Additional bibliographical information on works cited in these notes in shortened forms may be found in the bibliography, pp. 137–9.

1 Of recent studies, those which I have found most helpful are: Worcester *The Art of Satire*; Knox *The Word Irony and Its Context, 1500–1755*; Muecke *The Compass of Irony*; Booth *A Rhetoric of Irony*; D.H. Green 'Irony and Medieval Romance'; Green 'Alieniloquium: Zur Begriffsbestimmung der mittelalterlichen Ironie'; Green 'On Recognizing Medieval Irony' in *The Uses of Criticism* ed. A.P. Foulkes (Bern, Herbert Lang 1976) 11–55; Green *Irony in the Medieval Romance*. On Chaucerian irony the essay by Vance Ramsey in *Companion to Chaucer Studies* ed. Rowland remains unsurpassed.

2 See, for example, Batts 'Hartmann's Humanitas: A New Look at Iwein' 39; E. Reiss 'Chaucer and Medieval Irony' SAC 1 (1979) 67–82.

3 'Ars grammatica' in *Grammatici Latini* ed. Keil, IV 401, 30. See also Bede 'De schematibus et tropis' 615, 39; Isidore of Seville *Etymologiarum sive originum* I xxxvii 23.

4 Cicero *De oratore* trans. H. Rackham, II (London, Heinemann 1960) III, liii 203; Quintilian *Instititio oratoria* trans. H.E. Butler, III (London, Heinemann 1959) VIII vi 8; Pompeius 'Commentum de artis Donati' in *Grammatici Latini* ed. Keil, V 310, 29

5 *Ad C. Herennium* ed. Harry Caplan (London, Heinemann 1964) IV xxxiv 45–56. See also Quintilian and Pompeius, as cited above. The latter distinguishes between allegory and irony.

6 Quintilian *Institutio* VIII vi 8, IX ii 44–6; Rufinianus 'De schematis dianoeas' in *Rhetores Latini minores* ed. C. Halm (Leipzig, Teubner 1863) 61–2; Isidore *Etymologiarum* II xxi 41

7 Cicero *De oratore* II 67; Quintilian *Institutio* VIII vi 55–6, IX ii 43–53; Isidore *Etymologiarum* II xxi 41

8 *De officiis* trans. Walter Miller (London, Heinemann 1956) I xxx 108

9 See Earle Birney 'Structural Irony within the *Summoner's Tale' Ang* 78 (1960) 204–18 (below, 109–23).

10 St Augustine 'De doctrina Christiana' I xxxvii 23, *Patrologia Latina* 34, col. 81: 'Sed Ironia Pronuntiatione indicat quid velit intellegi, uti cum dicimus homini mala facienti, "res bonas facis." ' See also Diomedes, 'Ars grammatica' in *Grammatici Latini* ed. Keil, I 462, 16; Bede 'De schematibus' 616, I.

11 'Poetria nova' in *Les arts poétiques du XIIe et du XIIIe siècle* ed. Edmond Faral 210; trans. Jane Baltzell Kopp in *Three Medieval Rhetorical Arts* ed. James J. Murphy (Los Angeles, University of California Press 1971) 49

12 *Les arts poétiques* ed. Faral, 244, trans. Margaret F. Nims *Poetria nova of Geoffrey of Vinsauf* (Toronto, PIMS 1976) 71

13 *Les arts poétiques* ed. Faral, 226, trans. Kopp in Murphy *Three Medieval Rhetorical Arts* 66

14 Booth *Rhetoric of Irony* 28

15 E. Reyner *Government of the Tongue* (London, Newberry 1656) 227

16 Birney 'Chaucer's Irony' I 33

17 Robert A. Caldwell 'Chaucer's *taillynge ynough, Canterbury Tales,* B² 1624' 55 (1940) 262–5; Claude Jones 'Chaucer's *taillynge ynough'* MLN 52 (1937) 570; Albert H. Silverman 'Sex and Money in Chaucer's *Shipman's Tale' PQ* 32 (1953) 329–36

18 B. Rowland 'The Wife of Bath's Prologue, D. 389' *Expl* 24 (1965) 14; B. Rowland 'The Mill in Popular Metaphor from Chaucer to the Present Day' *SFQ* 33 (1969) 69–79

19 *Irony in the Medieval Romance* 216–19; 'Irony and Medieval Romance' 54. E. Talbot Donaldson, *Speaking of Chaucer* (New York, Norton 1970) 10, assumes that the courtly audience would have been 'aware of the similarities and dissimilarities between Chaucer, the man before them, and Chaucer the pilgrim, both of whom they could see with simultaneous vision.' See also Ramsey 'Modes of Irony' 357.

20 *The Compass of Irony* 87

21 Worcester *The Art of Satire* 90; Knox *The Word Irony* 45

22 E. Talbot Donaldson 'Chaucer the Pilgrim' *PMLA* 68 (1954) 928–36; Donaldson *Speaking of Chaucer* 11–20. See also Howard 'Chaucer the Man'; Ruggiers *The Art of the Canterbury Tales*; Ramsey 'Modes of Irony' 357; B. Rowland 'Chaucer's Speaking Voice and its Effect on his Listener's

Perceptions of Criseyde' *ESC* 7 (1981) 129–40; B. Rowland 'Pronuntiatio and its Effect on Chaucer's audience' *SAC* 4 (1982) 33–51.

23 *Dramatic Irony in Chaucer* 7–8
24 'Modes of Irony' 363
25 *The Art of Satire* 129
26 *The Compass of Irony* 150–1
27 'The Doctrine of Charity in Medieval Literary Gardens' *Spec* 26 (1951) 28
28 If one can trust the evidence of one's nose, the English daisy, *bellis perennis*, does have a smell, surpassing but not dissimilar to 'gomme, or herbe, or tre'
29 D.W. Robertson, Jr, and Bernard F. Huppé *Fruyt and Chaf: Studies in Chaucer's Allegories* (Princeton, NJ, Princeton University Press 1963) 143
30 'Chaucer's Irony' 1 63

ESSAYS ON CHAUCERIAN IRONY

The Two Worlds of Geoffrey Chaucer

I HAVE ALWAYS ADMIRED that anonymous freshman who wrote, in the heat of an examination, that Chaucer 'stood with one foot in the Middle Ages and with the other saluted the rising dawn of the Renaissance.' I think that, beneath the almost Shakespearian abandon of that imagery, there is an honest attempt to characterize Chaucer. I am not sure that the freshman knew what is meant by the Middle Ages and by the Renaissance, and I am not sure that I know, or that anyone knows. Yet the more we study Chaucer's poems, the more we realize that he lived in two worlds, that he is neither feudal nor modern, but a strange and perhaps unique synthesis of the two. All this may be assumed, but what is still neglected in Chaucer criticism is that the duality of his art reflected a duality in his life and times.

It is obvious, for example, and yet often forgotten, that Chaucer was in a position of literary and social dependence upon the feudal aristocracy of his day. By the time he was thirty-four, the poet and his wife had each been granted the modern equivalent of fifteen hundred dollars annually, for life, from John of Gaunt, Duke of Lancaster. Earlier, Chaucer had performed military service for the duke, in Picardy, and he was almost certainly Gaunt's brother-in-law. This may appear to be *political* patronage only, but there was no clear dividing line then – is there now? – between political and literary patronage; Chaucer's first long poem, his *Book of the Duchess*, was written as an elegy upon the death of Gaunt's first wife.

In addition to the Lancastrian records, we have now a long list of pensions, gifts, and appointments which came to Chaucer from other members of the reigning house or directly from the king himself. These favours went far beyond those which Chaucer would normally have received as an esquire of the king's household, and they tell us that Chaucer's real profession was, as Samuel Moore has phrased it, 'servant to the king,' and his avocation, literature. But again the two were not easily separable. Through social connections Chaucer, like Gower, Hoccleve, and the monk Lydgate, sought *literary* patronage and found it. In one ballade he sends political advice to Richard; in two others he sues for court favour. He dedicates his *Legends of Good Women* to Richard's queen, and his last known poem is an amusing and successful begging letter to the new King Henry.

Richard's spendthrift idleness, whatever else it did, created the most luxurious and leisurely court which had yet been seen in England, with a sophisticated if narrow culture, in the enjoyment of which the king shared. His patronage of Froissart is well known; he was also the first monarch personally to encourage authors to write in English. He was, says R.M. Garrett, 'accessible to poets'; it is a natural conclusion that Chaucer, most polished literary entertainer of his time, should have freest access of all. No doubt, of course, he was a busy and competent public official. The ironist of the *Canterbury Tales* could not have failed to be an excellent diplomat. And he had the shining versatility peculiar to the Italian artists of the next century. He was both poet and forester, philosophical student and courtier, humanist and customs collector, theological scholar and royal carpenter, astronomer and linguist – and a brilliant dabbler in law, medicine, and alchemy.

Yet it must have been poetry which increasingly absorbed his energies, and that poetry could not have taken an open stand either against the persons of power in the court, or against the beliefs which kept their power unquestioned. As with Gaunt and his circle, so with monarchy itself, Chaucer could not have received his living from them with the right hand of the esquire and struck against them with the left of the writer. It is worth noting, for example, that when Chaucer during the early years of Richard's reign translated *Melibeus* he made only one important omission, and that was the passage on the evils of being ruled by a boy-king.

Even if he had not depended on the patronage of aristocrats, he would still have shaped his work for their entertainment, since the gentility made up almost the whole of his possible readers and listeners. A miniature in the *Corpus Christi* manuscript pictures Chaucer reading his poetry aloud to a chivalric audience in a castle garden. An enlargement of this illumination should hang over the bed's head of every Chaucer scholar. To begin with, it would prevent him from being yearly puzzled by the poet's familiar, personally intrusive, digressive style, for that style is natural to oral delivery; more important, it would remind him that when Chaucer wrote of courtly love he wrote it to courtly lovers, and especially to their live, flesh-and-blood mistresses. The *Troilus* and many another work abound in phrases which reveal that Chaucer designed his poems to be 'read or elles sung' to audiences containing 'queenes, lyvinge in prosperitee, duchesses and ... ladyes everichone.'

The wives and attendant ladies of the warrior class must have dominated his audience. The lord himself spent much of his short life away from the castle in fighting of one kind or another; his lady was normally a grass widow, with time and need for entertainment. With no conventual *regulae* to fill up her day, she turned, like many modern women, to the arts, to music, poetry, needlework. Nor were these three diversions distinct. The interminable embroidery sessions were lightened by song and by the reading of romances.

When Chaucer was away from the ladies, on a continental campaign or mission, he might have carried a manuscript with him – but his audience would still be, for the most part, blue-blooded. As an esquire he was expected not only to 'make songes ... and wel endite,' like his Pilgrim Squire, but to read them to the assembled courtiers. It is possible, as well, that he may have followed in the footsteps of Giraldus Cambrensis who had proudly carried his *Topography of Ireland* to Oxford, there to recite it, he says, 'before a great audience ... where clergy and learning were most vigorous and eminent in England.' Certainly Chaucer's prose tales would have been welcome at Oxford in the days when Wiclif was its resident *enfant terrible*; later, he might have returned with verses from the *Canterbury Tales*, 'thilke that sounen into lere.' And no doubt the scholars would have enjoyed, as well, a private hearing of the goliardic deeds of their own undergraduates, Aleyn and John of the *Reeve's Tale*.

Concerning this we can only speculate. What we know is that Chaucer's works are stamped with the impress of oral delivery to the 'gentils everichone.' And this was true even of his fabliaux. Though their plots were such as thrived in bourgeois Flanders and were re-told in taproom by apprentice or Bath webstress, yet they became, with Chaucer, sophisticated short stories, flavoured with cautious balancing, allusive aphorism and with refined double-speaking even in the midst of earthy words and acts. Bawdiness did not denote the plebian; introduced with proper aplomb, it was quite to the spicy taste of lords in the short lethargic hours between banquet and bower, as Petit de Juleville testifies.

Such an audience determined more than the superficies of Chaucer's style; it required the poet to remain essentially a narrator, an entertainer, even though the tales themselves give every evidence that Chaucer was increasingly drawn away from mere story and towards dramatic action illustrating the realities of character and scene in his day. Above all, such an audience forced upon Chaucer that enigmatic spirit, that careful casualness, thoughtful innuendo, and mock impartiality, in short that *irony* which has come to be regarded as the distinguishing peculiarity of his art. For no matter how far Chaucer's eye might range beyond the world of chivalry, he could not allow his sophistications or boredoms to outstrip the pace of those who held his fortunes in their hands.

Circulation of his manuscripts could not have appreciably altered the class composition of Chaucer's audience, for his courtly listeners also represented most of those who could afford or who would wish to purchase books. A single manuscript might, according to H.L. Schramm, cost the equivalent of fifteen hundred dollars today. The poor clerk in the *Prologue* only *dreamed* of twenty, and it was a dream of wish-fulfilment. Chaucer's poems would certainly not be amongst the cheapest. Unless he were a noble, a high church official, or a rich merchant, a man could not buy a Chaucer manuscript in the fourteenth century any more than he can in the twentieth.

Even borrowers or 'browsers' must have been limited pretty largely to the lay aristocracy. A lucky few would see the first editions by virtue of being friends to Chaucer, or friends to friends, or pals of Adam Scrivener. But the majority would need to have access to the library of a wealthy buyer, and he would perforce be an aristocrat. What records we have indicate that the rich clergy, whatever their secret tastes, collected either works of holiness, or no books at all. As for the merchants, though there were many who could now afford to buy, we have as yet found no records of any of them doing so. The universities perhaps, the castles and the courts certainly, were the typical early homes of Chaucer manuscripts.

This did not, however, reduce Chaucer's reading public to a handful. The study of literature was one of the seven arts or *probitates* required of all graduates to knighthood. The average noble was not illiterate; he possessed a library; and though he was not present at the embroidery sessions yet he was capable of taking a manuscript to the battlefield, and reading it when there was time for frighted peace to pant, as the French King John brought a translation of Peter the Eater to the battlefield of Poitiers. The best library in all fourteenth-century England was probably the king's own, which had been accumulating since the days of the first Edward. The most natural immediate repository for the best Chaucer manuscripts was in the royal palace or the queen's retreats 'at Eltham or at Shene.'

That Chaucer was not a typical medieval poet is not therefore surprising but rather to be expected. Fashionable society in any age is not likely to be the most conservative any more than the most radical milieu for art and the world of ideas. In Chaucer's England this was intensely the fact, because feudal society had lost its unity and the whole of England was, in various ways, caught in the first sharp throes of transition from the old ways of inherited caste and inherited service to the modern ways of price and profit and individualistic competition. Chaucer may have stood with both feet in the Middle Ages but he nevertheless saluted the rising dawn of a renaissance, even though it was a false dawn to be followed by a century of gloomy reaction, inter-feudal strife, cynicism, and literary sterility.

It is in Chaucer's day, not Goldsmith's, that we see the first pronounced growth of the town system, of the flight of labour from the village, of bitter disputes about enclosure of land. It is in his century that merchant combines are developed, and that an embryonic factory-system is established in such important industries as wool-weaving and tin-manufacture. Manorial tenure, fundamental to feudalism, began to give place as far back as the previous century to leasehold and to commutation of labour dues for money, and the process is now greatly accelerated. The guilds wax; they stand for collective bargaining, and the right of the emancipated serf and artisan to share in the increasing surplus of wealth.

The rich merchants are climbing into the lower seats of government, into parliamentary representation, into control of London Town. In Chaucer's time a bourgeois City party was able for a while to force a new privy council upon the king, and to appoint two brash commoners, Walworth and Philpot, as official receivers of taxes, and watchdogs upon king and nobles. Trevelyan's summary of the times shows a parliament which was continually claiming and sometimes enforcing those rights which were not actually to be won until Cromwell's day. Even such powerful nobles as Gaunt and the king himself were forced to intrigue with the burghers, working upon their trade rivalries to cleave the united front of the guilds into two camps, those of the victuallers and those of the clothiers. Gaunt supported the latter for his own reactionary ends, and Richard utilized the former. It is not without significance then that Chaucer, patronized by both powers, should carefully select his guildsmen in the *Prologue* from the carpenters and other crafts who were among the few in neither camp.

The world of Thomas Aquinas, in which bargaining was sinful because everything had its natural, just price, where authority was never questioned and disputes concerned only the interrelations of authority, was passing; men of thought had to deal with the democratic theses of Marsiglio and the English William of Ockham, with the reformist theology of Wiclif, and the Lollardry of such as Chaucer's friend, Sir Lewis Clifford. 'In political and social history, in the history of commerce, and in the history of religion,' says Holdsworth, 'we can see the decay of old institutions and beliefs and ideas, and the beginning of a new order of things.'

Nevertheless the old order had by no means been displaced. The masses were yet chained to the land. Lords and abbots still owned the earth, still saddled the highways with ruinous toll-bridges. As a result ferment, indecision, and violent class struggle characterized Chaucer's age almost as much as they characterize the United States today. In both, literature as well as life tends to become preoccupied with such phenomena as the breaking of old mores, crime, social frivolity, profiteering and racketeering, labour 'troubles,' waste in the midst of poverty, civil war, and international war.

For the Hundred Years War *was* an international war, not just an interfeudal struggle. Behind it were the ships and gold of merchants such as Chaucer's, 'who wolde the see were kept for any thyng,' who were willing to risk all for entry into the woollen industries of Flanders and the vineyards of Gascony. A nationalistic spirit was already rife; it began to transform the long rivalry between church and state into a disillusioning international intrigue between rival popes and rival holy alliances, an intrigue in which the English court manoeuvred as trickily as any.

And the Peasant's Revolt of 1381, and succeeding uprisings, represented a greater civil rebellion, for all its sudden termination, than any since in England. For three days London was held by a mass of peasants and poor artisans which the contemporary *Anominale Chronicle* has estimated as 100,000 strong – one-third the active male population of all Chaucer's England. Chaucer's home over the vaulted Aldgate was no ivory tower when 'Jack Straw and his meynee' ran yelling through it, into his city and his Customs House. At the same time, half the countryside was overrun with bitter bands of the common people, whose battle cry was not, as it might be today, abolition of private property, but rather the right to create it. They asked only for 'personal freedom, and the commutation of all services for a rent of four pence an acre.' Their demands granted by the king, the peasants returned home, for they had no political plan and no permanent organization. They could only wait, to be betrayed *en masse* and hanged in detachments; for they were living in the fourteenth century of transition, not the seventeenth of revolution.

When he crossed the Channel, Chaucer must have found life even more invigorating and disturbing. The Flanders which he twice visited was the heart of the new commercial democracy, of capitalistic revolt, of heterodox religious thought whether of a mystical or of a reformist character, the home too of books, the centre of European manuscript production. In Italy, where Chaucer travelled widely and repeatedly, there was already the Renaissance – a land which must have both stimulated and alarmed him, even more than the USSR galvanized tourists in the 1920s. For Chaucer's Italy was not only the ancient home of art, music, architecture, and story, not only the living background for Petrarch and Boccaccio, but it was the country of the latest, extremist forms of government, of both democratic merchant states and dictators, benevolent or otherwise, and the eyrie of a new race of scholars and writers, men who were neither clerics nor aristocrats but exalted artist sons of the city, men of the new race to which Chaucer himself belonged.

Literature was equally in transition. On the one hand, saints' legends, homilies, interminable paraphrases, conventional romances, allegories, feudal chronicles, all continue; on the other hand there appear realistic satire in the sermons of Bromyard and the stories of Mannyng and Langland, the Bible in literal English and in secular play, politico-religious tract, pagan nature poetry, and Ovidian legend retold not as warped Christian prophecy but for its own sake. One man alone wrote in virtually all these forms – Chaucer. And he too alone spans almost the whole range of emotion and of form, from thirteenth-century impersonality and symbolism, serenity and simplicity, to sixteenth-century individuality, realism, and laughter. And in the difficult task of reconciling the opposites he developed his irony.

This irony, to be sure, has generally been regarded as something wholly and miraculously 'modern' in Chaucer, something at least Shakespearian, impartial, in him. The eminent Chaucer scholar, Root,

has declared that 'Chaucer is never touched by the spirit of the reformer,' and another modern editor is sure that the poet 'took even
the pardoner to his heart.' I think that old Elizabethan, Reginald Scot,
was more accurate when he said Chaucer looked upon men 'and derided
their folly in such manner as the time would suffer him.' The trouble
with Chaucer study today is that it has fallen into the hands of professors, who are such incorruptible fellows. In anything which involves
politics or history, that is, in the real problems of the present or the
vital lessons of the past, they never take sides. But unfortunately, just
as history is made by partisans before it is made over by professors, so
literature is created by men who had actual emotions and prejudices
of their own, even if, as in the case of Chaucer, they had need sometimes to conceal their feelings in a cloak of good-humoured equivo-
cation. The trusting teacher does not see this, however; himself born
without the capacity for prejudice, he is deluded by the artistic con-
cealment of it in the literary great whom he admires. And so he insists
that Chaucer and Shakespeare really were without bias, and even goes
on, with a touch of understandable vanity, to praise them for being
like himself. And all his students praise them so that they may grow
up to teach others to praise them.

Actually much of Chaucer's apparent impartiality was either an
inability to make up his mind or a fear of revealing that he had. The
deliberate inconclusiveness of medieval scholastic debate is stamped
upon the *Wife of Bath's Prologue* as clearly as it was upon the tractates
of such dialecticians as Chaucer's friend the 'philosophical Strode', or
the 'holy doctour Bradwardine'. The Wife herself is a champion of
marriage, yea of octogamy, so long as the wife may rule, but she is
made by her creator to present equally potent arguments either for
celibacy or for the domination of the male. Her debating technique
was interesting enough in itself to satisfy Chaucer's audience, and her
learned arguments would not be taken as persiflage but as a valuable
collection of ideas on one of the most hotly disputed questions of
medieval days – the social value of celibacy. It was precisely because
the question was on the top of the hour that Chaucer, who was neither
a cardinal, like Jerome, nor a militant feminist, like Christine de Pisan,
but a court man and literary entertainer, took care to balance the
disputes and satirize the satirizer.

Sometimes Chaucer's detachment, even his good humour, is the
most superficial of illusions. For a medieval reader the inverted gusto
of the Monk's portrait would but faintly camouflage a machine-gun

nest of satiric assault upon everything that was decadent in fourteenth-century monasticism. Elsewhere, Chaucer hides his critical self behind even thinner veils – the medieval conventions of a dazed dreamer, a simple-minded narrator, or an ignorant translator. To protect himself against the envious at court he takes care in all his later poems never to refer to himself as a lover. It was generally held that real love was an emotion reserved for the nobly born; so Chaucer never pretends to have experienced it. He is simply a slavish translator, a fellow whose very fatness testifies to his unromantic nature; if he seems to take liberties with his texts, if he presents a Criseyde who is pitiable and human even though she breaks the prime canon of courtly love, fidelity, blame it on his old and mysterious authorities, such as Lollius, an author known only to Chaucer. If he appears to make fun of the old romances, it is not he, it is another Chaucer, a pilgrim, an elvish chap, ill-favoured, ill-tempered, who is quickly put out of countenance by Harry Baillie. It was a trick as familiar to the author of Mandeville's *Travels* as it is to Barrie or Conrad. The author's McConnachie is a device to secure dexterity of treatment, delicacy of satire, removal from responsibility. We should not forget that Conrad was after all much the same sort of person as his Marlow.

Moreover, satiric subtlety was not something Chaucer had to learn from the 'modern' Italians. It is true that in Boccaccio Chaucer found a satirist who could conceal himself, whenever he wished, in the impartiality of the tale-teller. But Chaucer must have come to him as to a brother-spirit, not as to a master. For both had behind them a long and rich literature of irony. This tradition, as it led up to Chaucer, is little studied or known today, but its records exist, for those who wish to read, in the self-critical sermons of the tenth-century Rather; in the pages of that lively but cautious satirist, Walter Map, archdeacon and courtier; in that jocose polemist, Nigellus Wireker, in whose book of Daun Burnel the Asse Chaucer's Fox was so well read; in the insouciant fabliaux of Rutebeuf, great thirteenth-century 'janglere and goliardeys'; in the rich legacy of English proverb, and Anglo-Norman political song; in such self-ironists as the Provencal Arnaut Daniel; above all in the long saga of Reynard the Fox and in Jean de Meun. All these are as authentically medieval as any masters could be.

Furthermore, Chaucer, it should be remembered, was, like most great writers, shrewd enough to get himself born at the end of a long literary age, so that even if all previous preachers and satirists had been crude and forthright, the very accumulation of their strength would have prepared the way for subtlety. Ten years ago Hitler's was an unfamiliar face. Today an adept cartoonist can evoke it for us in twelve strokes of a pen. In Chaucer's day, a friar could be called up by as few symbols and with an even readier response in the audience, for his reputation had been delicate for two hundred years. As for Chaucer's prioress, the lips of a medieval reader would be set to smile, or to purse with disapproval, the moment she is recorded as one of a mixed throng of Canterbury pilgrims; for the medieval reader did not need footnotes in a College Chaucer to tell him that bishops were almost daily and publicly rebuking nuns – and of course especially their responsible superiors, the prioresses – who joined in these hodge-podge holidays to holy shrines. We have Etiènne de Bourbon and many others to witness for the bawdry of the talk on such journeys, the too obliging maidservants at the inns *en route*, the open drinking and gambling, even within the precincts of the wayside graveyards, through which various delights, says Etiènne, the clerical pilgrim 'lost both his virtue *and* his money.'

But there are many other things in Chaucer which are not explainable by parallels to the literary past, or in any medieval terms. There was often, for instance, a gentleness in his satire which was the direct product of the shifting values of a shifting age. The Franklin, for example, is not only a study in physiological fatalism, an objectifying of the sanguine temperament; he is also an embodiment of Gluttony, of all that 'high living' in middle-class life which constantly drew the fire of ecclesiastical disapproval. Yet he is not condemned, because Chaucer, and his courtly audience, looked upon him much as we would today. The extravagances of the fourteenth-century well-to-do were the direct products of certain economic facts – such as increased foreign trade – facts which no amount of moralizing, fitted to the rigours of a more primitive society, could overcome. It was much easier for those who shared in the new wealth to adjust their morality to the economics than to continue lashing themselves for a sin which had become general. Chaucer, whose rank was much like the Franklin's and whose own tastes were similar, if more varied, did not therefore portray his 'son of Epicurus' in accordance with the fulminations of poor parish priests, however much he might continue to glorify the latter for remaining poor and temperate themselves. Instead he writes an amused, temperate account of an amusing and slightly *in*temperate franklin.

There are other ways in which Chaucer does not fit into standard medieval patterns. He is almost entirely incapable, except in his earliest, most imitative works, of sentimentalism. He was not afraid to deal with the piteous, but he never sought for pathos falsely. The same can scarcely be said of any other medieval writer except Dante. And his realism is as burgherish as Frans Hals'; for even though he used it to impale merchants and burgesses' wives, he was always interested in them, in the new profitmakers, artisans, and weavers of Bath, as no Englishman had ever been interested before him.

And when the demands of his story material, and perhaps of his audience, drew the mature Chaucer back into the old land of allegory and romance, he took less and less trouble to conceal his doubts or his ennui. Scepticism was not by any means unknown to the Middle Ages; Chaucer could have acquired some forms of it from that champion of feudalism, Froissart himself; but the expression of it in the very midst of an intricate love-allegory or a stirring tale of chivalry *was* a new phenomenon in English verse, and so was whimsical boredom. Scattered throughout the *Canterbury Tales* are many casual jests upon a great number of ideas and things taken seriously by Chaucer's ancestors – upon Arthur and Lancelot and the fairies, magic, black or white, astrology and alchemy, and even, perhaps, upon heaven and hell:

> Men mosten axe at seyntes if it is
> Aught fair in hevene (Why? for they can telle)
> And axen feendes is it foul in helle.

So quiet are these asides that many are yet missed. I still wait for some modern pacifist to exploit those lines in which Chaucer notes the value of music in warfare:

> For in fight and blod-shedyinge
> Ys used gladly clarionynge.

Boethius and Dante thought of the universe as a whole whose parts were co-ordinated by Love. Chaucer was growing to think of it in the manner of an Elizabethan, as something bewilderingly disunited and diverse, a place too of indifference and even of mockery, where Love is not the rule but the solacing exception.

Did Chaucer's criticism ever reach so far as to a rejection of church doctrine? If an author unfailingly attacks pardoners and never portrays a good one, if he suggests that their curses and absolutions are equally valueless and their wallets always stuffed with lies, does he still believe in the theory of absolution? 'So heigh a doctrine I lete to divines', who may 'bult it to the bren.' All I know is that to have argued openly against church doctrine would have been to risk burning for heresy; and Chaucer was no Wiclif. Here, as always, his social position and the times were forcing him to choose between being a conventional court poet, or an outcast rhymer of the people, or an ironist. He chose the third and middle road, in art as in life.

This is the secret of the dualism in the *Troilus*. Readers have rightly complained of its 'confused fatalism'. Chaucer never clearly decided between Fate or Free Will, though he devotes so much of the poem to those problems. But neither did his times. Destiny, a concept natural to caste societies, was giving place to doctrines of Pluck and Luck; enterprise was being dealt a hand in the game of Chance. Boccaccio had modernized the Criseyde story into a simple study of capricious individualism. Chaucer, as C.S. Lewis has shown, actually restores some of its medievalism; he hampers free will with the doom of Troy, with fatal days, with astrology. The result is unsolved compromise.

Courtly love is similarly made debatable, just as earlier in the *Parliament of Fowls*. For the benefit of Queen Anne and her ladies, or ladies like them, Chaucer strips away from earlier versions all moralizations upon the inconstancy of women or even the inconstancy of Criseyde. Then, to hold also the men-of-the-world and of court, and his fellow-poets and scholars, Chaucer transforms Pandarus into a polished reconciling ambassador of two epochs. Pandarus is both Boccaccio's witty sceptic and the mentor of the love drama; he scoffs at, and teaches, the rules of the game; he actually carries on, in the background, a wistful orthodox affair of his own. When, for example, Pandarus at last brings Troilus to kneel at the feet of Criseyde, he cannot resist running for a cushion. Yet it is a gesture not of cynicism but of vivacious practical interference, born of the incongruity of the man who could remind his protegée always to blot love-letters with a few tears, and could yet shed them himself in anguish when sardonic Fate and the sliding heart of Criseyde destroy the lover's happiness. Pandarus is as near a self-portrait as Chaucer ever came. He is comic relief, not only for the sophisticates in Chaucer's audience, but for the poet himself. It was not, it should be remembered, a simple question of opposing reality to illusion; for the courtly love conventions, however rococo, were born of men and women and their unending ego-drive. If one doubts the reality of Troilus' sentiments, he need turn only to the love letters of John Keats, or perhaps no farther than to the epistles of his own adolescence. No, it was the inevitable opposition of two realities; the self-indulgent, charming amours of the leisured aristocrat, and the perforce more direct and practical matings of the common people, speaking through the gnomic proverb and the homely image.

In the *Knight's Tale*, similarly, a serious, poetic, at times very dignified treatment of chivalry is quickened by a raciness which in no way implies bad faith or the subtle, underhanded burlesque which so many modern sages allege. The vivacity is there to enliven manners which had become mannerisms. Therefore it is often only on the spur of the moment that Chaucer pops his 'hore heed' from behind the arras. When he came to translate Boccaccio's description of the ascent of Arcite's soul to heaven, he found that he had already used that grave and poetic passage in his *Troilus*. So what does he do? Replace it with another philosophical disquisition? No, he wants to get on with the story. Yet here was a space that had to be filled. When a waterspout or corbel needed ornamentation, or the bottom of a choir seat, the pious carver, left to his own devices, might shape a very unsaintly face with goggle eyes and protruding tongue. So Chaucer writes that Arcite's spirit

> chaunged hous and wente ther
> As I cam nevere, I kan nat tellen wher.
> Therefor I stynte, I nam no divinistre.
> Of souls fynde I nat in this registre –

and rushes on to tell about the heroine. Chaucer is thus continually filling the casual blanks of the narrative with his own literary gargoyles and misericords. And just as the puckish monsters which stare from the medieval churches neither burlesque nor mar the beauty of the whole structure, so the light releases of Chaucer's personality in the interstices of his poems should never be taken as calculated parodies upon the very material he shapes so brilliantly.

In the *Prologue* to his *Canterbury Tales* Chaucer draws back the curtains of a new play where for the first time that bourgeois world which elbowed for room in the crowded backgrounds of his earlier and essentially chivalric poetry pushes its garish, vigorous shapes into the forefront of the stage, there to strive or to mingle openly with the still living figures of feudalism. Chaucer the story-teller, the courtly poet, the wit, and the Boethian philosopher in enchanting verse, was no doubt God's plenty already to the narrower circles of Westminster. But to the inner Chaucer, the creator, the genius in sensitive observance of the shifting incongruities of his era, the versatile man of the world and the son of a Thames Street wholesaler in wines, this realm of Black Knights and classic Eagles and Dreamers, of Trojan princes and their epigrammatic cousins, of falcons and ducks and fair martyred lovers, was not enough. These were compromises with the past; here Chaucer compromises with the future – by adjusting himself to the actualities of his present. It was not new, of course, to parade the types of men in caricature before the reader. Gower and Deschamps had done it; and behind them all was the great literary chess book of Jacobus de Cessolis. But, precisely because it was an old device it was too cramping for Chaucer's purpose. John of Salisbury's simple three-layer world of fighters, workers, and pray-ers, was now a sagging framework within which moved a multiplicity of sub-classes, some, like pardoner and summoner, parasitic on the old, some, like the wife of Bath and the solemn merchant, evolving into an economic role and class-consciousness of their own. Chaucer must find a place for these too, so he adapts his genre to the real panorama of his day, a Canterbury pilgrimage, where the new and the old mingled as nowhere else.

But he does not let the bourgeoisie run away with him or his Tales, any more than they had made off with feudal society, as yet. Though he gives them the full width of the widest stage he could devise, he attaches them by strings, invisibly but firmly, to a long-established puppet machinery of medieval literature. In each character is still visible the moral type, the Sin or Virtue. Every vice is connected with its calling, for each of the pilgrims is made a Professional. Another strand leads to medieval physiognomy; Chaucer gives his moralities eyes, noses, feet, and gestures, and he clothes the professions in their appropriate garments and their peculiar prejudices. Still another puppet-wire leads not to types but, as Manly showed, direct to reality. Chaucer literally gives some of his pilgrims a local habitation and a name, and such names and habitations as must have furnished the merriest topical satire that any English audience has been privileged to hear.

Yet long before clever modern men saw fauns a-peeping through the green of the *Prologue*, discovering Sir Thomas Pynchbeck in a sergeant-at-law, readers had sensed something intrinsically new in the method. That is because the poet had attached a final thread to his most human of puppets, and that one led straight to Geoffrey Chaucer. The wooden objectivity of typical medieval satire disappears before the living, lurking presence of the author himself. He pursues a bewildering and essentially personal manner of careful haphazardness in the setting down of his details:

Bold was hir face, and fair, and reed of hewe.
She was a worthy womman al her lyve,
Housbondes at chirche dore she hadde fyve.

The various type-details are not marshalled, but capriciously intermingled so that the pilgrims shine out like photographic reproductions which, apparently just by chance, still recall the old familiar faces of the medieval categories. This is Chaucer's unique and characteristic method; the old is never discarded but rather utilized to the full; and at the same time it is quietly *played with* by a persistent but never rebellious innovator.

It is highly significant that, in this long portrait gallery, the authentic representatives of the ancient Three Estates alone are untouched by satire; Chaucer *could* not indulge in major criticism of the social structure; hence his knight, parson, and plowman are idealized beings, transfixed to their traditionally appointed stations. There is unadultered praise, also, it should be noted, for two new sub-classes, the yeoman-fighter – that archer upon whom English chivalry had now come to lean for the successful prosecution of its wars – and the university student, representative of the finest intellectual life of the church. The clerk is brushed only with the slightest and mildest of ironies. Though his poverty is odd, it is the mark of his professional respectability. But around the many-shaped heads of the rest, those who in the words of old Speght were 'giuen to deuotion rather of custome than of zeale', Chaucer flashes all those weapons which he had welded from the uniformed Sins, the medical Object Lessons, the allegorized Professionals, the astrological Types, and from the real men of fourteenth-century England, and which he had sharpened with shaded rhythm and rich, ambiguous vocabulary. Harry Baillie and his guests have become actual persons indeed, but they live only because they embody, in their various ways, all the clashing desires and hypocrisies and parasitisms which ate at the old life and yet hampered the fulfilment of the new, in the intense dialectic of this great English Transition.

There is not time here to dwell upon the brilliance of picture, the sweep of humour, of the separate Canterbury tales, though the strange exoticism which is their total effect is the finest flower of Chaucer's duality. I content myself with two instances, one from near the beginning, and the other from the end of his greatest work.

First, the portrait of Allison in the *Miller's Tale*, the new bourgeois heroine redescribed for the amusement but not for the scorn of the gentility:

> Fair was this yonge wyf, and therewithal
> As any wezele hir body gent and smal ...
> Ful smale ypulled were hire browes two,
> And tho were bent and blake as any sloo.
> She was ful moore blisful on to see
> Than is the newe pere-jonette tree,
> And softer than the wolle is of a wether ...
> Hir mouth was sweete as bragot or the meeth,
> Or hoord of apples leyd in hey or heeth.
> Wynsynge she was, as is a joly colt,
> Long as a mast, and upright as a bolt ...

The conventional genteel beauties, the slim, tall, graceful body of Blanche the Duchess, the joined eyebrows of Criseyde, the mouth of Canacee, are all still here, but they are made *real* by relation to an actual if humbler world of weazels and pear-trees and the wool of the sheep. Any fear that the original chivalric outlines will be coarsened dissolves in the concentrated beauty of this imagery. Here, as always, Chaucer was not opposing the graces of the old world with the vigour of the new, but fusing them. Contrast returns only with the significant class distinction of the concluding couplets:

> Hir shoes were laced on hir legges hye.
> She was a prymerole, a piggesnye,
> For any lord to leggen in his bedde,
> Or yet for any good yeman to wedde.

Finally we come to Chaucer's so-called 'Retractions', a sweeping revocation of all the literary riches we associate with his name. Some, including even such a stout knight of Catholicism as Chesterton, have thought it spurious. I do not think so. Chaucer never *repudiated* traditions, especially if they could free the poet from the responsibilities of his own utterances. Moreover he was quite capable of applying conventions with some sly adjustment which released him also from the gravity of the convention itself. It is only natural then that at the close of his life he should, like Jean de Meun and Boccaccio, placate Rome with a traditional author's confession, and yet attach that solemnity to a work which is itself indissolubly linked with the *Manciple's Tale*, which in turn is as plain a 'worldly vanity' as one can find in all Chaucer's writings. There is a much more personally *religious* renunciation at the end of the *Troilus*, but it did not prevent Chaucer from surviving to write the *Canterbury Tales*. In fact the whole of Chaucer's poetry, the richest and broadest comic poetry ever set down in our language, is sprinkled with just such sudden humilities and hoary pieties. The most we can rightly suspect then is that Chaucer sought to appease Holy Church with a penitential farewell, secured, it may even be, by the pertinacity of the monks of Westminster, as Chaucer lay in a troubled dying within the shadow of their cloisters. But whether that eased Chaucer's conscience, or whether he had one, is not written in my source, 'therefore I lete it goon'. The tapestries of those courtly chambers in which our tales, chivalric or bourgeois, were told, have parted once more, this time to the solemn robes of an abbot. Chaucer and his company pause to cross themselves and bow with low, suave, but acceptable deference. Only, on this occasion, the tales are not resumed, and the teller disappears in silence. Nevertheless, it is possible that here, too,

... may ye se, myn owene deere brother,
The carl spak oo thing, but he thoghte another.

English Irony
before Chaucer[1]

ONE FEELS THE NEED to apologize for being concerned with irony
at all, and more especially with irony so far away and long ago. But
while Ottawa remains unbombed, we continue to read English literature, or literature about English literature. The excuse for the present
essay lies in the fact that if we confine our studies to the second
category, as too many wise men continue to do for the centuries on
the far side of 1400, we shall have no knowledge whatever of a long
tradition of English irony worthy of notice in itself, and doubly interesting because it may have helped to form the style of that most pervasive of all English ironists, Geoffrey Chaucer.

If, for example, we turn to the only monograph yet published on the
history of English irony, Mr F.McD. Turner's *The Element of Irony in
English Literature* (1926), we find his chronicle beginning with Milton,
and the statement that irony in English was 'but faintly apparent' before
the Commonwealth. Mr J.A.K. Thomson, author of one of the few
books of authority upon the form itself, *Irony: An Historical Introduction* (1926), is no kindlier to the Middle Ages. Irony, to him, is a
marble goddess whom 'Erasmus brought ... from Greece. This is not a
matter of opinion but of fact.'

Readers of Chaucer, of course, know better, but none of them has
yet thought it urgent to publish any extended study of that quality
which all seem united in praising as the essence of Chaucer's genius.
And into the reaches behind Chaucer not even the most wandering
student of English irony seems to have strayed. It is still the custom
to assume that his sly witticisms and his satiric adroitness were either
mysteriously born within him near the close of the fourteenth century,
or were achieved by his reaching back, perhaps with the help of Jean

de Meun, across a waste of time to the forgotten subtleties of Horace and Ovid. The truth is rather that in the rich accumulation of political satires, beast stories, fabliaux, in the parodies of church literature, the burlesques of romance, the proverbs, and even in the older epics, romances, and chronicles, and the writings of the Church Fathers themselves, irony, in varying degrees but in nearly all the admired forms, has descended with little interruption from the golden days of Aristophanes and Lucian. This tradition came to Chaucer in at least four languages – French, Italian, Latin, and English – and of these *l'esprit gaulois* was undoubtedly the richest and the most influential. There is room within the scope of these pages, however, only for brief notice of some ironies in authentically English literature before Chaucer.

The word *irony* is itself so protean a cliché that I must begin with a warning that I shall use it as loosely as the dictionaries allow. 'Indirect satire' may serve as a working definition and it is one which I should be prepared to defend for even the 'irony of fate' and 'dramatic irony.' A more discriminating analysis of ironic forms is now to be found in the excellent studies in dramatic irony recently published by Dr G.G. Sedgewick of the University of British Columbia.[2] If, in the meantime, someone should push me to stand solemnly upon an independent definition, I should venture that, in all uses of the word today, there is this unity of meaning: an illusion has been created that a real incongruity or conflict is non-existent, and the illusion has been so shaped that a bystander may, immediately or ultimately, see through it and be thereby surprised into a more vivid awareness of that very conflict. One of Chaucer's contemporaries described the same thing more neatly as 'wit graced with pointed wings.'[3]

BATTLE-IRONY

The first use of the word was, as is well known, limited to Socratic understatement, that is, understatement with satiric or didactic intention. This is also the first form to appear in what survives to us of Anglo-Saxon literature. The exultations of victors are regularly couched in sardonic taunts. The *Beowulf* scop rejoices that the slain sea-monster 'was slower in swimming in the ocean when death overtook him.'[4] The same primitive jeering of the vanquished enemy swells in the epithets of Constantine at Brunanburh, and in the insults hurled against the Northmen at Maldon. 'Massive' and 'savage' to the French ear of M. Emile Legouis, it is nevertheless a form of irony which was to continue smouldering in English poetry, from Chaucer's epitaphs upon

Nero and Nebuchadnezzar, to the republican Shelley's sonnet upon Ozymandias, and the witticisms of Kipling's imperialist soldiers. English medieval narrative is seldom without it. Listen to the gloatings of Layamon and his hero upon the slaying of two invaders:

> He smote him over the head so that he fell down,
> And he put the sword into his mouth – such meat was new to him –
> Until the point of the sword sank through into the earth.
> Then said Uther: 'Now, Pascent, lie there.
> Now hast thou Brut-land [Britain] all clutched in thine hand.
> Dwell here you shall, thou and thy friend Gillomar.
> And enjoy well Brut-land for now I deliver it into your hand
> So that you may dwell together with us here.
> And ever have no fear of who shall feed you.'[5]

The same elaborate battle-irony reaches even into the pious lives of saints, when an English chronicler tells them. The Devil visits St Dunstan in his smithy-hermitage and tempts him in the guise of a wanton. The fiend, seized suddenly in the nose by the hot tongs of the holy man, is utterly routed, for, says the poet, 'since the Saint he found at home, who blew his nose so sore, / Thither to cure him of his cold, he hied him never more.'[6] In the *Purgatory of St Patrick* it is the fiends who 'gleek' at the good man. They lead Sir Owain to hell's pit and jocularly invite him to descend and 'find solace' with the other 'birds in our cage.' For 'this is our court and our castle tower.'[7]

Beneath Minot's varnish of Norman sprightliness there is the same ponderous and pitiless jeering, as of David the Bruce, who marched doughtily against the English at Neville's Cross but got 'the faire tower of London for reward.'[8] With the same old epic fierceness the hero-worshipping Barbour crows over the English warriors whom David's father had vanquished. The most playful and perhaps the most consistent of all these gladiatorial ironists is the author of the *Tale of Gamelyn*. He does not merely tell us that his hero cudgels clerics; he says that Gamelyn made a new order of monks and friars by the laying on of hands. Gamelyn's comrade Adam counsels him to do no harm to the clerics, scratch not their holy tonsures – 'but break both their legs and then their arms.' Gamelyn shares this storm-trooper humour; when he vanquished the wrestling champion

> And kaste him on the lefte syde that thre ribbes tobrak,

And thereto his oon arm that yaf [gave] a gret crak
Thanne seyde Gamelyn smertely anoon,
'Schal it be holde for a cast [throw] or elles for noon [none]?'[9]

This tradition of literary sadism explains those elaborations of the Christ-tauntings which appear in the mystery plays, and which Chaucer himself may have heard bellowed from a pageant-wagon. In the York Tilemakers' Play, when Jesus faints under scourging, one of the soldiers complains: 'Despite our care, this dastard dozes.'[10] A mere crowning with thorns is not enough; the single mocking 'Hail, King of the Jews' recorded by the Evangelists must be almost lovingly improvised upon:

FIRST SOLDIER
Hail! comely King, who no kingdom hast known.
Hail! undoughty duke ...
FOURTH SOLDIER
Hail! strong one, who may scarcely stand up
        To fight.
Whee! rascal, heave up thine hand
And thank us all who are worshipping thee ...[11]

PROVERB-IRONY
The riddles and the rare proverbs of the Anglo-Saxon, in their concealments and involutions and their racy realism, contain the germs of ironic wit, but little more than the germs. There was a certain pedantic coldness about the Anglo-Saxon folksay which needed to be clarified by Latin incisiveness and warmed by French gaiety. When that had happened, laconic rusticity became a guise for that barbed posing and punning which has been preserved to us in such collections as the *Demaundes Joyous*, or 'Merry Questions:'

DEMAUNDE
Why dryve men dogges out of the chyrche?
RESPONSE
Bycause they come not up and offre.[12]

Much of what seems to be very 'personal' humour in Chaucer is spun out of just such homely village aphorism, which had become by this time definitely integrated with English literature. 'The cock is brave on his own dunghill,' puts us in Pandarus' world – but it occurs in the pious *Ancren Riwle*.[13] These proverbs, from Alfred and Hendyng and Alanus de Insulis to Chaucer and Gower and George Eliot's Mrs Poyser, consistently reflect the ironic view of life. They are a distillation of the sour jokes fate plays on man, comments upon the capricious contradictions of life which were ready formed for Chaucer. 'A beguiler shall himself beguilëd be' appears not only in his contemporaries, Langland and Gower, but harks back through the *Roman de la Rose* and Dionysius Cato to the *Psalms* and the dim East.[14] There is a similar history for the phrasing of some of Chaucer's most 'Chaucerian' broodings upon chance or the inconsistencies of men. He had but to bend an ear to the common speech of his day to learn the trick of casting sophisticated meditations in memorable form. When Troilus said 'Nettle in, dok out, now this, now that ...'[15] he was using the words of an ancient charm which accompanied the application of dock-leaves.

IRONY OF FATE

Many proverbs evoked that deeper irony which views life as a show 'that passeth sone as floures faire.'[16] This was more than an attitude cultivated by monks for the disprizing of the fleshly world. Some medieval Englishmen were still pagan enough to suggest that even what was done 'for God's love' drew no reward.[17] Life was topsy-turvy and the sooner one faced it the better. Chaucer's contemporaries brought Fortune's wheel into the lullabies:

> Lollai, lollai, little child!
> The foot is in the wheel.
> Thou knowest not if it will turn
> To woe or weal.[18]

Such lugubrious pessimism, given narrative form, supplies the typical medieval 'irony of fate,' that extension of dramatic irony to the theatre of life, where all the actors walk trustingly to unexpected and often undeserved catastrophes, and where the gods are the subtle and sardonic deceivers.

There is little of it in the *Beowulf*, for though Wyrd is Fate, it is a Fate which tends to side with the hero and even to be susceptible to his influence. Philosophic irony, when it does appear, is generally limited to moral comments upon the pursuit of riches. The scop is at pains to contrast the sordid end of the Bad King who assembled much wealth and hoarded it, with the golden sunset of his successor, the Good King, who promptly began to disburse the treasure – presumably being careful to include the poet among the beneficiaries. A deeper irony lies in the symbolism of the epic's ending; the gold which Beowulf lost his life to obtain is burned on his pyre: 'There it still lives, ancient, useless as it was before.'[19] The Norman hero of the epoch's close receives the same brooding epitaph: 'He who was formerly a mighty king and lord of much land had now of all his land but seven foot space; and he who was whilom clothed with gold and with gems, now lay over-wrought with mold.'[20]

This savouring of the tragic ironies which dwell in all human action becomes curiously blended with the old battle-irony. The unknown Englishman who celebrated the Flemish burghers when, in 1301, they cut to pieces the knightly forces of Philip the Fair, begins sardonically enough:

Lustneth, lordinges, bothe yonge ant olde,
Of the Freynssh-men that were so proude ant bolde,
Hou the Flemmyssh-men bohten hem ant solde,
        Upon a Wednesday.

But the consciousness of human woe has crept in before the first stanza is ended:

Betere hem were at home in huere londe
Then for to seche Flemmyssh by the see stronde,
Wherethourh moni Frenshe wyf wryngeth hire honde,
        Ant singeth, weylaway.[21]

There is no pity here, perhaps, but there is humane realization of the ironies, exultation with a sigh. There is the same fusion of moods in the more familiar ballad of *Sir Patrick Spens*:

O our Scots nobles wer richt laith
    To weet their cork-heild schoone;
Bot lang owre a' the play were playd,
    Thair hats they swam aboone.[22]

We come closer here to the 'classical' notion of the irony of fate as a visitation by the gods upon one who committed that indiscretion, that initial sin, which the Greeks called *hubris*, a conscious or unconscious emulation of the deities themselves, Agamemnon's treading of the purple. In English, as in other medieval literatures, *hubris* is simplified into the formula: Pride goeth before a fall. In the Chester cycle – whose extant version may antedate Chaucer – there is a play, the *Fall of Lucifer*, which dramatically exemplifies the formula. It is not enough for Lucifer to revolt. The playwright must seat him upon God's own throne – in the temporary absence of that potentate – and make him appeal to other angels for confirmation that he becomes it as well as his Maker. Significantly, too, the seraphs who fall with him are those who, at the opening of the play, were self-consciously exulting in their brightness and beauty, in plain contrast to the sedately mystical majority who ignored themselves in contemplation of the Godhead.

If the irony of fate may be said to be dramatic irony magnified to the dimensions of the world's stage, it is equally true that dramatic irony is the irony of fate reduced to the microcosm of a single poem or play. Dramatic irony is to be taken for granted in most narrative literature, and though it is singularly absent in the *Beowulf* and in Old English literature generally, it provides the essential story interest in the sagas of Horn and of Havelok, in many incidents of the *Cursor Mundi*, in such 'thrillers' as *Gawain and the Green Knight*, and in romances like *Sir Orfeo*; and it is the stuff out of which most of the finest and simplest ballads were woven.[23] Moreover, the fashioners of Chaucer's contemporary drama were often quite 'modern' in their alertness to dramatic irony; they made, for example, a complete and strangely moving play out of the slight situation furnished in the *New Testament* when the risen Jesus talks unrecognized to travellers from Emmaus.[24]

At the other extreme of tone, but because of that much closer to the author of the *Nun's Priest's Tale*, is the fable *Of the Fox and of the Wolf*, from the reign of Edward I. Like the villain of Chaucer's mock-epic, this fox uses ambiguities to deceive Chanticleer, though here with less success. He tells the rooster, for example, that he has only 'let they hens' blood' as any good neighbour or physician would, and suggests that Chanticleer has the same sickness 'under the spleen' and needs the same doctor.[25]

It was in comedy that the dramatic ironist of medieval England felt most at home. His impress is upon that finest of English pre-Chaucerian fabliaux, *Dame Siriz, or the Weeping Bitch*. Of the brotherhood, too, is Chaucer's anonymous contemporary, the poet of the alliterative *Patience*, who accepts the Jonah story as a satiric fable upon a foolish sinner who tried to escape Jehovah, and develops its latent laughter in a manner sufficiently startling but not perhaps unfaithful to the original Hebraic conception. Jonah's relief when he has secured passage on the boat (by which he intends to elude God) is carefully played upon. 'Was never so joyful a Jew as Jonas was then'; but 'Lo!' says the poet, smacking the irony, 'the witless wretch – because he would not suffer, now has he put himself in peril all the more.' The storm's fury increases. All assemble for the lot-drawing, all except the banal 'Jonas the Jew who had joked in secret. He had flown, for fear ... down to the boat's bottom, and clung to a plank.'[26] But even there he does not escape the Lord and His Whale.

The same mixture of clowning realism and gay sarcasm sharpens the well-known combats between the Chester Noah and his music-hall wife. Another source less quoted by historians of comedy, the ballad, provides similar humours. A peculiar 'practical-joke irony' permeates such stories as the *Gay Goshawk*[27] and gives memorable form to the deceptions practised by priests and wives upon husbands or upon each other; it is an irony often underlined by *contrasti* or satirical wit combats, the medieval comic equivalent of the Greek *stichomythia*.[28] Practical-joke irony is one of the breezy charms of Robin Hood himself, that discreeter English Paul Bunyan; when the Great Outlaw captures the Sheriff of Nottingham he entertains him at a banquet furnished under the greenwood with vessels stolen from the sheriff's own table.

IRONY OF THE UNDERDOG

A great measure of the artistic satisfaction supplied by such ballads, particularly in their own times, lay in a wish-fulfilment, the imagined or actual triumph of the exploited over the traditional exploiter. In the 'political ballad' this irony of the underdog becomes the essence of the form. The pages of Thomas Wright's collections are charged with the bitterness of peasant and struggling burgher and all those not yet strong enough to strike openly. Nor is such satire confined to the stray ballad. For example, in the midst of a symbolic representation of the awful Day of Doom, the Towneley play *Juditium*, suddenly appears a page of low comedy, a lampoon of the upper classes. If monks and even friars were lumped with knights and barons it was for the reason that churchmen were also now land-owners and tax-gatherers. 'Holy chi-reche is vnder fote' is the doleful title of one song whose punning refrain concentrates the protest of the English masses against clerical exploitation: 'Once Simon was here, but now is Simony.'[29] In the four-teenth century religious satire was class satire, just because the church-had become identical with feudal rule and the most obvious compendium of the resulting social injustices.

There are, of course, numerous poems which make subrisive assault upon secular feudalism only. Such is that pungent allegory *On the King's Breaking his Confirmation of Magna Charta*, which mildly suggests that the great charter has been held too near the fire and, being of wax, has melted away.[30] But at other times the class protest speaks so broadly as to attack all learning. Under the mock-simple allegory of *Piers the Plowman's Creed*, written before Chaucer's death, lies a reproach against peasants who, by allowing themselves to be 'corrupted' with a zeal for knowledge, become priests and thereby remove themselves into the ranks of the lettered enemy.

It is easy, of course, to over-simplify the class elements in medieval irony, for not only were there satirists in both camps, feudal and bourgeois, but there were men like Langland who were not really conscious of which side they championed, while such intellectual pioneers as Wiclif were not aware of the profundity of the political issues which they raised. Moreover, internal dissensions within the classes had their own reflection in ironic literature. *Richard the Redeless*, a court man's attack upon Richard II, became of necessity also a series of guarded puns directed against other courtiers. Until the fourteenth century, too, in England skilled 'literary' satire was predominantly clerical in origin, since the clergy had almost a monopoly of learning. The major exception, the gleeman, entered the field of social satire only, as ten Brink has remarked, to denounce the gluttony and bawdry of pages, grooms, and any others who might be his professional rivals for court favour. It is natural, then, that the folk attacks on the clergy and their feudal rôle should arouse learned counter-attack. But when the cleric per se becomes ironic, it is with a different smile on the face – contemptuous rather than savage, mocking rather than snarling. Such is the *Satire of the Men of Stockton*, a burlesque account of a council which had been held by serf leaders on the eve of their attempt to force legal concessions from their local monastery. The attempt failed, much to the satisfaction of the poet.[31]

PARODY AND BURLESQUE

Such burlesques deserve independent place in any survey of irony. Like its cousin Parody, with which it is generally confused, Burlesque is a Brobdignagian variant of the satire of overstatement. Parody mocks a literary form by exaggerating its defects at the very moment it pretends a docile imitation. Of such is Beerbohm's *Christmas Garland* and Chaucer's *Sir Thopas*. The more jovial Burlesque draws laughter not from the form it affects but from the material which it pretends to consider worthy of that form. This is the spirit of the mock-heroic *Nun's Priest's Tale*. Though Chaucer may have found his finest models, for both poems, in the Latin of the goliards or the *sottes chansons* of the French, yet each was already at home on English soil. The St George of that ancient folk-piece the *Mummer's Play* is a fustian Quixote, as willing to be bought off as to fight.[32] There is a fine bourgeois 'romance of prys,' the *Turnament of Totenham*, where heavy-footed yokels engage in knightly tilt; as a prize, the reeve has offered his daughter, with a spotted sow thrown in.[33] The word *gesta* is rapidly becoming jests.

Unknightly woodcarvers, in the same century, were venting similar humour in the misericords of Bristol Cathedral, where chivalric combatants are mounted on geese and hogs.[34] Indeed, burlesque was tolerated in the holiest places of medieval Britain. Those mock-religious carnivals variously known as the feasts of the Ass, the Fool, or the Innocents were permitted to troop into the English churches as into those of the continent. In spirit and perhaps even origin these festivals extended back to the Roman Saturnalia.[35] Lords of Misrule, Abbots of Unreason, Popes of Folly were, under the amazing catholicity of the One Catholic Church, allowed to preside over macaronic parodies of the mass, to the accompaniment of ludicrous music, costume, dumb show, feasting – and even, it is said, of dicing upon the altars. Such travesties, edged with satire of clerical shortcomings, were evidently to the humour of those clerics themselves. 'It was,' says F.H. Hedge, 'the irony of the Church herself, the Nemesis of faith, religion resenting its own sanctities.'[36]

Perhaps the finest piece of comic irony before Chaucer, the *Land of Cockaygne*,[37] is a fusion of the two forms, burlesque and parody. The sustained dexterity with which the mirage of the Earthly Paradise is scaled to the lowest level of monkish desire is given added comicality by a close adaptation of the poem's form to the most pious phrases of the standard medieval vision, with its catalogue of the flowers, fruits, and birds of the standard heaven. The poem is at the same time the most devastating and the best humoured of all the attacks on monastic sensuality – perhaps because written by someone 'on the inside' of monastery walls, someone who could dream of a land where hot-roasted geese fly unaided through the sky to the platters of holy men, and where Sister Water is used only for washing or for ornament. The humour is compact of traditions which wander back to Lucian and forward to the 'Rock-Candy Mountains' of the American hobo.

IRONISTS

In all this irony there are few ironists. It is not simply that satirists wisely preferred anonymity even if it were not conferred upon them by the 'ravage of six long sad hundred years,' but that the consciousness of irony as a continued personal method, stamped with the individuality of the author, seems lacking from writers in English, as it was not lacking in the Provençal Arnaut Daniel, or in Rutebeuf. This is partly explainable by the fact that those who strove for irony consciously as for any artistic grace were likely to be scholars who wrote in Latin. So the great English names of Becket's secretary, the Ovidian John of Salisbury, of Neckham, of that saturnine Canterbury precentor Nigellus Wireker, and of Walter Map are only names to those who do not read medieval Latin. But they were undoubtedly more than that to Chaucer, and perhaps also to two or three men who preceded him in the known ranks of English ironists, to Mannyng, to John of Trevisa, and perhaps even to Wiclif. Whatever their literary models these last were conscious ironists. Another, whose name has not survived, is the author of a goliardic *Satire on the People of Kildare* (written c. 1300). Here is the shameless intrusion of the jesting 'maker,' that effervescence which provides the link with Chaucer, though this Anglo-Irishman's irony is of the boastful rather than the sly order. At the end of each racy stanza he appends a couplet in which he gazes, with unabashed delight, upon the skill of his own raillery:

> Hail to ye, brewsters, with your gallons,
> Your pottles and quarterns, all around the town:
> Your thumbs take much away, shame to your guile;
> Beware of the cucking-stool, the lake is deep and hoary.
> (Certainly he was a clerk
> Who so slyly wrote this work!)[38]

For Mannyng and Trevisa, sarcasm was a regular form of annotation, the escape of men who, though incensed by abuses, were scrupulous in dogma. So Mannyng pauses in the midst of his holy exempla for rapier thrusts at the Women and the Landlords; Trevisa amplifies his author Higden with solemn sneers at all fat begging priests. As for Wiclif, he was too earnestly the fighter to risk irony except when he had already bound his victim securely with the strong cords of denunciation. But no preacher was then more expert in the solemn anticlimax than the wily rector of Lutterworth. He concludes a painstaking examination of the inefficacy of 'letters of fraternity' sold by wandering friars with the grave deduction: 'Be siche resouns thinken many men that thes lettris mai do good for to covere mostard pottis.'[39]

The hoax of Mandeville's *Travels* is well known; as a work of irony it belongs to the department of literary fraudulency, with *The Strange Case of Mrs Veal* and the wilder adventures of Richard Halliburton. But it stands above its descendants in the impertinency of its coney-catching. Purporting to be a humble guide-book for pilgrims to Jerusalem, and opening with a sanctimonious prologue urging reverence for the Holy Land, it rapidly develops into a collection of the most impossible geographical gossip and anthropological superstition of which those times were capable, all carefully integrated and made respectable by a process of documentary lying unsurpassed till Defoe. We now know that its origins were French, but its fame and its influence were English.

Langland – or whoever wrote *Piers Plowman* – was potentially a great ironist. Any man who has the dramatic sense to cloak his teaching and his denunciation under an allegory so gigantic and yet so completely humanized as *Piers Plowman* had the poise of irony. But Langland saw too clearly the need for strenuous indignation, was too sensitive to the tempo of the times, to the swiftly succeeding rebellions of Wiclif, the peasants, the parliament, to allow his voice to be weakened with philosophic apathy or courtly mildness. Chaucer was amused by the contradictory society of his day, but Langland looked upon this same world as something infinitely worse than ever had been or would be. Neither was the clear spokesman for a class. Chaucer climbed from the vigour of the awakening burghers into the fading glory of a feudal court and never quite resolves his own dualism even by irony; Langland, though he impresses one as having been born of the people, and though he certainly spoke with their accents, did not announce or even suspect the impending advance of the artisan and trader. While the merchants and small country land-owners were opening that long parliamentary struggle which was to reach its triumphant conclusion only by the arms of Cromwell, Langland dreamed of the Christian re-establishment of early 'ideal' feudalism. While Chaucer entertained a society to which he did not fully belong and whose decadence never really infected him, Langland stood amid a labouring mass which was historically incapable of political leadership, and from it he thundered in splendour, impotently yet with perfect self-confidence.

Only rarely does he pause for direct irony, and never if his own position would be the least obscured by it. In the first seven *passus* and prologue of *Piers Plowman* there are less than a score of examples; and these are either proverbial understatements, or allegory become, for the moment, subtle and even fiercely comic. The most bitterly absurd of the latter is the confession of Covetousness. That worthy is represented as having a long rascally experience in banking and trading (forms of robbery as yet but imperfectly legalized):

> 'Dids't never repent,' quoth Repentance, 'nor restitution make?'
> 'Yes, once I was at an inn,' quoth he, 'with a heap of merchants.
> I rose when they were asleep and rifled their packs.'
> 'That was no restitution,' quoth Repentance, 'but a robber's theft.
> Thou deserves better to be hanged for this
> Than for all else that thou hast here revealed.'

Covetousness is sorry; he never went to school and so knows not this new-fangled word *restitution*:

> 'I thought rifling was "restitution"' quoth he, 'for I never studied in books,
> And I know no French, 'ifaith, except of Norfolk's farthest corner.'[40]

Chaucer, being Chaucer, had little to learn from these rare grim jests of Langland, nor can we be sure that he went to school to any one ironist, English or continental; but he could scarcely escape the influence of this long tradition of ironic speech in the language and literature of his own country. No one has rightly savoured the great ironies of the *Prologue to the Canterbury Tales* if he has not also tasted the coltish wit of Gamelyn, or the elaborately guarded assaults of the political ballad-mongers, or the *saeva indignatio* of Bromyard and Wiclif. Even the Italianate *Troilus* can be better understood if we catch echoes, behind its perfect cadences, of those mournful overtones of Fate in the *Anglo-Saxon Chronicle*, or of Hendyng's wry and slangy wisdom.

There are, of course, still more important ancestral ghosts of Chaucer's irony to be conjured from other literatures – the Latin and Italian and French worthies whose names we have been compelled to hurry over, or to leave unmentioned. There are the anecdotal elegances of

Ovid and Appolinarus Sidonus and Ekkehard IV, and of John of Brid-
lington and Jean de Hauteville; the ironies, tragic and comic, of the
Vulgate; the edged praises of Dante for his birthplace, Florence; the
subtle malices of Jean de Meun and Jean de Condé and Deschamps;
the dramatic intricacies of the French fabliaux; and the wit of that
greatest and most delightful treasury of all medieval irony, the multiple
saga of Reynard the Fox. But that is another, and still longer, story.

NOTES

1 For the reader's convenience I have modernized a number of my quotations. In two cases I have drawn from M.H. Shackford, ed. *Legends and
   Satires from Medieval Literature* (Boston, Ginn and Co. 1913) and once
   from Jessie L. Weston's *Chief Middle English Poets* (London, Harrap
   1922). Other notes refer the reader to the best printed text of the original.
2 *Of Irony, Especially in Drama* (Toronto, University of Toronto Press
   1935); see also his essay on 'Dramatic Irony' *University Magazine* (Mon-
   treal) 12 (1913) 116–34.
3 'Contention of Phillis and Flora' trans. Shackford
4 Lines 1435–6; cf. 2277.
5 Trans. from *Layamon's Brut* ed. F. Madden (London, Society of Anti-
   quaries 1847) II 334–5 (MS. Cott. Calig. A. ix)
6 Trans. Weston, 39, lines 91–2
7 Trans. Shackford
8 *Poems* ed. Joseph Hall (Oxford, Oxford University Press 1887) no. 9,
   lines 35–40
9 Ed. W.W. Skeat (Oxford, Oxford UniversityPress 1884) lines 521–33,
   245–8; cf. 135–6.
10 Trans. from *York Plays* ed. Lucy Toulmin Smith (Oxford, Oxford University Press 1885) no. 33, line 365
11 Ibid., lines 409–20 (modernized)
12 *Reliquiae Antiquae* ed. Thomas Wright and J.D. Halliwell, 2 vols (London, William Pickering 1841–3) II 73
13 'Thet coc is kene on his owune mixenne'; *The Ancren Riwle* trans. and
   ed. James Morton 140
14 *Canterbury Tales* ed. F.N. Robinson (Boston, Houghton Mifflin 1933) I
   4321. Cf. *T&C* I 740–1, IV 1585; and W.W. Skeat's *Early English Proverbs*
   (Oxford, Oxford University Press 1910) nos. 237, 153.

15 *T&C* IV 461; see *N&Q* ser. I III 368.

16 *T&C* V 1840–1; cf. Skeat *Early English Proverbs* 205.

17 See the fragment 'Al it is fantam ... ' in *Reliquiae Antiquae* ed. Wright and Halliwell, II 20.

18 Modernized from the fourteenth-century Anglo-Irish poem in F.E. Budd *A Book of Lullabies 1300–1900* (London, Scholaris Press 1930) no. 1,p. 27

19 *Beowulf* ed. Wyatt (Cambridge: Cambridge University Press 1908) lines 3167–8

20 Trans. from *Anglo-Saxon Chronicle* (Bodl. Laud 636) ed. Benjamin Thorpe (London, Rerum Britannicorum medii aevi Scriptores 1861) I 354

21 Joseph Ritson *Ancient Songs and Ballads* 2 vols (London, n.p. 1829) I 44, lines 1–8

22 *Child's English and Scottish Popular Ballads* ed. Helen C. Sargent and George L. Kittredge (Boston, Houghton Mifflin 1904) 104, no. A. 8. The date of composition may be as early as the thirteenth century.

23 Germaine Dempster's scholarly, if limited, study of *Dramatic Irony in Chaucer* (Stanford, Stanford University Press 1932) has revealed some less familiar models which lay close to Chaucer's hand, in his own language as well as in the French.

24 'The Sledman's Play' *York Plays* ed. Toulmin Smith 426

25 *Reliquiae Antiquae* ed. Wright and Halliwell, II 273

26 Modernized from *Early English Alliterative Poems* ed. Richard Morris (London, EETS 1872) 89; lines 109–14, 182ff.

27 See Winnifred Smith 'Elements of Comedy in English and Scottish Ballads' (Vassar Medieval Studies 1923) 104–7.

28 Cf. the ironic wit in *The Owl and the Nightingale* (Mätzner *Mittelenglische ... Literaturproben*) ed. 2, p. 125, esp. lines 1177ff.

29 *Old English Miscellany* ed. Richard Morris (London, Early English Text Society 1872) 89

30 *Political Songs* ed. Thomas Wright (London. Camden Society 1839) I 253

31 *Anecdota Literaria* ed. Thomas Wright (London, J.R.S. Smith 1844) 49–51

32 See lines 46–9 of the normalized text, in E.K. Chambers *The English Folk-Play* (Oxford, Clarendon Press 1933) 7.

33 See *Cambridge History of English Literature* ed. A. Ward and A.R. Waller, 14 vols. (Cambridge, Cambridge University Press) I 366.

34 See F. Bond *Wood-Carvings in English Churches* (London, Oxford University Press 1910) I 159–60.

35 See Thomas Wright *History of Caricature and Grotesque in Literature and Art* (1865, rpt F. Unger 1968) 207.

36 'Irony' *Atheism in Philosophy* ... 1884, 327
37 Karl Goldbeck and Eduard Mätzner *Altenglische Sprachproben* (Berlin, Weidmannsche 1867) 1 147ff. For the classical 'cockaygne' tradition see *Transactions of the American Philological Association* XLI (1910) 175; and C. Lenient *La Satire en France au Moyen Age* (Paris, Hachette 1893) 92.
38 Modernized from *Reliquiae Antiquae* ed. Wright and Halliwell, II 176
39 *Select English Works* ed. T. Arnold, 3 vols. (Oxford, Oxford University Press 1869–71) 1 381
40 Modernized from Skeat's edition, Text B: V 232–9. Cf. the last line with Chaucer's famous remark on the French of his Prioress.

Is Chaucer's Irony
a Modern Discovery?

'℡HE GAY, incomparably felicitous irony of Chaucer is as precious to us today as any other mark of his genius, yet between his generation and our own it lay unregarded, a quality which there were few to know, and very few to love.'[1] This recent picturing of Chaucer's irony as a violet only now uncovered from the moss of the centuries deserves to be scrutinized, if only in fairness to our ancestors, and all the more as it seems to represent an opinion widely held. In one of the latest monographs on Chaucer, Professor Patch writes: 'In the long history of the appreciation of Chaucer's poetry, as it is spread before us in Miss Spurgeon's *Five Hundred Years of Chaucer Criticism and Allusion*, one may see that understanding of his humour has been slow in developing. "It is not ... until well on in the nineteenth century," Miss Spurgeon observes, "not indeed until Leigh Hunt wrote on it in 1846, that Chaucer's humour seems to have met with any adequate recognition." '[2] Now it is possible, though unprovable, that we of this century recognize more of Chaucer's jokes – more, perhaps, than he made – but it is certain that the invaluable roster of references which Miss Spurgeon herself collected, and those which others have since supplied, offer abundant proof that not only Chaucer's broad mirth but his slyest innuendo never at any time dwelt among the untrodden ways of criticism.

Since it is the ironic flavour of Chaucer's humor which is felt to be the modern discovery I shall concern myself here mainly with the history of its recognition. In doing so I shall keep in mind that both 'irony' and 'humour' did not develop their complex present-day meanings until at least the mid-eighteenth century. When Miss Spurgeon stated that Thomas Warton was the first to associate the poet's art

with our idea of humour she was writing not about Chaucer appreciation, but about semantics.[3] 'Irony,' even in the narrower senses of
verbal ambiguity and understatement, is a rare pedant's term in English
until the Victorian age. The NED lists one appearance as early as 1502
but the word is not popular until after the writings of Bishop Thirlwall.
With reference to Chaucer I find no earlier use of the term than in a
note of Thomas Gray's, about 1760, where, ironically enough, the immediate application is to Lydgate.[4] Nevertheless, long before Gray,
readers were smiling with Chaucer at the incongruities of his pilgrims,
exploring his hidden satire, and experiencing the curious grim elation
that comes from the witnessing of an irony of circumstance.

Among Chaucer's contemporaries or immediate successors, the il-
luminator of the Ellesmere manuscript, at least, was aware of the poet's
humour. Mr Edward F. Piper, in his study of the illustrations to the
Prologue, stresses the artist's appreciation of 'Chaucer's use of costume
to express personality,' of his realism and his comic drama. As if to
ensure that readers should not be misled by the quietness of Chaucer's
reference to the monk's jingling bridle, the embellisher hangs on the
monk's horse a profusion of bells and bosses from ears to crupper. The
cook's mormal is a major wound, and both the miller's thumbs are
gilded.[5] One might add to Mr Piper's observations that the most prom-
inent object in the physician's miniature is not simply a 'green flask ...
introduced ... as a professional object' (p. 248) but a 'hippocras' shining
with *gold cordial*; the pardoner is made distinctly effeminate, by an
exaggeration of his vernicle and his locks, and his 'male' is so big it
hangs like a feed-bag around his horse's neck; the monk's hounds are
large, sleek, and expensively adorned; and the prioress' forehead is
almost grotesquely broad, and her red beads very conspicuous – though
curiously the brooch is missing.[6] Having in mind the limitations of
manuscript illumination, one is inclined to credit the illustrator with
the determination to see that Chaucer's subtleties were properly appreciated. In one instance it may even be that he has caught a joke we
have all since missed. He drew the shipman's beard as nothing more
than a small drooping 'ounce.' Is it possible that the line so often quoted
simply for its picturesqueness, 'With many a tempest hadde his berd
been shake,' carries as well the jest that the whiskers of Peter Rys-
shenden, or whoever he was, looked as wispy as if the North Sea gales
had blown most of them away?[7]

Fifteenth-century allusions tend, it is true, to present a solemn Chaucer, a learned and moral rhetorician. It is not certain, however, that

Lydgate 'ascribed most qualities to Chaucer except imagination and humour' (Spurgeon xciv). When, in the Prologue to his *Seige of Thebes*, Lydgate spoke of the 'crafty writinge of his sawes swete' and his 'Sugrid mouthe,' he may have been thinking of Chaucer's irony as well as of his polished artistry, and certainly, in the same poem, Lydgate, who was more than Ritson's 'drivelling monk,' contrives a very fair resurrection of Harry Bailly, including his chaffing humour.[8] In his *Bycorne and Chichevache*, too, he refers appreciatively to the Wife of Bath and makes good use of the ironical envoy to the *Clerk's Tale*. Like Lydgate was the author of the *Tale of Beryn*; scarcely a humorist in his own right, he yet missed few of the subtleties of comic characterization in the *General Prologue*.[9]

Among the Scottish Chaucerians, Dunbar was certainly influenced by the robust humour of the Wife of Bath, and Henryson, however heavily he approached the story of Criseyde, nevertheless owed something to the anthropomorphic laughter of the *Nun's Priest's Tale* for his *Fables* and as Miss Eleanor Hammond has phrased it, generally reflected a 'quiet amused penetration' which took 'something of its form and pressure from Chaucer.'[10]

As for the more elaborate ironies, we should remember that John Shirley, long before Professor Braddy, suspected satiric allegories in some of Chaucer's earlier poems, and would appear to have been recording traditions which went back to Chaucer's own day.[11] It is also possible to deduce, from the numerous marginalia in Chaucer manuscript and incunabula, that many of Chaucer's early readers were especially attracted to his humour. A great many, perhaps most, of the *nota bene*'s, and other marks of emphasis occur opposite the witty proverbs of Pandarus or the Wife of Bath, and a number are plainly there to call attention to ironies, as when the friar in the *Summoner's Tale* protests 'But that I nolde no beest for me were deed.'[12] For the sixteenth century Miss Spurgeon herself presented sufficient examples to contradict her own conclusions. Hawes detected that, however moral Chaucer might be, he often taught through satire 'for he was expert/ In eloquent terms subtyll and couert,' and Hawes distinguished between sententious tales and those which were simply 'glade and mery.'[13] Even the tough Skelton delighted in such a nice touch as Thopas' 'semely nose' and borrowed it to affix to a flyting rival.[14] That the satires of Douglas and Lyndesay, for all their crudeness, are still in part entertaining is a testimony to the pervasive influence of Chaucer's humour. The author of *The Pilgryms Tale* (ante 1540) quotes with obvious relish one of the Wife of Bath's most disarming ironies, the opening lines of her story.[15] And all this is a generation before the first recognition, according to Miss Spurgeon, of anything even 'pleasant, lively, amusing' in Chaucer (I xcvi).

Leland, who has been regularly listed with the dullards who saw in Chaucer only the crude theological reformer (Spurgeon xx), was actually the first recorded critic who wrote specifically of the characteristically masked and playful quality of Chaucer's satire. Recounting the story that Chaucer lived in France during the last years of Richard's reign, Leland remarked: 'tum praeterea eadem opera omnes veneres, lepores, delicias sales, ac postremo gratias linguae *Gallicae* tam alte coimbibisse, quam cuiquam vix credibile.'[16] Two hundred years before Warton, at least one critic spoke of Chaucer's wit in terms of delicacy, lightsome saltiness, and *l'esprit gaulois*.

From the Elizabethans Miss Spurgeon withheld any deeper understanding of Chaucer's temperament than that he was 'lively' and 'amusing'. Actually many of them delighted not only in recalling Chaucerian examples of what Puttenham called 'the dry mock'[17] but also in analysing the essentially ironic flavour of Chaucer's mature work. They thought of him as 'a right Wiclevian,' it is true (and so should we if we believed he had written *The Plowman's Tale*), but as a Wiclifite who, like Erasmus, was compelled by the times to conceal his criticism in disarming pleasantries and cautious ambiguities. Foxe is typical:

vnder shadowes couertly, as vnder a visoure, he suborneth truth, in such sorte, as both priuely she may profite the godly-minded, and yet not be espyed of the craftye aduersarie: And therefore the Byshops, belike, takyng hys workes but for iestes and toyes, in condemnying other bookes, yet permitted his bookes to be read.[18]

Reginald Scot, similarly, describes Chaucer as, in the opening of the *Wife of Bath's Tale*, deriding clerical folly 'as the time would suffer him.'[19] The Elizabethan view is most fully stated by William Webbe:

He by his delightsome vayne, so gulled the eares of men with his deuises, that ... without controllment, myght hee gyrde at the vices and abuses of all states, and gawle with very sharp and eger inuentions, which he did so learnedly and pleasantly, that none therefore would call him into question. For such was his bolde spyrit, that what enormities he saw in any he would not spare to pay them home, eyther in playne words, or els in some prety and pleasant couert, that the simplest might espy him.[20]

We today would be more inclined to apply such a description to Swift than to Chaucer, but Webbe's insistence that Chaucer's ironic method had a critical motive is implicit in much recent criticism[21] and has quite as much textual and historical evidence to support it as the popular Victorian interpretation of Chaucer's irony as the reflection of a philosophic aloofness. It is partly because the latter view tends to persist as a tradition that the Elizabethan critics have been slighted.

We are likewise unduly patronizing towards the seventeenth-century commentators. It is not true that they did not recognize the 'lightness and delicacy' of Chaucer's humour.[22] Though Chaucer is now, said Edward Phillips in 1675, to many simply 'not unpleasing for his facetious way, which joyn'd with his old *English* intertains them with a kind of Drollery,' yet he is still 'by some few admir'd for his real worth.'[23] And there were many more in the century than Phillips probably knew of, who laughed with Chaucer rather than at him and continued to delight in that strange mixture of insouciance and seriousness which the Elizabethans had found in him. Just before the century's beginning Speght had written: 'In the Tales is shewed the state of the Church, the Court, and Countrey; with such Art and cunning, that although none could denie himselfe to be touched, yet none durst complaine that he was wronged.'[24] In his 1602 edition Speght introduced marginal 'hands' pointing to specific 'touches' as well as to proverbs admired by the times.[25] John Davies, in his *Microcosmos*, similarly spoke of Chaucer as loving 'to *Iest* ... in earnest,'[26] and Thomas Fuller conceives of him as 'so *tickling* Religious-Orders with his *tales*, and yet so *pinching* them with his *truths*, that Friers in reading his books, know not how to dispose their faces betwixt *crying* and *laughing*.'[27] In a 'Historiola de nostro Chaucero' written probably as early as 1687 but first published in the 1740 edition of Cave's *Scriptorum Ecclesiasticorum Historia Litteraria*, Henry Wharton (one of the really learned scholars of the Restoration) said of Chaucer that 'primus enim omnium Linguae nostrati sordes exussit, *nitorem* intulit, & largâ vocum molliorum aliundè invectarum supellectile ditavit ... Hinc graviores Ecclesiæ Romanæ superstitiones & errores acerbè saepiùs *vellicat*; corruptam *ineptissimis commentis* Disciplinam Ecclesiasticam luget' (my emphasis).[28]

Moreover, the comments of the century record continued appreciation of specific nuances. Ben Jonson understood and adapted Chaucer's jokes about the Prioress' French and the old friendship between doctors and apothecaries,[29] and as the century continues, such allusions become, together with references to the over-busy lawyer and the physician's 'gold in cordial,' clichés of the humorists.[30] That bland glutton and merry gloser of texts, the friar of the *Summoner's Tale*, was naturally a favourite with the religious disputants. The great Wentworth made use of him, and the precocious Cambridge rector, Henry Foulis.[31] In 1643 an anonymous Roundhead exclaimed, 'This is like old *Chaucers* tale of a Fryar, whose belly was his god, he would feed upon the sweetest, Mutton, Goose and Pig, but a pitifull man! he would have no creature killed for him, not he.'[32] The Cavaliers read their Chaucer too and dressed themselves in the feathers of his wit. 'I. Chaucer junior' lampooned a dull Puritan versifier with a mock-biography partly composed of some of the best shafts from the *Prologue*:

A Clerke of Oxenford he was tho,
That vnto Logicke had long ygoe ...
Now is it not of God a ful fayre grace,
That such a lewde mans wit shall pace
The wisdome of an heape of learned men ... [33]

That industrious squire of Westmoreland, Richard Brathwait, had early in the century written and in 1665 published some *Comments upon Chaucer's Tales of the Miller & the Wife of Bath* which, though mainly paraphrases of the obvious, include a number of enthusiastic notations upon ironies that he is anxious other readers should enjoy. A typical example is his suggestion that Chaucer, in picturing the leisurely toilet of Nicholas, 'glauncheth wittily at the delicacy or effeminate privacy of this Scholer,' and Brathwait draws a moral which, if pat for the Protestants, might yet have been present in Chaucer's mind: '[By inference he] glanceth at the pride of the Clergy ... For if a poor Parish-Clerk must be curiously dressed, as to have his hair curled ... what may we think of those, whose Revenues were greater ...?'[34]

There were readers too who savoured the structural ironies of Chaucer's stories. Bryan Twyne, the Oxford antiquarian, succinctly if ungrammatically described the *Pardoner's Tale* as 'of 3 drunken gluttons y^t went about to kill death, and was killed by it,'[35] and Samuel Butler planned to adapt the central contretemps of the *Shipman's Tale* by drawing the character of a banker who 'borrows the King's money of his officers to break his laws with, as Chaucer's fryar borrow'd money of a merchant to corrupt his wife with, and makes him pay for his own injury.[36] Thomas Nash enjoyed the ironies of plot in the tales of the summoner, merchant, nun's priest, manciple, and others,[37] and some appreciation of the use of allegory for humorous effect, in the *House of Fame*, was shown by Bishop John Hacket, who analysed the third book to reveal how by 'pretty Fiction' and 'pleasant Art' Chaucer made fun of 'the Giddiness of Common Talk.'[38]

Some of our misconceptions about seventeenth-century criticism may spring from too ready an assumption that Dryden's preface to his *Fables* represents the 'first ... careful criticism of Chaucer'[39] or even the most appreciative comment of his period. It is true that here and elsewhere Dryden left a memorable testimony to Chaucer's healthy vigour and breadth of vision (finding in Chaucer many of the qualities which Professor Patch feels to be characteristic of his humour); it is also true that in sensitivity to the characteristic irony of Chaucer, as to his melody and his tenderness, Dryden was singularly behind his own and Elizabethan times. It was Dryden, certainly, who said of Chaucer that 'As he knew what to say, so he knows also when to leave off,' but it was also Dryden who, a few pages later, added that 'Sometimes ... he runs riot, like *Ovid*, and knows not when he has said enough.'[40] Dryden could not have been Dryden without being a lover of irony, of 'fine Raillery ... the nicest and most delicate touches of satire':

How easie it is to call Rogue and Villain, and that wittily? But how hard to make a Man appear a Fool, a Blockhead, or a Knave without using any of those opprobrious terms? To spare the grossness of the Names, and to do the thing yet more severely, is to draw a full Face, and to make the Nose and Cheeks stand out, and yet not to employ any depths of shadowing.[41]

But these remarks were not made apropros of Chaucer, or even of the Romans (though they appeared in his dedication to the Juvenal translations), but in flattery of the lordly nonentity whose patronage he sought. 'This [Raillery], my Lord, is your particular Talent, to which even Juvenal could not arrive.' When Dryden sought a classical affinity for Chaucer he found him not in Horace, who 'barely grins ... and, as *Scaliger* says, only shews his white teeth,' but in the rough pioneer, Ennius, or the 'well-natur'd' but garrulous Ovid.[42] Far more than other seventeenth-century commentators Dryden coarsened or oversimplified Chaucer's humour. The *Troilus*, for example, is primarily 'a Satyr on the Inconstancy of Women,'[43] and the fabliaux are simply 'gross ribaldry.' This insensibility naturally interfered with the accuracy of his modernizations. Thomas Warton pointed out how Dryden entirely misrepresented an image in the *Knight's Tale* and 'turned it to a satire on the church.' Where Chaucer had written

Contek, with blody knyf and sharp manace,
Al ful of chirkyng was that sory place,

Dryden translated,

Contest with sharpen'd knives in cloysters drawn,
And all with blood bespread the holy lawn.[44]

Significantly, those lines in the tale which are most likely to be touched with irony were by Dryden either obscured or entirely omitted.[45]

Dryden's failure to catch the delicacies of Chaucer's humour tended temporarily to lower the quality of Chaucer criticism in the early part of the next century, for Dryden's remarks were taken to be the final word by the scribbling 'transmogrifiers.' To many Chaucer was nothing more than 'our *English Ennius*,'[46] noted for 'Crotchets, Puns, and merry Stories.'[47] and 'leering Glee.'[48] As Miss Spurgeon herself observed, however (liii), the neo-classicists had already begun to apply to Chaucer the word *wit* apparently with its modern connotation of an ingenious and polished joker. What has not been sufficiently stressed is that a far broader appreciation of Chaucer's humour appeared in the biographical preface to the Urry edition of 1721. Written by John Dart, another antiquarian curate, it is dismissed by the *Dictionary of National Biography* as a 'ridiculous memoir,' and in part it is; yet in respect to Chaucer's humour, Dart fused the best judgement of his own time, that Chaucer was 'a pleasant Wit' who wrote with 'gay humour' and 'gallantry,' with the Elizabethan interpretation of him as a subtle and cautious satirist. 'He was a true Master of Satyr ... not incapable of writing in the Horation way,' but

the Persons levelled against, and the Crimes exposed, would not allow of the severe Scourge *Juvenal* made use of, nor was there such a variety of Follies as *Horace* facetiously exploded: Not but that *Chaucer* had a Scene of Vice in the Court of that time, capable of supplying him with matter sufficient for the sharpest strokes of Satyr: but he was wise enough not to exasperate a Court by which he was supported, and in which he had interest little enough to skreen himself from malice without provoking it.[49]

After Urry's edition there is a steady growth in appreciation of Chaucer's 'archness,'[50] his 'quaint Festivity,'[51] and the'cunning hand'[52] of his satire. Addison, it is true, cannot be said to have perceived the literary kinship between himself and Chaucer, but Pope was more appreciative than is generally thought. Like Dryden, of course, his modernizations were patronizing in spirit and in general blunted the delicacies of Chaucer's humour, but at least the selections he 'polished' were chosen to display the very finest examples of Chaucer's satiric art. Though his 'January and May' played havoc with the ironic framework of the *Merchant's Tale*, it is a remarkable example of Pope's precocious juvenilia in its recreation of this, the most sardonic and 'contrived' of Chaucer's works. In the course of his rendition, too, Pope can often be seen carefully preserving some of Chaucer's most characteristic and adroit turns of phrase.[53] Later (1714), he made a free and fluent adaptation of the third book of the *House of Fame*, to which he had been attracted by Chaucer's neat allegory of the ironies of Fame's rewards. His *Wife of Bath's Prologue*, however, failed to catch some of the nicer ambiguities,[54] and Dame Allison is 'transmogrified' into a mere flippant apologist for her sex. Pope retained an interest in Chaucer throughout his life, and on his deathbed, in one of his last letters, he could still make a spontaneous and amusing adaptation of an apparent whimsy in the *Knight's Tale*.[55]

Further evidence of neo-classical interest in Chaucer's humour could be drawn from the several other modernizations of the time, and the translations of the latter into French after the mid-century. Here there is space only to mention a contributor to the 1741 *Tales of Chaucer modernized by several hands*, George Ogle. Himself a translator and imitator of Horace, he boldly ranked Chaucer with the latter, and in an earlier essay had made copious notes on most of those 'strokes' in the *Prologue* whose understanding is assumed so readily to be a modern discovery.[56]

In the light of all these examples, most of which Miss Spurgeon herself assembled, it is difficult to agree with her that a new age in Chaucer criticism began slowly to dawn with Thomas Warton's remark, in 1754, that Chaucer 'was the first who gave the English nation, in its own language, an idea of HUMOUR.'[57] Even if Warton meant more by the word than had that judicious compiler Mrs Elizabeth Cooper, in 1737, when she said that Chaucer 'blended the acutest Raillery, with the most insinuating Humour,'[58] what was happening was simply that a single word was now capable of expressing the connotations of a group, of 'wit,' 'raillery,' 'archness,' 'drollery,' 'glee,' 'tickling,' and 'pinching,' which earlier critics had already gathered to describe Chaucer's preference for passages which convey satire through irony. Later, in his *History of English Poetry*, he ranges more widely, though even his appreciative analysis of *Sir Thopas* and his comparison of its spirit to that of Don Quixote was an extension of what Bishop Hurd had already written: 'I call it a *manifest banter* ... so managed as with infinite humour to expose the leading impertinences of chivalry, and their impertinencies only.'[59]

Thomas Warton's very real claim to respect as a Chaucer critic does not lie in his discovery of Chaucer's humour, for that had never been undiscovered, but in his application of the method of historical approach to extend the general boundaries of Chaucer appreciation. By quotations from Wiclif and from priory records, for example, he uncovered hitherto unguessed nuances in the Monk's portrait, and by parallels from Langland he made clear not only the stock medieval satire of friars but the 'new strokes of humour' which Chaucer had added.[60] His superior knowledge of medieval literature made him a pioneer in perceiving the nice balance Chaucer seems to have maintained between imitation and parody, as of the medieval rhetoricians and romancers and pedants, and the curious 'mixture of sublime and comic ideas' in Chaucer's Italianate stories.[61]

There remains to be instanced, for those who assume that we moderns rescued Chaucer's ambiguities from oblivion, Thomas Tyrwhitt's edition of the *Canterbury Tales* (1775). This is a work which deserves to rank with the labours of Child among the products of pre-romantic antiquarianism. Here it is only pertinent to recall that Tyrwhitt, both in preface and in notes, regarded Chaucer's genius as essentially one of comedy (observing that Chaucer followed his sources much more closely in the serious tales), and that he confirmed and multiplied by independent research many of the 'flings' and 'ridicules' suspected by Warton. He was especially responsive to the dramatic subtleties of the Links in the *Canterbury Tales*, and was the first critic, so far as I know, to apply the favourite modern word *irony* to a Chaucer passage.[62]

It must be admitted that there is one notable difference between pre-nineteenth-century interpretation of Chaucer's humour and the critique of Leigh Hunt (which Miss Spurgeon considered the first 'adequate recognition' of Chaucer's humour). Hunt, who began to formulate his opinions of Chaucer in a preface to his 'Story of Rimini' in 1816,[63] tacitly abandoned the view that Chaucer's irony was a protective colouring for social and religious satire and substituted the belief that Chaucer was essentially non-partisan, laughing because tolerant, 'tranquil,' given by nature to 'fair play' and 'bonhomie.'[64] In a later paper I hope to show that Hunt's views, which came to dominate Victorian criticism and much still of ours, were not based on a widening knowledge of Chaucer and his times but were primarily a reflection of German romantic criticism, and in particular of the cult of *Romantische Ironie*. Here there is only space to remark that, when we consider the evidence which Manly and many others[65] have uncovered to show the sharp topical satire underneath so many of Chaucer's apparently casual details, we should not be quick to assume that the Elizabethans understood their Chaucer less than did the Victorians.

It would be blind to deny, of course, that there is in Chaucer also 'insight, sympathy and tender seriousness, all brought into play upon the ever-present sense of the incongruous' but it is easy also to trace the recognition of this 'deeper and more delicate quality alone deserving the name of "humour"'[66] in the comments from Leland down. The earlier critics differed only in feeling that Chaucer could be tough as well as 'tender.' They did not suffer the Victorian compulsion to picture Chaucer as 'a second Shakespeare ... a Human Catholic ... who never adds his voice to the mere party cries of his day, whose sound taste shrank from every form of caricature.'[67] It was not entirely unfair of Lounsbury and Miss Spurgeon to say that the Elizabethans found morality in Chaucer, and the seventeenth century found bawdiness, because they sought for these things; but it may not be entirely unfair also to suggest that the Victorians found a peculiar kind of innocuous impartiality and aloofness in Chaucer because they, in turn, sought for those things. What is certain is that the essential irony of Chaucer, the 'subtle, shifting, delicate and all-pervading humour' which was the 'distinguishing quality of [his] mind,'[68] was, far from being unrecognized, never forgotten. Chaucer's earlier critics did not use our terms; but they knew when someone had 'pulled a fynche' and they responded as warmly as we do to a man who could

> write in such a maner wise
> Which may be wisdom to the wise
> And pley to hem that lust to pleye.[69]

NOTES

1 David Worcester *The Art of Satire* (Cambridge, Mass., Harvard University Press 1940) 95

2 *On Rereading Chaucer* (Cambridge, Mass., Harvard University Press 1939) 5

3 Caroline F.E. Spurgeon *Five Hundred Years of Chaucer Criticism and Allusion 1357–1900* (Cambridge, Cambridge University Press 1925) 1 cxxxix; Warton *Observations on the Faerie Queene of Spenser* (London 1754) 228. For the history of the word *irony* see G.G. Sedgewick *Of Irony, Especially in Drama* (Toronto: University of Toronto Press 1935) ch.1. The basis of Spurgeon's generalizations about this phase of Chaucer appreciation may be traced in T.R. Lounsbury *Studies in Chaucer* (New York, Harper 1892) III ch. 7.

4 Thomas Gray 'Metrum. Some Remarks on the Poems of John Lydgate' dated by Spurgeon 1760–61, first published in *Works* ed. T.J. Mathias (London, Shakespeare Press 1814) II 70ff: 'Lydgate seems to have been by nature of a more serious and melancholy turn of mind than Chaucer; yet one here and there meets with a stroke of satire and irony which does not want humour ...'

5 'The Miniatures of the Ellesmere Chaucer' *PQ* 3 (1924) 241–56

6 The Ellesmere Chaucer, B.M. MS Facs. 158, vol. I 137 II 142, 73, 152

7 Ibid. II 147; *CT* I 406 F.N. Robinson *Chaucer's Complete Works* (Boston, Houghton-Mifflin 1933)

8 Ed. Erdmann *EETS* e.s. 108 (1911) lines 57, 52

9 His knight is more of an ironist than Chaucer's; see ed. Furnivall *EETS* e.s. 105 (1909) lines 263–6. For an appreciative analysis of the Chaucerian elements, see E.J. Bashe 'The Prologue of *The Tale of Beryn PQ* 12 (1933) 1–16.

10 *English Verse Between Chaucer and Surrey* (Durham, Duke University Press 1927) 25

11 See Robinson *Chaucer's Complete Works* 971b.

12 There is a mark opposite this line (*CT* III 1842), in old ink, in a Rylands copy, 13880, of Speght's edition of Chaucer (Islip 1598), fol. 41. The marginalia are ascribed to William Trone. Especially interesting for its marginalia is a B.M. copy of William Thynne's edition (1532), with a MS date 1540, in the same hand, on the title-page (B.M. 644.m.2). See also below, note 25.

13 See extract from 'Example of Vertu' (1504) in Spurgeon *Five Hundred Years* and *Passetyme of Pleasure* (1506) ed. Mead *EETS* o.s. 173 (1928) line 1330; cp. Spurgeon xciv.

14 'Skelton Lauriate Defend Agenst M. Garnesche Challenger, et Cetera' (1510); John Skelton *Works* ed. Dyce (London, Rodd 1843) I 117, lines 39–40; cp. *CT* VII 729.

15 Francis Thynne *Animadversions upon Speght's First (1598) Edition of Chaucer's Workes* (1599) ed. G.H. Kingsley *EETS* o.s. 9 (1865), rev. ed. Frederick J. Furnivall (1875) 2–13, app. I, p. 79, line 93ff., and cp. *CT* III 857–81.

16 *Commentarii de Scriptoribus Britannicis* (c. 1545), first printed in Hall's edition (Oxford 1709) 420

17 E.g., (1) John Ferne *Blazon of Gentrie* (1586) refers to 'purchase being better than rentes,' recorded by F.B. Williams, Jr 'Unnoted Chaucer Allusions 1550–1650' *PQ* 16 (1937) 68; (2) Unknown (c. 1590) refers to Prioress's French, recorded Williams, ibid. 69; (3) George Gascoigne *Posies* 2nd ed. (London, Smith 1575), sign. Eiiij (flippant allusion to Criseyde's doubtful virginity, and Lollius); (4) Gabriel Harvey *Marginalia* ed. Moore Smith (Stratford, Shakespeare Head 1913) app. II, p. 228, marginalium beside *CYT* in a first edition of Speght's Chaucer: 'Two notable discourses of cunning withowt effect' – an admirable summary of the essential structural ironies of the tale. See ibid. 228 for a similar remark of the *MancT*.

18 John Foxe *Ecclesiasticall History Contaynyng the Actes & Monumentes ...* 2nd ed. (London, Daye 1570) II 965

19 *Discouerie of Witchcraft* (London, Brome 1584) bk. 4, ch. 12, p. 88. Cp. Thomas Lodge: 'Chaucer in pleasant vain can rebuke sin vncontrold, & though he be lauish in the letter, his sence is serious'; 'Reply to Stephen Gosson's Schoole of Abuse' (1579) *Works* ed. E. Gosse (Glasgow, Hunterian Club 1883) I 15.

20 *A Discourse of English Poetrie* (1586) Arber Reprint (Westminster, Constable 1895) 32

21 E.g., in the criticism of J.M. Manly, Edith Rickert, A. Brandl, H.B. Hinckley, and G.K. Chesterton. It is explicit in the following studies: G.R. Stewart 'The Moral Chaucer' *Essays in Criticism, UCPES* I (1929) 92 seq.; Fritz Krog *Studien zur Chaucer und Langland* Angl. Forsch. (Heidelberg 1928); G. Lange 'Geoffrey Chaucer als Hof- und Gelegensheitdichter' *Archiv* 158 (1930) 36–54.

22 See Spurgeon *Five Hundred Years* liii–liv and Lounsbury *Studies in Chaucer* III 238.

23 *Theatrum Poetarum* (London, Smith n.d., rpt. New York, George Olms. 1976) 'prefatory Discourse' sign. **2b

24 Thomas Speght *The Works of ... Geffrey Chaucer ...* (1598). I quote from

the second edition (London, Islip 1602), 'The Argument to the Prologues' sign. A. ii.

25 E.g., Speght, fols. 35, 39. See L.B. Wright 'William Painter and the Vogue of Chaucer as a Moral Teacher' *MP* 31 (1934) 166. Wright shows that Painter, in *Chaucer New Painted* (c. 1623), used Chaucer's reputation as a quipster to sell a haphazard collection of wisesaws.

26 In 1603. Noted by R.P. Bond, J.W. Bowyer, etc.: 'A Collection of Chaucer Allusions' *SP* 28 (1931) 483.

27 *Church-History of Britain* (London, Williams 1655) bk. IV, p. 152. Fuller himself used the phrase 'iest-earnest' to describe an irony; see ibid 'Note to the Reader.'

28 William Cave *Scriptorum Ecclesiasticorum Historia Litteraria* 3rd ed. (Oxford 1740) II, app., 13–14. The 'Historiola' is here ascribed to Archbishop Tenison, but for authorship and date see Spurgeon *Five Hundred Years* I 261, III iv A 78–80, and *DNB* 'Henry Wharton'.

29 *The New Inne* (London, Harper 1631) (acted 1629) act II, sc. ii; 'The Magnetick Lady' (acted 1632) III iv, *Workes* (London, Meighen 1640) II, sign. E2b. Gifford, in his 1875 edition of Jonson, commenting on the latter passage remarks that 'Jonson seems to have had Chaucer at his finger's end' (Gifford VI 60).

30 For men who 'semed bisier' than they were see (1) Jonson 'Loves Welcome at Bolsover' (acted 1634) *Workes* II 282, sign. PP (ed. Gifford-Cunningham III 221) – first recorded by T.S. Graves 'Some Chaucer Allusions (1561–1700)' *SP* 20 (1923) 472; (2) Wentworth's letter to Coke, 14 December 1635, printed in Thomas Wentworth (Earl of Strafforde) *Letters and Dispatches* ed. W. Knowler (London, Bowyer 1740) I 497; (3) Richard Flecknoe (1653) – see Spurgeon III iv 72.

31 Wentworth, ibid. II 145; Foulis *The History of ... our Pretended Saints* (1662) 80, 99 recorded by B. Harris 'Some Seventeenth-century Chaucer Allusions' *PQ* 18 (1939) 399. See also ibid. 402 for a similar reference by Henry Care (1682) and 400 for an adaptation by Foulis of Chaucer's lines about the dieting doctor.

32 'Powers to be Resisted: or A Dialogue ... (London, Overton) 39–40; see B.M. Collection of Pamphlets no. 136. Milton quoted the lines about the Friar's 'sweet' hearing of confession (*CT* I 221–3) in *Of Reformation Touching Church-Discipline* (1641); see *Works* ed. William Hale 35–6.

33 Recorded by Louis B. Wright 'A "Character" from Chaucer in a Seventeenth Century Satire' *MLN* 44 (1929) 365–6

34 (London 1665) 13 (*CT* I 3312–24). For date of writing see Spurgeon *Five Hundred Years* xxxvi, and her introduction to the Chaucer Society re-

print of Brathwait, ser. 2, no. 33 (1901). See also his comments on CT I 3284–6 (p. 12), 3308 (p. 13), 3328–30 (p. 14), and his notation of the dramatic irony of the anticipated kiss in 3679–84 (p. 25). These passages are not displayed in Spurgeon's *Five Hundred Years*. T.R. Lounsbury dismissed Brathwait's comments as 'barren'; *Studies in Chaucer* III 90.

35 Recorded by Spurgeon, ibid. I 182, where the allusion is dated 1608–44

36 Recorded by Spurgeon, ibid. I 243, where the allusion is dated c. 1667

37 *Quaternio* ... (1633); see L.B. Wright 'William Painter' 171n.

38 *Scrinia Reserata* ... (London, Lowndes 1693) II 221–2. The date of composition is nearer 1650 (see DNB 'John Hacket').

39 Spurgeon *Five Hundred Years* introduction, xxxvii; cp. Mark van Doren *The Poetry of John Dryden* (New York, Harcourt 1920) 276ff. Over-praise of Dryden as a Chaucer critic reaches its peak in J.H. Hippisley *Chapters on Early English Literature* (London, Moxon 1837) II 42, q.v. and Lounsbury's protests, *Studies in Chaucer* III 103, 360.

40 'Preface' *Fables Ancient and Modern* (London, Tonson 1700), sign. *B2 *C2; reprinted in W.P. Ker *Essays of John Dryden* (Oxford, Clarendon Press 1926) II 258, 265

41 'Discourse Concerning ... Satire' *Satires of Juvenal and Persius* (London, Tonson 1693) xli (dedication to the Earl of Dorset); reprinted in Ker, ibid. 92–3

42 See preface to *Fables*, sign *B1 and *passim*, and 'Postcript to the Reader' *The Works of Virgil* (London, Tonson 1697) 621; Ker, ibid. II 254, 241. Even the comparison to Ovid was not new; Deschamps had made it three hundred years before; see *Œuvres* ed. Emile Saint-Hilaire (Paris, Didot 1880) II 138, line 3, 'Autre Balade.'

43 'Preface' *Troilus and Cressida* ... (London, Tonson 1679), sign. A4b; Ker, ibid. I 203

44 Warton *History of English Poetry* (London, Dodsley 1774) I 358n; Chaucer CT I 2003–4; Dryden 'Palamon and Arcite' bk. II, lines 571–2, *Works* ed. G.R. Noyes (Cambridge, Riverside Press 1909) 767

45 E.g., the characteristic Chaucerism 'With many a florin he the hewes boughte' is omitted, and the most realistic of the murals in the Temple of Mars are deprived of their hearty grotesqueness (with Sir Walter Scott's approval; see his edition of Dryden's *Works* [Edinburgh, Ballantyne 1808] I 498–9). See 'Palamon and Arcite' II 524ff. Similarly, Dryden missed the mock-heroic comedy in the NPT and excised the rooster's pedantries. See 'The Cock and the Fox' *passim*, and G. Saintsbury *Dryden* (London, Macmillan 1912) 159.

46 Samuel Cobb 'Poetae Britannici. A Poem' *British Poets* B.M. pamphl. 643.1.24.(5), p. 10, dated by Spurgeon 1700

47 See Richmond P. Bond 'Some Eighteenth Century Chaucer Allusions' *SP* 25 (1928) 319, 'A Letter from the Dead Thomas Brown to the Living Heraclitus' (London 1704).

48 See 'An Excellent Ballad. To the Tune of Chevy-Chace' by 'Dr. Darrell' in William Hone *Every-Day Book and Table Book* (London, Tegg 1831) II 298–9. The 'ballad' was written ante 1760 and first printed in 1764 (see Spurgeon *Five Hundred Years* I 417).

49 'Life of Geoffrey Chaucer' *Chaucer's Works* (London, Lintot 1721) sign. b2, e3, E3-f. Spurgeon's extract omits some of the pertinent phrases here (ibid. I 360). See also *DNB* 'John Dart.'

50 See 'The Apotheosis of Milton' *Gentleman's Magazine* 8 (1738) 233.

51 William Hawkins 'An Essay on Genius' *Dramatic and Other Poems* (Oxford, Jackson 1758) II 231. See also the comparison of Chaucer and Marot in *The Universal Museum* ... (1765) 422, recorded by Richard C. Boys 'Some Chaucer Allusions, 1705–98' *PQ* 17 (1938) 266.

52 Mark Akenside 'For a Statue of Chaucer at Woodstock' (R. Dodsley) *A Collection of Poems ... by Several Hands* (London, Hughs 1758) VI 31

53 See W. Elwin and W.J. Courthope *The Works of Alexander Pope* 10 vols (London, Murray 1871–98) I 125, esp. lines 57–8 (cp. *CT* IV 1317–18) and Gifford's comments, 123n–124n.

54 E.g., *CT* III 20, 46, 429–30; see Elwin, Whitwell, and Courthope edition, 163ff.; Austin Warren *Alexander Pope as Critic* (Princeton, Princeton University Press 1940) 125; and Lounsbury *Studies in Chaucer* III 180–1.

55 *CT* I 2835–6 (in a letter to Lord Orrery, 10 April 1744, *Works* ed. Elwin, Whitwell and Courthope VIII 518). Austin Warren, ibid. 226, feels that 'we would hardly, today, think it in the best taste to paraphrase lines from the *Knight's Tale* for humorous purpose' – a remark which reveals a profound ignorance both of the tone of the *Knight's Tale* and of good taste in dying. Someone, probably Henry Fielding, in this period adapted Chanticleer's mistranslation of *mulier est hominis confusio*; see 'A Pleasant Balade ...' by 'Dan Jeffrey Chaucer' in *The Covent Garden Journal* 50 (23 June 1752) and Spurgeon *Five Hundred Years* III iv 90–1. For Addison's pitying attitude, see his 'Account of the Greatest English Poets' *Works* ed. Richard Hurd (London, Bohn's British Classics 1854–6) I 23.

56 See his 'Letter to a Friend' prefixed to his *Gualtherus and Griselda* (London, Dodsley 1739) ix. First French appreciations of Chaucer's satire ap-

peared in the *Journal Etranger* (1755). In the May number a portion of the *PardT* was translated to exhibit Chaucer's Gallic wit. Most French translations of the period (including Voltaire's) drew from Dryden not Chaucer but at least introduced such characters as the Wife of Bath. See A.C. Hunter 'Le "Conte de la Femme de Bath" en francais au xviiie siécle' *Rev. Litt. Comp.* 9 (1929) 117–40.

57 See above, note 3, also Thomas Warton *Observations* (London, n.p. 1754) 141. Spurgeon *Five Hundred Years* cxxxix: 'After Warton, the idea began very gradually to creep in that a sense of humour was one of the qualities of [Chaucer].'

58 Preface *The Muses Library* (London, Hodges 1737) xi

59 Richard Hurd *Letters on Chivalry and Romance* (London, Millar 1762) letter xi, 107–8, and 3rd ed. (1765) 325; cp. Thomas Warton *History of English Poetry* (London, Payne 1774–81) I 433. Sir Thomas Wyatt may have anticipated Hurd in noting that *Thop* is to be taken ironically; see Lounsbury *Studies in Chaucer* III 243–4.

60 Warton, ibid. 445–6n, 164–5n, 278; see *CT* I 167, 203, III 2099ff.

61 E.g., ibid. 333–4 (*CT* I 2197–205, II 701–7, V 63ff.), 360 (*CT* I 1177, 1261, 1995–2050, 2519, 2760), 367 (general comment on *KnT*, 395 (*HF* III), 420 (*CT* VII 2923ff.), 423 (*MilT*), 426 (*CT* I 3233ff.), 433 (*Thop*), 435 (*Prol*, 436 (*PriorT*), 443 (*PhysT*), 445 (*SumT*), 452 [misnumbered] 451 (*Man of Law*).

62 (London, Payne 1775) III 284–5, note to 'tragedie,' *CT* VII 2783: 'the Host quotes the fine-sounding word with some irony'; see also Tyrwhitt III 276, where an emendation of *CT* III 1932 is rightly rejected for the original, which 'may stand, if it be understood ironically.' For his comments on Chaucer's use of sources see IV 143; his remarks are repeated without acknowledgment by Richard Morris, ed. *Poetical Works of ... Chaucer* (London, Bell 1866) I 221. See also Tyrwhitt IV 143–4 (Ch. *CT* VII 3346ff. and *Mel Prol*), 175 (*Thop Prol*), 200 (*CT* I 203), 224 (re *CT* I 2016–30), 232–3 (Arcite's soul, *CT* I 2809ff.), 240 (Absolon's dancing, *CT* I 3328).

63 Not 1846, as Miss Spurgeon wrote in the passage quoted by Patch, above; see Leigh Hunt, preface to 'The Story of Rimini' *Poetical Works* 3rd ed. (London, Ollier 1819) I.

64 Hunt, ibid. x–xi; also *Wit and Humour Selected from the English Poets* (London, Smith 1846) 76–7

65 E.g., Koch, Lowes, Curry, and Tupper. Some of the evidence for this contention is embodied in my unpublished doctoral thesis, 'Chaucer's Irony,' University of Toronto Library.

66 See Spurgeon *Five Hundred Years* cxxxix.

67 J.W. Hales 'Chaucer and Shakespeare' *Quart. Rev.* 134 (1873) 126, 123n.
68 Spurgeon *Five Hundred Years* cxxxviii
69 John Gower 'Confessio Amantis' Prologue to first version 83–5; *Complete Works* ed. G.C. Macaulay (Oxford, Oxford University Press 1899–1902) II 6

The Beginnings of
Chaucer's Irony

Ⓒ HAUCER'S POETRY is generally felt to be distinguished by 'an irony so quiet, so delicate, that many readers never notice it is there at all or mistake it for naïvete.'[1] Granting, of course, the danger that 'naïveté' may in turn be mistaken for irony, we may still suspect, with G.K. Chesterton, that Chaucer 'made a good many more jokes than his critics have ever seen.'[2] Whatever disputes continue about certain passages, no one is likely to deny today that the *Prologue to the Canterbury Tales* is rich in subtle and satiric ambiguities. A more debatable and more neglected question, and one which I wish to pose here, is: How early did the ironic spirit manifest itself in Chaucer's works?

The tendency in criticism is to assume that irony is a quality of the mature Chaucer only. One of Brusendorff's arguments for deriving the lost *Boke of the Leoun* from Deschamps rather than from Machaut is that, since the English poet evidently wrote his version in later life, he would then have been attracted to the delicate satire of Deschamps rather than to the sentimentalism of the elder Frenchman.[3] Germaine Dempster, studying the special field of dramatic irony, concludes that, though Chaucer had a 'latent taste' for the form, the taste was temporarily subdued by early readings in French allegory and Latin classics, and developed only when he came under the spell of Boccaccio.[4] Canon Looten similarly pictures Chaucer turning from an early docile following of Dante to the spirit 'ironique' and 'narquoise' of the author of *Il Filostrato*.[5] Even in such minor matters as the use of verse-tags and other clichés critics have sought to show a gradual development in Chaucer from humourless acceptance to dramatic and humorous exploitation.[6]

What is neglected by most of the commentators is the simple fact that Chaucer did not need to be graduated into an 'Italian period' to read ironic literature. I have elsewhere sought to indicate something of that fine long tradition of irony, in English medieval writings, to which Chaucer was heir.[7] Much of this might have been familiar to him from childhood. In addition, G.R. Owst has lately reminded us that the technique of indirect satire, as of direct denunciation, was weekly demonstrated in a superior fashion by the vigorous and ubiquitous preachers of fourteenth-century England.[8]

Neither should it be assumed so readily that Chaucer's first foreign models were devoid of encouragement to the ironic style and the ironic attitude. Tolerance and restraint, attitudes fundamental to irony, characterize the Roman literature of his early reading.[9] In French, as in all medieval literature, understatement (the oldest form of verbal irony) and humorous overstatement were normal rhetorical devices,[10] as was also a peculiarly sophisticated use of homely proverb and folk-wit. These were traditions of which Chaucer made full and, as we shall show, early use.[11] Medieval rhetoric in fact recognized officially the curious value of saying something different from what is meant, not to deceive with a lie but to awaken to a truth. This effect, which is not likely to be called irony, gave the savour to such formal literary dishes as the *circumlocutio* and the *conduplicatio* (in amplification) and the *prosecutio con proverbiis*. Irony hovered about such recommended styles as the *humilis* and the *œnigma (stilus ornatus difficilis)* and occasionally even about the *sententia, dubitatio,* and *diminutio (ornatus facilis)*. Such tricks Chaucer could have learned as an esquire pursuing the obligatory *ars versificandi;* certainly, as Traugott Naunin has remarked, they appeared in his earliest writings and (like many other artifices of his trade) were not cast aside but instead more firmly integrated with his technique as Chaucer matured.[12]

Equally familiar to feudal rhetoric was Chaucer's penchant for hollow self-depreciation[13] and his not unrelated habit of presenting both sides of a philosophical argument and then (like Erasmus later) sliding cannily away from the onus of a verdict. The latter device reflected not only Chaucer's native prudence but also the time-honoured procedure in both the teacher's *lectio* and the student's complementary *disputatio* – nor is it indeed a practice unknown to present-day professors and the earnest compilers of seminar papers. So far as Chaucer acquired the lecture-manner consciously, he may have learned it, as Looten thinks, either from Oxford directly or from such Oxonian dialecticians as Strode and the disciples of Bradwardine,[14] but the briefest acquaintance with fourteenth-century literature is sufficient to provide arguments that Chaucer could have lisped in this petrified 'dialectic' as easily as in rhyme. In any case, the method was one potent to fructify not only verbal ironies but the habit of ironic detachment from life itself. Finally, medieval 'tragedy' by definition was a story of irony in the larger sense of the word, 'the overthrow of overweening pride, infatuation, an unexpected change from better to worse, a contradiction of what is anticipated by the tragic hero.'[15] This too was a concept Chaucer would appropriate as easily as he breathed the medieval air, and it was one, as we shall see, to make an early appearance in his writings and to constitute, among other things, the unifying thesis of his comparatively youthful *Monk's Tale*.

Evidence for the first appearances of irony in Chaucer is obscured, of course, by continued uncertainty as to the chronology of his works. For the purposes of this paper, however, it will be sufficient to examine the poems which the latest editor has tentatively ascribed to the period before 1380, since there seems to be little serious disagreement with his arrangement. Excluding the *Balade of Complaint* as of very doubtful authorship, the *juvenilia* of Chaucer may be listed as follows: ABC (before 1370), *Complaint to Pity, Complaint to his Lady, Complaint d'Amours, Against Women Unconstant, Merciles Beaute, To Rosemounde* (perhaps later), *Book of the Duchess* (1369–72), *The Second Nun's Prologue and Tale* (1372–80), *The Parson's Tale, The Monk's Tale* (c. 1374; except the Barnabo stanza, c. 1386), and *Womanly Noblesse* (c. 1380).[16] Of these only the first and the last seem quite devoid of any of the common forms of irony, whether verbal innuendo, indirect satire, dramatic ambiguity, or the reversals of fate.

COMPLAINT TO PITY

The *Pity*, although one of the most conventional of his love lyrics, contains definite anticipations of the manner of the 'mature' Chaucer. The central allegory of the poem is a dramatic irony. The lover comes with an elaborate bill of complaint against Pity, only to find her dead. The contretemps is toyed with in a manner that is almost lugubrious:

> But yet encreseth me this wonder newe,
> That no wight woot that she is ded, but I.   (29–30)

The lover is really joking at his own misprized affections:

> For wel I wot, although I wake or wynke,

Ye rekke not whether I flete or synke. (109–10)

There seems here to be a deliberate dropping of the legal-chivalric diction in favour of the homely style and detached mood native to Jove's eagle and to Pandarus.

A COMPLAINT TO HIS LADY

In *A Complaint to his Lady* the same irony of unrequited love becomes the central topic. 'The more I love, the more she doth me smerte' (20) is the virtual refrain. The god who so plagues men is prettily berated with mock praise:

Now hath not Love me bestowed weel
To love ther I never shal have part (33–4)

The lady who causes both the passion and its frustration is logically addressed in oxymorons; she is his 'best beloved fo' whose 'swete herte of stele' makes him wake when he should sleep, quake when he should dance. Such conceits are, as in the *Pity*, bromides of the courtly erotica and parallels to the familiar Boethian musings upon life in general,[17] but they are expressed with an unusual grace, a playful savouring of the situation, and with a singleness of ironic effect which is scarcely surpassed in the very latest of Chaucer's shorter poems.

COMPLAINT D'AMOURS

However doubtful the data and even the authorship of this poem may be, it can easily stand as a designed supplement to the two lyrics just examined. The same paradox – that because he loves truly he is likely to die for his truth[18] – is dallied with and in exactly the same insouciant manner. But now the lady herself enjoys the irony and laughs like Fortuna at those who pine for her (10, 62–3), and the lover draws the conclusion, withheld from the first two complaints yet dictated by logic and good manners, that his mistress is really not responsible for his suffering (35): 'Hit is nat with hir wil that I hir serve!' This thought too is developed with adroit exaggerations and pretty modesties, and with abrupt reversals of mood, impulsive transitions from the conventionally mournful to the personally *gay*, which set the tone to the later *Legend of Good Women:*

> I may wel singe, 'in sory tyme I spende
> My lyf'; that song may have confusioun! (24–5)

If the *Complaint d'Amours* be not Chaucer's, it is the most remarkable imitation of his early style which has ever been written.

AGAINST WOMEN UNCONSTANT

This is more pedestrian, but even here there are glimpses of the sly, cryptic, 'later' Chaucer. His lady is faithful only in her fickleness (17); she should wear green in summer, not blue, 'ye woot wel what I mean' (20–1). The language in which the poet repudiates her falls repeatedly from aristocratic grace; she is full of 'newefangelnesse' – a homely epithet,[19] she is as changeable as a 'wedercock' (12). Such a simile was already proverbial – but not in *courtly* poetry, to judge by Skeat's examples.[20] The word is a bourgeois intrusion of the precise sort which was to make Pandarus so unpredictable and memorable a wit.

TO ROSEMOUNDE

Both the *Merciles Beaute* and *Rosemounde* contain ironies so marked as to have led at least one critic to classify the poems among the utterances of Chaucer's disillusioned old age,[21] and another to expel them from the Chaucer canon as examples of 'the more primitive forms of humour employed by lesser men.'[22] It is true there is more patent whimsy here than in the poems referred to above, but the difference is one of degree rather than kind. *Rosemounde*, if the evidence of irony means anything, may easily be as early as Miss Rickert thinks, that is, produced on the occasion of Richard's return from France with his child-queen, Isabel.[23] There are only four apparent grotesqueries in style:

a The poet declares his passion is now 'refreyd' (21). Skeat translates this as 'refrigerated,' which makes it a flippant modernism, not to say anachronism. Actually the word was good medieval English for 'cooled' and used as such by Chaucer in serious passages elsewhere and by Wiclif in his Bible.[24]

b The lover boasts he is True Tristram the Second. This was a commonplace comparison probably waggish only to modern ears.[25]

c 'For thogh I wepe of teres ful a tyne' (9). Here Skeat conjures up a picture of 'brawny porters, staggering beneath the "*stang*" on which is slung the "tine" containing the "four or five pailfuls" of the poet's tears.' One should remember that this expansion of the image is Skeat's, not Chaucer's. The poet is repeating an exaggeration current in conventional and not very humorous balades, at a point where he must surely have been grateful for the rhyme.[26]

d 'Nas never pyk walwed in galauntyne
  As I in love am walwed and ywounde.'   (17–18)

This is the only obvious sally in the poem. It is true there is little *lèse majesté* in the use of 'walwed,' which was then 'the almost official word for the lover's condition,'[27] but the general simile undoubtedly smacks of the cook-book. As such it is quite in key with the puckishness of Pandarus or of the Pilgrim-observer in the *Canterbury Tales*.

Elsewhere the poem is graceful but orthodox. Far from parodying the form or burlesquing the viewpoint of the courtly balade, as some have thought,[28] Chaucer enlivens both by the economical use of the more vivacious metaphors already dared by his masters. Chaucer had not yet prepared the court, or himself, for the out-and-out burlesqueries of *Sir Thopas*; but it is plain that he was already willing to relieve his ennui, and perhaps theirs, with an occasional whimsicality which would not necessarily cancel the good faith of his longing for Rosemounde, whoever she may have been.

MERCILES BEAUTE

In this there is also 'Spott statt weichhertzigem Verzicht'[29] but the joke is not nearly so broad as some have made out. To say, with Kitchin, that 'the vulgar diction and imagery betray the burlesque intention' is to misread the poem. Only one image appears even superficially to be plebeian in the setting, that of the lover escaping fat from Love's lean prison. However flippant the allegory may appear today, it evidently struck the ears of the courtly Duc de Berry, in 1389, as worthy of literal translation into an orthodox French balade.[30] Chaucer's poem is the expression of a gallant in holiday mood, not the grimaces of a professional clown. As in all these early verses, the poet is engaged in skilful rhythmic exercises which he executes with no great seriousness and yet carefully. Whenever he can lighten an arpeggio with a tinkle of his own he does so, but never at the expense of a discord, or a transition to jazz.

THE BOOK OF THE DUCHESS

The *Duchess* is not an ironical poem, yet is there any other elegy in the language with such playful passages and with such a general effect of lightheartedness? From what we know of Gaunt's character, and specifically of his readiness to remarry, it is likely of course that the husband's grief was more chivalric than intense; certainly Chaucer's lament seems delicately adapted to just such polite mourning. All the conventions of the dream genre and the lover's threnody are not so much obeyed as they are lightly greeted and quickly forgotten.

The poem opens with what would appear at first to be the traditional complaint of an ailing lover.[31] Chaucer, however, is carefully mysterious about his ailment, nowhere acknowledging it as love-longing. Perhaps a medieval reader would have inferred but one cause for his symptoms, just as easily as a modern would connect alcoholism with phantasies described in terms of pink snakes. Chaucer's delicacy of allusion would nevertheless be conspicuous. Froissart, whom the English poet is evidently imitating here, opens his *Paradis d'Amour* in much the same manner but later in the poem makes it quite clear that his sickness is the ordinary lover's malady.[32] Why is Chaucer reticent? Andrew Lang's notion that the poet was suffering from war-veteran's insomnia may be properly discarded along with Fleay's theory that the illness is the poet's married life.[33] The Godwin myth that Chaucer suffered from a long, hopeless passion for a lady of high rank, though it still receives some credence, fails to explain the absence of references to love.[34] If the poet were burlesquing the love-sickness, like Deschamps, to describe the fever arising from 'pou d'argent,'[35] we have the evidence of the *Complaint to his Empty Purse* to show that he knew how to make such jokes quite clear. If he had wished, like Gower, to record a prosaic physical illness he would have avoided, of necessity, all courtly love terms.[36]

The most plausible current explanation is still not wholly satisfactory. According to Cowling, Chaucer is indicating that, since eight years ago when he first met Blanche, she has been his 'ideal' lady; he avoids the terms of love in order that he might not appear in the false position of an actual lover of the duchess.[37] The difficulty with the interpretation is that the typical medieval love-poet was never deterred by such considerations. Poetical declarations of love were simply the normal form of literary compliment and carried no breath of scandal, no evidence even that the poet was personally acquainted with the lady.

The neglected point is that, however impeccable a lady Blanche was, Chaucer though a poet was not quite a gentleman. He was the son of a Thames Street wholesaler, and for all his squirehood and his military service and his court favour, it was vital for him to guard himself continually – in fact, I believe, throughout his life — from the envious tongues who would be quick to accuse him of trying to assume the airs of a true 'gentle.' Chaucer, the bourgeois, could become a court poet only by avoiding the pretensions of a courtier. In the outside world of fourteenth-century London he, and many another plebeian, could by now rise to positions of wealth and political influence; but the narrower circles of Westminster and of the nobles' castles maintained (all the more rigorously because of this) the feudal barriers. And nowhere was the time-lag more marked than in the literature of the aristocracy, and most of all in the predominating literature of courtly love.

This necessity to avoid the ostracism meted out to the low-born who dared to step into the enchanted circle of courtly love Chaucer gradually made into a virtue. The little coy heresies of the early complaints may be the beginning of it. Certainly by the time of the *Duchess* he has hit upon that self-depreciatory pose in love matters which he was to develop, far beyond the customary literary humilities, in the direction of whimsy and personal caricature. Ultimately the pose leads, as in the *House of Fame* and the *Troilus*, to a complete denial of his capacity to love (that is, to be a courtly lover) and even to the elvish and misogynic fat man of the *Canterbury Tales* and the *Envoy to Scogan*.

All this self-depreciation is not ironic in the Socratic sense; that is Chaucer is not minimizing himself in order to prove his superiority over an opponent, but it is definitely ironic in so far as it is a sly ambiguity which is nevertheless not meant to deceive. Chaucer is, in the *Duchess*, steering a subtly devious course between dutiful elegiacs and light entertainment. Without declaring his purpose he must yet have managed to entertain Gaunt highly, and if necessary to solace him, without at any time pretending to the role of official elegist to the Duchess of Lancaster.

As the poem progresses the author becomes a Dreamer and in this capacity assumes another pose of lighthearted self-abasement. Like all dreamers he is 'daswed' and 'lewd,' as later in the *House of Fame* (for example, 658). This was consistent both with psychological realism and with medieval literary practice; the author represents himself as wrong-headed and dull to facilitate a story or sermon from the wise and loquacious teacher encountered in the vision. The teacher must be furnished a pupil obviously in need of advice or ignorant of what is probably a familiar story. When such material involves, as in this case, descriptions of the beauties of a lady, it is only gallant that Dream-teacher as well as Dreamer must confess himself dull in one thing – in the ability to find words to match her loveliness.

The parallels in the stupidity of the dreamers in the *Duchess* and the *House of Fame* are sufficiently familiar,[33] and their likeness to medieval dream-literature in general is too obvious to need elaboration here.[39] Nowhere does Chaucer, in his use of the device, approach the symbolic integration of Dante and Langland, but he does manipulate it for narrative suspense and variety and for something more relevant to the present discussion; an admirably dreamy sort of dramatic irony. For it appears that the Dreamer is only simulating ignorance of the lady's beauty in order to draw out the Knight, who can more properly essay to describe her. If it is not simulation, nothing at all can be made of the poem's opening. Has he not there already hinted that, so far as his worm-like soul is capable, he has been held in thrall for eight long years by the charms of this very angel?[40]

However whimsical, the poem is nevertheless an elegy, and it is not surprising to find running through it threads also of tragic irony. The very device of the 'daswed' dreamer heightens the knight's sorrows by sharpening his loneliness; he has but one listener, and between even them there is a gulf, as between Tolstoi's Ivan Ilyitch and those who listen by his deathbed. Chaucer never emphasizes these darker ironies here, however; he manages to draw more attention to his Dreamer-self than to the black mourner. We are distracted, a little shocked, but yet amused and permanently interested in a Dreamer who is such a bourgeois as to blame Dido because she died for love (734), be delighted and surprised to find neither holes nor cracks in his dream-windows (321–5),[41] imagine that a lady's beauty is relative to the observer (1047ff), and think that a knight could conceivably regret having loved intensely (1112ff.) These social 'breaks' of the Dreamer have narrative function, of course, but their mildly ludicrous effect must have been calculated. Chaucer is developing the role he was to play throughout his literary life, that of amateur entertainer to a courtly audience in a time when bourgeois heresies were common enough to be amusing and yet not influential enough to be treated with alarm.

On the other hand, there is no need to assume that Chaucer here pushes his playfulness to the point of parody or burlesque. The lively passage in which Morpheus is wakened has actually been listed among Chaucer's 'parodyings' of the classical gods.[42] Actually it is, as Shannon has shown, a free imitation of Machaut, who drew in turn from Ovid.[43] None of these authors was attempting the mocking of literary *form* (that is, parody) or of literary *material* (that is, burlesque). Both Chaucer and his models recount the Seys legend unencumbered either by religious allegiance to or religious contempt for the gods who appear. The English poet is simply alert to the ordinary humours of a cave of sleep, and glad to lighten his material with the jokes his predecessors have evolved in the picturing of such a bower. His only contribution to the gaiety is that very vigorous and efficient messenger who swishes into the realms of slumber and blows his horn precisely in Morpheus' ear (178–81). At other times Chaucer actually subdues some of Machaut's frivolity, as Lowes has noted.[44] The Seys episode is after all not included primarily for comedy; it is there to form a complimentary classical parallel to introduce the main theme of the poem.

Just how ingenious that parallel is has not, I think, been appreciated. Cowling thinks that 'a delicate compliment to Gaunt is conveyed by the implication that if Halcyone died of grief, Gaunt's existence must be a living death,'[45] But this is a gloomy suggestion which the poem itself does not leave with us. The effect of the passage is rather *consolatory* than mournful. Juno, out of pity for the weeping Alcioune, sends her ghostly image of the dead king, 'That lyeth ful pale and nothyng rody (143).' So Chaucer, out of respectful sympathy for the bereaved Gaunt, 'Ful pitous pale, and nothyng red (470),' brings him a pleasing memory-picture of the dead queen, to comfort rather than to renew his sorrow. If Chaucer had wished to make the parallel definitely tragic he would not have stripped Ovid's tale of the forebodings which Alcioune expresses at the departure of her husband, and of the concept of *hubris* which dominates both the classical and medieval formulations of the legend[46] (a concept to which Chaucer was ordinarily strongly attracted, as we shall see in the *Monk's Tale*).

The whole poem is in fact singularly free from the heavier ironies, of the despairing lover or of Fortune's fool, which Chaucer elsewhere conjures so readily from Boethian literature. There is one long tirade against the wheel-goddess, who checked the knight's 'fers' at chess (even here the image has playful connotations) and lulled him into happiness the better to plunge him into its reverse. The passage is, however, one of the most imitative in the poem, without a phrase or a thought for which parallels have not already been found.[47] It seems almost to have been thrown in out of hasty duty to the allegedly solemn purpose of the poem. Wherever else his sources pause for tragic utterance, Chaucer either summarizes perfunctorily or skips.

In contrast, whenever his models permit a moment of lightness, Chaucer, with the exception already noted, is quick to respond with like gaieties and even with a few unobtrusive jests of his own. He does not, for example, simply say that his dream is strange, as all narrators' dreams must be; he flirts with hyperbole which, conventional in basis, yet seems to be mildly amused at its own pedantries (276–90). Even the solemn knight is made to share occasionally in graceful heresies. He praises his lady for *not* encouraging crusading and knight-errant suitors, who would 'Goo hoodles to the Drye Se' (1027–9). Unfortunately for him, she favours none at all, counts his tale worth 'nat a stree,' and answers, in short, 'nay' (1236–43). Apparently we are to understand she is like Criseyde and other ladies past and present who refuse in order to be asked again.[48]

The abrupt climax and resolution of the poem (1308–10) is not so bewildering if one has followed it so far as *consolatory entertainment* rather than serious lament.[49] It is perhaps an extreme example of the casualness of the whole work. Langhans has shown that the conclusion is closely parallelled in a section of *Floris and Blanchefleur*.[50] In the latter it is not a finale; but Chaucer had no really tragic summary to make. His models carry him no further and there is no real demand from the patron of his poem that he rise to independent heights of solemnity. He has completed a flattering memory-picture of the duchess and presented it to Gaunt, without flippancy but with as light and gay a gesture as the subject could allow. This done, the poem is rounded off without more ado, perhaps even a little ironically, lest the reader shift his interest to the not very serious sorrows of the ducal widower.

THE SECOND NUN'S PROLOGUE AND TALE

The poems later assigned as Prologue and Tale to the Second Nun are, in consonance with their religious purpose, lacking in any of the 'game' or slangy slyness of other Chaucerian works of this period. A possible, but doubtful, exception appears in the brief mention of the bridal night:

> The nyght cam, and to bedde most she gon
> With hire husbonde, as *ofte* is the manere. (141–2)

Both Chaucer and the second nun knew it was a custom which brides followed a good deal more frequently than 'ofte.' If the understatement is intentional it is as striking an example as can be found anywhere of Chaucer's inability to sustain gravity even when all the dictates of art and religion demanded it.

The tale is not utterly bare of the more thoughtful ironies, Mrs Dempster to the contrary.[51] Cecilie speaks with the modest directness becoming a Christian martyr but Chaucer manages her debate with Almachius in such a way that the latter is in effect taunted sardonically for his worldly blindness. He is led to insist on his princely power 'To maken folk to dyen or to lyven' (472), and immediately we are shown that, in a theological use of the words, this is exactly the power he lacks. To kill the body of a Christian is to ensure everlasting life to its spiritual possessor, a paradox of which Cecilie is shown to be aware and Almachius by nature ignorant. The narrator deliberately encourages Almachius in his boasting until he becomes the staring fool the virgin sees in him.

For a moment there is even some reverse irony – an intimation that those who fix their eyes on a visionary life may by that very preoccupation come to lose the one sure life which is on this side of the grave. The thought is allowed to pass through the mind of Tiburce, struggling unsuccessfully against conversion; but the doubt is recorded only that it may be crushed, and the story ends with all paradoxes dissolved in the clear solution of martyrdom.

THE PARSON'S TALE

This would seem to be as barren a field for irony as the previous story, since it is a handbook on Penitence which follows closely upon pious originals. In view of the continued uncertainty regarding its exact sources we cannot even be sure that the few apparent deviations are really Chaucer's. Nevertheless, the tale is a sermon and (like good sermons everywhere, and particularly in the age of Wiclif and Bromyard) not without its moments of vivid scorn, sardonic question, and racy abuse.

The preacher's lips twist as he thinks of the folly of the Christian who earnestly does good deeds, and yet remains in deadly sin. Since, from the viewpoint of eternal judgement, he has so far accomplished nothing, 'wel may that man that no good werk no dooth synge thilke newe Frenshe song, "Jay tout perdu mon temps et mon labour" '(¶247).

It is a refrain which Chaucer will quote again later, and once more with ironic effect, in his balade of *Fortune*.[52]

Generally the preacher of the *Parson's Tale* is wrathful rather than coldly scornful, expressing himself in rank metaphor and free ridicule, as in the much-quoted and magnificent attack upon 'disordinat scantnesse' of clothing (421–8). Worthy of equal notice but neglected by prudish comentators is the cryptic comparison of lecherous old impotents to hounds who lift their legs, by habit, 'by the roser or by othere beautees.' And, continues the caustic divine, if an old fellow thinks 'that he may nat synne, for no likerousnesse that he dooth with his wyf, certes, that opinion is fals. God woot, a man may sleen hymself with his owene knyf, and make hymselven dronken of his owene tonne.'[53]

For the most part the parson hits from the shoulder, scorning sly pokes, but there is an economy in his metaphors and a careful restraint from glossing them, which is surely in the spirit of irony. He indulges in a sour pun upon 'amercimentz,' 'whiche myghten moore resonably ben cleped extorcions than amercimentz' (751). Occasionally he comments, in the manner of the *Monk's Tale*, upon the irony of fortune, as in the case of Adam (324) or of the man who prides himself on his goods: 'some tyme is a man a greet lord by the morwe, that is a caytyf and a wrecche er it be nyght; and somtyme ... the delices of a man ben cause of the grevous maladye thurgh which he dyeth' (470–1).

Finally, there is an author's aside whose good faith is questionable: 'Now, after that I have declared yow, as I kan, the sevene deedly synnes, and somme of hire braunches and hire remedies, soothly, if I koude, I wolde telle yow the ten comandementz. But so heigh a doctrine I lete to divines. Nathelees, I hope to God, they been touched in this tretice, everich of hem alle.' (955–6). Since Chaucer was later to leave to 'divines' or 'grete clerkes' or other imposing authorities the solution of questions which he had already suggested might not be solvable, one's suspicions are aroused. There is of course a sober prudence in disclaiming, whether one be poor parson or court poet, any attempt to rival the holy doctors; the work after all is meant only to be a primer. Even if it were a contribution to high scholastic controversy the author would end with a denial of his own knowledge, in the form of an 'envyepilogue.' But here the occasion for the disclaimer is the least plausible one to be found in the whole Tale. The ten commandments did not stand for remote and difficult doctrine, by any means! As for meekly hoping that he has 'touched' on them, his whole sermon has been expounding the Decalogue by relating it, item by item, with his exposition of the seven deadly sins. Here it is surely Chaucer speaking, unable to resist a sportive poke at pedantic divines; the parson *in propria persona* has his own formal humility-prologue and epilogue quite apart from this passage. If the reader is doubtful that Chaucer ever intrudes into the parish priest's sermons, let him turn over the leaf and study the following aside: 'The exposicioun of this hooly preyere, that is so excellent and digne, I bitake to thise maistres of theologie.' The holy prayer thus referred for elucidation to the great experts is nothing more than the ABC of Christianity, the Paternoster.[54]

THE MONK'S TALE

Although written for the most part probably as early as 1374, several years before the *House of Fame* and the so-called 'Italian period,' the series of miniature tragedies which Chaucer later awarded to the Monk contains, like the other early works we have examined, a number of ironies typical of Chaucer's final productions.

Mrs Dempster has rightly remarked that the Monk's stories are too concentrated to leave room for good dramatic irony, but I cannot agree with her that they are quite devoid of it or that Chaucer was here interested in the abstract theme of Fortune's mutability 'rather than in his heroes.'[55] In any case, the conception of tragedy which the poet here epitomizes is inseparable from that larger dramatic irony which we term 'the irony of fate,' in which the gods (and the author) are the all-seeing observers and the human players act and speak in a manner which they would shun if they were aware of the real fortune awaiting them. 'Tragedye is to seyn a dite of a prosperite for a tyme, that endeth in wrecchidnesse,' says Chaucer,[56] but in the majority of the Monk's tragedies he is attracted not simply to the contretemps but to the psychology of prosperity itself. He sees that the keenest happiness of the man in great power is his false belief in the indestructibility of that power, a delusion which in turn often acts to precipitate the peripeteia. In other words Chaucer is concerned with precisely the same phenomenon which preoccupied the great Greek ironists, the sin or compulsion of hubris, the inevitability of that Pride which goeth before a fall.

Of Chaucer's eighteen unfortunates only seven fall without personal erro: Hercules, Hugolino, Alexander, Pompey, Caesar, and the two Pedros. In the case of the last two there is shrewd policy behind the discrimination. The king of Cyprus, we are very carefully told, was slain 'for no thyng but for (his) chivalrie' (2395). Later historians incline to agree that he was rather understandably assassinated at the height of a vicious and bloody rule. The king of Cyprus, however, was not only Chaucer's contemporary but also a much lamented friend and ally of Chaucer's own king, Edward III. The other murdered King Pedro, of Spain, also appears without tragic fault; he was the father-in-law of Chaucer's most powerful early patron, John of Gaunt. The choice of the other five guiltless is less easy to explain. An uncritical attitude to Hugolino results perhaps from Chaucer's concentration upon the children. As for Alexander, Pompey, and Caesar, they were pagan saints of literature. But the inclusion of Hercules seems to show a caprice on Chaucer's part as unexpected as that which he ascribes to Fortune. Hercules, stock medieval example of the champion destroyed by trusting a woman, is here simply the victim of the Wheel, with Dianira's complicity denied or at least 'not proven' (2127–9). On the other hand, the parallel case of Samson is presented as a tragedy of misjudgement as well as of fate, a warning 'That no men telle hir conseil til hir wyves.'[57]

Six others are explicitly made ironic victims of their own pride: 'Nabugodonosor,' Balthasar, Nero, Holofernes, 'Kyng Antiochus,' and Cresus. To this list might be added both Lucifer, since his unspecified 'synne' (2002) was known to be that by biblical authority, and Adam, who falls through his 'mysgovernaunce' (2012). The choice of those overturned by Superbia is obviously influenced by the emphasis upon that conception in the Scriptures. Whether or not Cenobia and Barnabo contribute to their descent is left in doubt. Cenobia's refusal to permit her husband normal sex relations is told at some length, and in a manner which approaches the colloquial slyness of the later Chaucer,[58] but the narrator does not definitely blame her for this though he links her pugnacity with her fall. When he comes to record this, he feels pity, and concludes by presenting in strong, quick contrasts the symbols of her tragic reversal:

> And she that helmed was in starke stoures,
> And wan by force townes stronge and toures,
> Shal on hir heed now were a vitremyte;
> And she that bar the ceptre ful of floures
> Shal bere a distaf, hire cost for to quyte.[59]

It is this swift juxtaposition of the concrete symbols of past glory and present misery which provides the finest ironies of the *Monk's Tale*. Especially grim examples are the line of Sampsoun, 'Now maystow wepen with thyne eyen blynde' (2077) and the very Anglo-Saxon gibe at the King of Antioch, stricken by God with incurable wounds in his 'guttes':

> And certeinly the wreche was resonable,
> For many a mannes guttes did *he* peyne, (2603–4)

Similarly the poet can be felt quietly exulting over the deserved reversal of Nero, desperately at the end seeking for loyal followers:

> He knokked faste, and ay the moore he cried,
> The fastere shette they the dores alle.[60]

In the background there echoes regularly, and with increasing effectiveness, the mocking laughter of Fortune who, when she has chosen, in her caprice, to be deceitful

> Thanne wayteth she her man to overthrowe
> By swich a wey as he wolde leest suppose. (2141–2)

At times the sportive malice of the goddess is pictured with a raciness which anticipates the style of Pandarus: she determines to upset Nero,

> For though that he were strong, yet was she strenger,
> She thoughte thus, 'By God! I am to nyce
> To sette a man that is fulfild of vice
> In heigh degree, and emperour hym calle,
> By God! out of his sete I wol hym trice;
> *Whan he leest weneth*, sonnest shal he falle.'[61]

Such ironies spring from a delight in justice unexpectedly dealt; others, of a more verbal sort, occur when Chaucer dwells upon *in*justice. When Nero rips open the womb of his dead mother and remarks, 'A fair womman was she!', the poet adds the contemptuous rider:

> Greet wonder is how that he koude or myghte
> Be domesman of hire dede beautee. (2489–90)

The two following lines are in the same key:

> The wyn to bryngen hym comanded he,
> And drank anon – *noon other wo* he made.

There is the same twisted indignation, Chaucer's tempered equivalent to the *saeva indignatio*, in an exclamation on the imprisonment of Hugolino's children:

> Allas, Fortune! it was greet crueltee
> Swiche briddes for to putte in swich a cage![62]

The lighter ironies intrude less into this 'tale' than into almost any of the works so far examined. With the exception of Fortune's exclamations on Nero, and the colloquial allusions to Cenobia's married life, there is no whimsy. Wilhelm Ewald thinks there is 'eine Ironie auf die Quelle' in lines 2709–10 on the death of Caesar and 'starke Humor' in the picture of Julius covering 'his privetee' as he lay bleeding.[63] These details however were recorded with sobriety in Chaucer's sources and imitated by him a trifle awkwardly. To suppose that he is here parodying his models is to ignore the universal homage paid to the memory of Julius Caesar in medieval times, to misunderstand the medieval fidelity to the minutiae of sources, and to find 'strong humour' in imagined pruriency. The mistake of Ewald, and of Frau Korsch, in approaching the whole of the *Monk's Tale*, is to assume that what is incongruous today was necessarily so in an entirely different society.[64] Ewald's final and most fantastic anachronism is to describe as 'humorvoll' the stanza with which Chaucer terminates the measured gravity of his tragedies – on the ground that 'Tragödien sind also nur möglich, wenn das Geschick willens ist, einen stolzen König unvermutet dahinzustrecken.'[65] Chaucer's conception of tragedy if seriously advanced today would of course be considered snobbery so limited as to be laughable; but in an age where only a very few possessed either worldly goods or power, only a very few could 'fall,' and in a time when nobility was the peculiar perquisite of the governing class, there could be no other kind of tragedy than the eclipse of illustrious lords and ladies. The Monk's definition of tragedy is a natural product of feudalism; to be even 'half-parodying' it, as Frau Korsch suggests,[66] would be to challenge the whole ideological basis of that system, and this Chaucer by no means attempted, here or later. Even the warning which the tragedies constituted to those still in high places was sufficiently unwelcome, though without satire of the tragic figures, to impel the Knight to interrupt; and it may well be that one of the reasons Chaucer did not amplify his collection was that the reaction of a pleasure-loving court to the gloomy 'dites' already written was identical with the Knight's.

That gentleman's distaste should not persuade modern readers to turn over the leaf too. Though the Monk is allowed no striking dramatic ironies, and never wanders far from his sources, he catches in almost every tragedy the tragic essence, by pictorial brevity, imagination, pity, and above all by a rich and free development of the ironies of fate.

So far, then, as our approximate knowledge of the Chaucer chronology allows us to judge, Chaucer was always an ironist. The vein of sportive self-depreciation which is so much a part of his individuality as a writer begins with the earliest complaints and runs through the *Duchess* and even the *Parson's Tale*. From the start it is identified with a pretended inability to avoid bourgeois love-heresies and kindred violations of consecrated literary codes. In the *Duchess* it is possible to see that these flippancies in thought and comic ambiguities in diction are motivated at least partly by an ambiguity in Chaucer's own life, an in-between social position which he was never to escape. In the *Parson's Tale* the same cautious combination of casual jokes at authority and coy humilities makes its appearance in connection with theological pedantries and points the way to the satiric portraits of clerics in the *Prologue to the Canterbury Tales*. The scornful invectives embedded in the latter are also to be matched occasionally in the parish priest's sermon and, frequently and strikingly, in the tragedies later to be assigned to the Monk. Ambiguities more structural in character – the ironies of fate and of drama – are likewise discoverable in the early Chaucer. In the Complaints there is holiday play with the plight of misprized love; in the *Duchess* there is a toying, still curiously light-hearted, with the dramatic contradictions of the dream world; in the Monk's tragedies Chaucer is already demonstrating his characteristic interest in the ironies of tragic drama and of fate.

On the other hand, Chaucer's irony is, in these works, still only in process of formation. Subtlety is already here, and merriness, but not breadth. For richly comic social allegory his audience had to await the *Parliament of Fowls*; for the perfection of his jovial self-depreciation, the *House of Fame*. There are yet no consistent active ironists like the Eagle or Pandarus, the Clerk of Oxford or Harry Baillie, nor is there any hint of the Chaucer who will create a series, in the *Prologue to the Canterbury Tales,* of the most intricate personalized type-satires in the language. It will be some years too before his little literary jokes will evolve into the frank burlesque of the *Purse,* the mock-heroics of the *Nun's Priest's Tale* or the exuberant parody of *Sir Thopas.* Irony in the sense of unconscious self-betrayal by a tale-teller will also not appear until the great conception of the Canterbury pilgrimage is born. Finally, in all the early works, irony is only an incidental grace or a spontaneous byplay which runs the risk of being also an artistic intrusion; not until the *Troilus* will the spirit of irony take possession of an entire poem.

NOTES

1 J.B. Priestley *English Humour* (London, Longmans 1929) 63

2 *Geoffrey Chaucer* (New York, Faber and Faber 1932) 20

3 *The Chaucer Tradition* (London, Oxford University Press 1925) 429–30

4 *Dramatic Irony in Chaucer* (Stanford, Stanford University Press 1932) 94ff. Similarly G.H. Cowling lists 'Chaucer's love of trickery' among the peculiar results of an Italian influence; *Chaucer* (London, Methuen 1927) 138.

5 *Chaucer, ses modèles ...* 'Mémoires et travaux ... des Facultés catholiques de Lille' fasc. xxxviii (1931) 35–6. Cp. the theory of E.K. Kellett that the later adaptations of Dante by Chaucer are burlesques; 'Chaucer as a Critic of Dante' *London Mercury* 4 (1921) 287–91.

6 E.g., C.M. Hathaway, Jr. 'Chaucer's Verse-Tags as a Part of his Narrative Machinery' JEGP 5 (1906) 476–84

7 'English Irony before Chaucer' UTQ 6 (1937) 538–57

8 *Literature and Pulpit in Medieval England* (Cambridge, Cambridge University Press 1933) 229ff.

9 See E.F. Shannon *Chaucer and the Roman Poets* (Harvard, Harvard University Press 1929) 371ff.

10 See J.M. Manly 'Chaucer and the Rhetoricians' *British Academy Proceedings* 12 (1926) 95–113.

11 See B.J. Whiting *Chaucer's Use of Proverbs* (Harvard, Harvard University Press 1934) 74–5 and *passim.*

12 *Der Einfluss der mittelalterlichen Rhetorik auf Chaucers Dichtung* (Bonn diss. 1929) 57–60

13 See F. Tupper 'The Envy Theme in Prologues and Epilogues' *JEGP* 16 (1917) 555–7.

14 *Chaucer, ses modèles* ... 167–8; cf. his 'Chaucer et la dialectique' *RA-A* 6 (1930) 199–205.

15 M.H. Shackford 'Sources of Irony in Hamlet' *SR* 34 (1926) 20

16 See F.N. Robinson *Chaucer's Complete Works* (Boston, Houghton Mifflin 1933) xxv, 853, 881, 887–8, 969ff., 981–3. Textual references in this article are to this edition.

17 Robinson, ibid., compares lines 43–5 with *Boece* III pr. 3; *Pity* 99ff.; *PF* 90–1.

18 Line 7; cp. *Lady* 29. W.W. Skeat, ed. *The Complete Works of Geoffrey Chaucer* 7 vols. (Oxford, Clarendon Press 1894–7) I 566) compares *FrankT* 1322.

19 Cp. its use in *AA* 141 and *SqT* 610.

20 *Early English Proverbs* (Oxford, Oxford University Press 1910) 61, no. 147

21 G.G. Coulton *Chaucer and his England* 4th ed. (London, Methuen 1927) 68

22 Aage Brusendorff *The Chaucer Tradition* 439–40; he compares the 'pyk' simile with some lines of Hoccleve.

23 See her 'Leaf from a Fourteenth-Century Letter Book' *MP* 25 (1927) 255, and later articles by the same author.

24 *OED, refried*; cp. *T&C* II 1343 – *OED* '1294–5' erroneously –; v. 507; *ParsT* 341. See Skeat *Works* I 550.

25 J.L. Lowes compares a line in Froissart; *vide* his 'Illustrations of Chaucer ... ' *RR* 2 (1911) 128.

26 Skeat himself notes a parallel in the unironic *Chevalier au cigne*; *Works* I 549.

27 George Kitchin *A Survey of Burlesque and Parody in England* (Edinburgh, Oliver and Boyd 1931) 15n.

28 E.g., Kitchin, ibid. 14 and D. Patrick 'The Satire in Chaucer's Parliament of Birds' *PQ* 9 (1930) 64n.

29 J. Koch 'Ausgewählte kleinere Dichtungen Chaucers' *ES* 49 (1934) 80

30 Kitchin *Survey* 14.Cf. W.G. Dodd *Courtly Love in Chaucer and Gower* (Harvard Studies in English 1913) 29; W.L. Renwick 'Chaucer's Triple Roundel ... ' *MLR* 16 (1921) 322–3. Renwick assumes, however, that Chaucer borrowed from Berry.

31 See W.O. Sypherd 'Chaucer's Eight Years' Sickness' *MLN* 20 (1905) 240–3.

32 Machaut, from whom Froissart was borrowing, also made clear the love-motif. See George Lyman Kittredge 'Chaucer and Froissart' *ES* 26 (1899) 336, and *Froissart Oeuvres: Poésies* ed. Jean Auguste Scheler (Brussels, M.A. Scheler 1870) I 1ff.

33 See Andrew Lang *History of English Literature* (London, Longmans 1912) 84, and Robinson *Chaucer's Complete Works* 881.

34 Godwin's influence may be seen in the comments of Skeat, I 463; Coulton *Chaucer and His England* 23–9; V. Langhans *Untersuchungen zu Chaucer* (Halle, Niemeyer 1918) 280ff. See also T.R. Lounsbury *Studies in Chaucer* (New York, Osgoode and Millvaine 1892) I 211, and Robinson, ibid. 881.

35 E. Deschamps *Oeuvres* ed. Q. de Saint-Hilaire (Paris, n.p. 1887) v 93–4

36 *CA* VIII 3106–37, *Works* ed. G.C. Macaulay (Oxford, Early English Text Society 1901) III 474–6. Though Gower does not specify his illness he links it with old age and uses it as a plea for the favourable reception of his book.

37 *Chaucer* 15 n. Miss Galway's suggestion that Chaucer's 'sovereign lady' was Joan of Kent does not affect the argument here; see *MLR* 33 (1938) 145–9.

38 See G.L. Kittredge *Chaucer and his Poetry* (Cambridge, Mass. Harvard, University Press 1915) 53, 70, and *passim*.

39 See W.O. Sypherd *Studies in Chaucer's 'House of Fame'* Chaucer Society ser. 2, no. 39 (1907) 1–11. On the other hand, C.S. Lewis says that the dreamer is a 'fool' only because Chaucer is 'clumsy.' I believe Mr Lewis overlooks here both the traditional basis and the functional necessity for a 'daswed' Dreamer. See his *Allegory of Love* (Oxford, Clarendon Press, 1936) 170.

40 See Dempster, *Dramatic Irony* 14 n.

41 The functional purpose of the lines is of course to introduce an indirect acknowledgement to the *Romance of the Rose* from which Chaucer is about to borrow at length; *vide* Robinson's note to 291.

42 By Kitchin, *Survey* 16; he compares *KnT* 2925–6, etc.

43 *Chaucer and the Roman Poets* 3–12; *vide* also John Livingston Lowes *Geoffrey Chaucer and the Development of his Genius* (Cambridge, Mass., Harvard University Press 1926) 120, and Skeat's note to 184.

44 Lowes, ibid. 121

45 *Chaucer* 95

46 See Skeat's note to 62.

47 See Robinson's note to 617, and Skeat's note to 634.

48 Cp. *T&C* I 491–7.

49 For the latter interpretation *vide* Kittredge *Chaucer and his Poetry* 53–4; for the view that the poem is 'an out and out bid' for Gaunt's literary patronage *vide* F.C. Riedel 'The Meaning of Chaucer's *House of Fame*' *JEGP* 27 (1928) 456–8.

50 See Langhans *Untersuchungen zu Chaucer* 300.

51 *Dramatic Irony* 91–3

52 Line 7; for an example of the sardonic question *vide ParsT* 196.

53 858. I have preserved the word *beautees*, rejected since Tyrwhitt, because it seems to me to make excellent sense in the context, in addition to being the reading of all the manuscripts. A somewhat similar contemptuous figure occurs in 897–8.

54 1042. Robinson notes the similarity here with 956–7 but adds that the parson would not include himself among the 'maistres.' The point is that even the humblest priest was expected not only to know but to expound the paternoster.

55 *Dramatic Irony* 86. W.E. Farnham similarly underestimates the tale after assuming the 'main theme is ... causeless misfortune'; see his *Medieval Heritage of Elizabethan Tragedy* (Berkeley, University of California Press 1936) 136.

56 *Boece* II. pr. 2.80

57 Line 2092; cp. 2052–4.

58 E.g., lines 2285–94

59 Lines 2370–4. The idea of the distaff is from Boccaccio but not apparently the still mysterious 'vitremyte.' For the effect of the passage cp. the lines on Lucifer, 2004–6.

60 Lines 2531–2. There is a touch of dramatic irony, inherent in the material, of course, when the glittering dream of proud Cresus is rightly interpreted by his daughter to mean the exact opposite of what he believes (2740–56). Cp. the ironic use of 'gerdoun' in 2630.

61 Lines 2521–6; cp. 2556–8.

62 Lines 2413–14; cp. 2395.

63 Wilhelm Ewald *Der Humor in Chaucers Canterbury Tales* Studien zur englischen Philologie 43 (Halle, Niemeyer 1911) 94; he compares *CT* IV 456ff.

64 So Ewald, ibid. 54 finds 'tragikomischer Emphase' where Chaucer is actually softening the usual medieval moralizings upon Samson's fall, lines 2052–4. See Hedwig Korsch *Chaucer als Kritiker* (Berlin diss. 1916) 85–7 and *passim*.

65 Ewald, ibid. 91–2

66 *Chaucer als Kritiker* 52

The Inhibited and the Uninhibited: Ironic Structure in the *Miller's Tale*

PATTERN OF STRUCTURAL IRONY in the *Miller's Tale* which seems not to have been noted is nevertheless one which the poet himself evidently kept very much in mind. The plot which Chaucer is presumed to have inherited involved two suitors of a young wife; one succeeded, but at the cost of being 'scalded in the towte'; the other succeeds only in kissing his lady's 'nether ye.'[1] What Chaucer adds, essentially, to this 'kiss-and-burn motif'[2] is an intricate craftsmanship designed to make the differing fates of the rivals proceed inevitably from their contrasting characters as lovers.[3] In the process he transforms the rough wool of this comedy into cloth presumably pleasing to the sophisticated courtier by an interweaving of symbolic detail, sly image, and verbal play. In particular, preparations for the irony of the misdirected kiss are observable from the story's opening, in casual phrases which have to do either with the mouth, the instrument of kissing, or with related sensory areas, the palate, nose, and throat, and with their pleasures: sweet tastes, stimulating scents, and even the more physical delights of singing.

Nicholas, the successful lover, to whom we are first introduced, not only keeps his room decorated and fresh with 'herbes swoote'[4], but is himself 'sweete as is the roote Of lycorys, or any cetewale' (3205-7). And 'sweetely' he sings there, 'this sweete clerk', so that 'Ful often blessed was his myrie throte' (3215-9). Chaucer avoids any hint of affectation or effeminacy, however, in the sweetness of Nicholas. His throat will prove equally adept at downing his share of a 'large quart ... of myghty ale' with the lady's husband (3497-8), or at sustained, histrionic 'capyng', when the stratagems of love demand such feats (3444ff). He is the devil-may-care, pleasure-loving, uninhibited young male, the lusty and unstudious student; he walks alert for amorous adventure, with the tang of strong wild herbs about him.

As such he is dramatically fitted to succeed with the girl in the bower below. For she too is 'wylde and yong' (3225); she has the voice of a swallow (3258); and she too evokes epithets of sweetness and bucolic fragrance. She is more delightful to look upon than a pear-tree in bloom (3248); her mouth is 'sweete as bragot or the meeth, Or hoord of apples leyd in hey or heeth' (3261–2).⁵ And, in a tale where there is a good deal of verbal play, we may be justified in suspecting a punning parallelism between the 'lycorys' sweetness of Nicholas and the 'likerous ye' that Alisoun 'sikerly' possessed (3244). True, she is the wife of a prospering village carpenter, and he is a traditionally subtle clerk of Oxford, but they both emerge as essentially country types – at least as these would be conceived by the *gentils*,⁶ from whose viewpoint such sophisticated fabliaux as this must be observed.

Their coming together is as certain and unthinking as spring; they take thought of nothing but how to achieve immediate and zestful satisfaction. The pollen-spicy bee seeks out the scented field-flower, 'a prymerole, a piggesnye' (3268). The roving eye detects the 'likerous' one – and the roving hand of 'hende Nicholas' reaches at once for the 'nether.' Nicholas's clerkly capacity for deviousness, upon which he will need to draw later, is referred to, at the moment of the first sexual advance, only to effect an ironic and punning anti-climax. Nicholas, finding the husband away,

> Fil with this yonge wyf to rage and pleye, ...
> As clerkes ben ful subtile and ful queynte;
> And prively he caughte hire by the queynte.⁷ (3273–6)

It is country pleasures he is intent upon and, though he is not so bestial as to neglect the preliminary gallantry of a kiss, he is not at all put off when she makes a show of refusing him even that; in no time he has spoken 'so faire' that he has won her total consent, and need now only devise the opportunity. Whereupon he smacks her 'aboute the lendes weel', kisses her 'sweete,' and withdraws temporarily from the scene singing to a fast tune on his minstrel's psaltery, the happy unaccommodated man (3284ff.).

Chaucer now introduces us to the luckless second lover. The essence of Absolon's contrasting failure lies in his *un*naturalness. That this small-town cleric and part-time barber fancies himself in the part of a courtly lover has often been pointed out;[8] but his perversity is more comically complex than this. Robert Bowen has recently observed, with somewhat disingenuous gravity, that Chaucer enriched the irony of Absolon's fate by making him the inhibited 'flatulatee' in contrast to Nicholas, the 'natural' man, the 'flatulator'; Absolon, who is 'somdeel squaymous/Of fartyng" (3337–8) and of all crasser manifestations of the flesh, suffers the ignominy of a 'thonder-dent' in the face, the calamity most suited to blast both his peculiar foppery and all his pretensions and hopes to a 'more-than-human' love.[9] What remains to be noted is that Chaucer has woven even more intricate threads of preparation for Absolon's earlier humiliation, his unintentional kissing of the nether eye. They are threads, moreover, which continue, in contrasting colours, the patterns of oral sensuousness begun in the portraits of his rival and the lady.

Absolon, for example, is also given to singing – but in a high, feminine voice, a 'quynyble' (3332),[10] a 'voys gentil and smal' (3360),[11] quavering, 'brokkynge as a nyghtyngale' (3377).[12] Such vocal endowments, applied to the serenading of an Alisoun, are fated to ineffectuality in competition with Nicholas, who sings simply in order to make his own chamber ring (3215), and trusts, in love-making, to plain speech and 'thakkyng' hands. Even under the lady's window Absolon's preliminary cough to gain her attention comes out with a thin, 'semy' sound (3697); he is by nature 'of speche daungerous' (3338), an oral as well as 'anal retentive,'[13] and for all his efforts he might as well have blown 'the bukkes horn' (3387).

Even more ironically futile are his preparations for wooing, and here the contrast with his rival is most marked. Where Nicholas is sweet, 'sweete as is the roote/Of lycorys,'' Absolon feels the need to chew cardamom and 'lycorys, To *smellen* sweete,' and to slip 'Under his tonge a trewe-love,' a leaf of an aromatic herb with sentimental associations (3690–2). His preoccupation with the gaining of a kiss is, of course, in keeping with his parody role as the courtly lover, for whom such a reward, as Bialacoil said, is 'the beste and most avenaunt ... Of loves payne ... And ernest of the remenaunt'[14]; but his concentration on oral matters has the quality of a fixation, an infantilism in direct contrast to the uncomplicated male maturity of Nicholas. Though Absolon is equally conscious of Alisoun as the essence of sweetness, he is no honey-bee raging at once about the honey-flower; he takes his stand lugubriously outside her window and addresses his 'hony-comb, sweete Alisoun, ... my sweete cynamome' (3698–9). The images identify him with the larder, not the meadows; and they are also in keeping with the coy sensuousness of a parish clerk who loves to swing his censer towards the young wives in his church (3340–1). Where Nicholas at the start demanded to have his will of the lady, Absolon bleats out an orally bathetic conceit: 'I moorne as dooth a lamb after the tete' (3704). Nicholas woos with no gifts but himself; Absolon not only 'So woweth hire that hym is wo begon' (3372) – the verbal echo deepening the bathos – but he sends presents to titillate *her* palate, 'pyment, meeth, and spiced ale,/And wafres, pipyng hoot out of the gleede' (3378–9). To this wild weazel-bodied wench, whose mouth was naturally 'sweete as ... the meeth,' he proffers more 'meeth.' Also he tries 'meede,' cash, because *he* thinks of her as being 'of town' (3380). 'For som folk,' Chaucer adds with straight face, 'wol ben wonnen for richesse,/And somme for strokes, and somme for gentillesse' (3381–2). These alternatives are fascinating in their inaptness, since most of Absolon's gift-making was neither luxurious nor sadistic nor courtly, but only a rather footling bestowal of artificial sweets upon the naturally sweet – upon a carpenter's 'hony deere' (3617), moreover, who had already been won by a fourth method not mentioned: simple frontal assault.

Absolon is granted no premonition of all this; his oral solicitudes betray him, indeed, into the most optimistic deductions:

> 'My mouth hath icched al this longe day;
> That is a signe of kissyng atte leeste.
> Al nyght me mette eek I was at a feeste.'   (3682–4)

From this he predicts 'That at the leeste wey I shal hire kisse' (3680), a prophecy which will have only a treacherous Delphic fulfilment, in the least and lowest way.[15] For Alisoun crudely repulses him from her window; he will have no 'com pa me' from her. Her curious phrase, usually explained as a snatch from a song, and meaning 'come kiss me,'[16] is linked in rhyme with *blame*, creating a sound which may also be intended as a baaing mockery of this falsetto lover, prompted by his own bleating image. But Absolon is too compulsive to desist; he pleads for the kiss that has become his fetish, promising to go if he gets it. Ceremoniously he sinks to his knees, a proper Troilus,[17] and begins to 'wype his mouth ful drie' (3730) to taste at last his 'hony-comb'; then 'ful savourly' (3735) and unaware, he offers up his sweetened effeminate lips to the unsavory bearded female fact. 'Who rubbeth now, who froteth now his lippes,' and with what? No longer with sweet herbs and licorice, but 'With dust, with sond, with straw, with clooth, with chippes' (3747–8).

Chaucer is not quite done with this theme. Absolon is shocked out of his synthetic passion but not out of his oral-anal personality. It serves him now to conceive his revenge. Armed with the hot coulter, ironic symbol of his sexual inadequacy,[18] he returns to the fatal window, calls once more, now with bitterness in his mouth, upon his 'sweete leef,' and promises her this time a gift of real 'richesse,' a gold ring, 'if thou me kisse' (3792–7). He can think of no other gambit, and whether he hoped to lure Alisoun again to repeat her insult, or this time to smoke out Nicholas, whose punning taunt on beards he had heard (3742–4), we are not told. It is Nicholas who looms and who promptly adds, to the lady's souring of Absolon's artificial sweetness, the blast that blows his scentedness away.[19]

Yet if inhibitions render men vulnerable, so also do the impulses of the uninhibited. 'Hende Nicholas,' whose hands and mind leap so quickly to the nether regions, is now recklessly presenting his own, naked to the blow. Smitten, agonized, he bellows out the words that bring the carpenter tumbling down and the story to its carefully anticipated end.

And Alisoun? Only she remains unscathed, and entirely successful,[20] Nature's female, neither inhibited nor lacking in primitive caution. She knew when to delay an ordinary kiss, to spur on the fit suitor, and when to contrive an extraordinary one, to discourage forever the unfit.

NOTES

1 *Works* ed. F.N. Robinson, 2nd ed. (Boston, Houghton-Mifflin 1957) *CT* I 3852–3. For the tale's history see Stith Thompson 'The Miller's Tale' in W.F. Bryan and G. Dempster *Sources and Analogues of Chaucer's Canterbury Tales* (Chicago, University of Chicago Press, 1941) 106–7.
2 The chaste phrase is Mrs Dempster's, *Dramatic Irony in Chaucer* (Stanford, Stanford University Press, 1932) 35.
3 For contrasting characteristics, in addition to those dealt with in this paper, see C.A. Owen, Jr 'Chaucer's *Canterbury Tales*: Aesthetic Design in Stories of the First Day' *ES* 35 (1954) 52ff.
4 Sweet-smelling herbs were sometimes hung from bedroom beams, or even intermingled with the floor rushes. See Sister M.E. Whitmore *Medieval Domestic Life ... in ... Chaucer* (Washington, DC, Catholic University of America Press 1937) 14, 35–6, 68. She suggests they may have

come fresh from Alison's garden (l.3572).

5 Too much emphasis has been laid on a single untypical detail, Alisoun's 'ypulled' eyebrows, by interpreters who would see her as a fashionable town flirt. 'Images of wild or young animals, ... suggestions of fruitfulness and natural growth' dominate her portrait, as J. Speirs has pointed out, *Chaucer the Maker* (London, Faber and Faber 1951) 129. See also my 'The Two Worlds of Geoffrey Chaucer' *Manitoba Arts Review* 2, no. 4 (Winnipeg 1941) 15 [pp. 3–19 above].

6 As Per Nykrog has established in *Les Fabliaux* (Copenhagen, 1957; new ed. Geneva, Droz 1960); cf C. Muscatine *Chaucer and the French Tradition* (Berkeley, California, University of California Press, 1957) 227ff.

7 *Queynte* seems to be punned on twice again: 3605, 3754.

8 See E.T. Donaldson 'Idiom of Popular Poetry in the *Miller's Tale*' EIE 1950 (New York 1951) 135ff.; and G. Stillwell 'The Language of Love in Chaucer's Miller's and Reeve's Tales ...' *JEGP* 54 (1955) 693–9.

9 'The Flatus Symbol in Chaucer' *Inland* (Salt Lake City) 2 (1959) 19–20. Although Bowen's article contains some parody of recent Chaucerian pedantics, it is here making valid interpretations.

10 See Robinson's note to this line.

11 *Gentil*, of course, carries also the parodic theme of courtly love; see D.D. Griffith 'On Word-Studies in Chaucer' *Philologica: The Malone Anniversary Studies* (Baltimore, Johns Hopkins Press 1949) 198.

12 See Robinson's glossary, *brokkinge*; also F. Klaeber *Das Bild bei Chaucer* (Berlin, R. Heinrich 1893) 435. The cacaphony of this strange word is intensified by the jingling preparation for it in the equally odd *brocage*, two lines before. Puns and verbal echoes occur frequently throughout in relation to the singing and general noise-making of the characters; cp. the use of *solas* in 3200 and 3335, and see Donaldson 'Idiom of Popular Poetry' 138.

13 The phrase, in its application, is Muscatine's, *Chaucer and the French Tradition* 228.

14 Robinson *Works*, *Romance of the Rose* lines 3677–80

15 An irony first noted by Richard Brathwait, *A Comment upon the Two Tales ... The Miller's Tale, and the Wife of Bath* (London, W. Godbid 1665) 44.

16 See Robinson's note to line 3709. A few lines later there is another sort of ironic echo, presumably meant to be unconscious on the part of the speaker, when Absolon uses the phrase 'trewe love'; cp. 3715 with 3692.

17 The parallel with the *Troilus* is noted by N. Coghill, *Geoffrey Chaucer* (London, Oxford University Press 1956) 47.

18 As Owen has observed, 'Chaucer's *Canterbury Tales* 53.
19 Or, as Muscatine more impressively if more punningly phrased it, *Chaucer and the French Tradition* 228, his 'anal-retentive squeamish spotlessness [is] punished with terrible aptness at the end'.
20 As J.Y.T. Greig noted, *The Psychology of Laughter and Comedy* (London, Allen & Unwin 1926), 104–5.

'After his Ymage':
The Central Ironies of the *Friar's Tale*

*S*O UNAPPRECIATED is the *Friar's Tale* that popular works on Chaucer still dismiss it, along with its companion *Summoner's Tale*, as a 'particularly coarse' affair,[1] or 'tedious as those horse-play medieval stories usually are.'[2] Even critics who have actually considered the work, and know that there is not a bawdy line in it, have been weak witnesses to the fact that there is not a tedious line either. Interpretation has dwelt too largely on the undoubtedly fascinating relations of the tale to the Canterbury framework and to the warfare of the summoners and friars, to the neglect of the story itself.[3] Yet the *conte*, considered quite apart from its frame, is one of Chaucer's most carefully worked and closely unified poems, and, in its sardonic development of the ironies latent in a Faustian situation, one of his most dramatic. Above all, in its unusual withholding of the denouement,[4] and in the subtlety of its moral implications, it is one of his most original compositions.

The tale idea as it came to Chaucer's ears – we have no source and no close analogues, and the weight of critical opinion is on the side of oral transmission to him[5] – was probably less like a fabliau than like one of those *facetiae* of Poggio, in the next century, short humorous anecdotes in which, to quote Edmund Storer, who has investigated the tradition apart from Chaucer, 'the matter is ninety per cent.'[6] A professional type – in one fourteenth-century telling he was a farmer,[7] in others a seneschal or a lawyer, but never a summoner – enters by chance into companionship with a devil who is roaming about to pick up whatever is consigned to him. The human rascal urges the devil to seize various objects or people apparently wished upon him by speakers in anger, but the devil refuses to accept anything not given him from the heart. Eventually they meet a professional victim of the human rascal who curses him to hell, and the devil carries him off. Embedded in the situation is ancient folk belief in the efficacy of curses uttered with intention.[8]

Chaucer, in elaborating this *facetia*, transforms it into a *novellino*, into a story where characterization and, even more, style – a pervasive duality of phrasing, an irony of attitude – achieve dominance without in any way reducing, but on the contrary extending, the grim comedies of the plot. And these comedies take on a curious complexity, half medieval, half Aristophanic, a playing of *Alazon* against *Eiron* in a series of scenes which, unobtrusively but harmoniously, build towards an orthodox Christian moral. To the primitive theme which Chaucer inherited, the rough justice of professional avarice rebuked and punished by a devil in disguise, is added poetic justice, the spectacle of a great but over-proud human hunter of sinners brought to bay unawares by a diabolic hunter whom he had sought to deceive and then to out-rival. The irony is deepened by the interweaving of a third theme: the human villain swears brotherhood with the satanic one to increase his own takings, only to create the conditions by which his own soul is taken. And the failure of his attempt to out-do, by masquerade and by imitation, the devil himself leads us directly to the moral of the tale which, as we shall see, is not primarily concerned with summoners or friars or even, as Coghill would have it, with the 'importance if Intention' in oaths,[9] but with masks and 'ymages.'

From the opening, Chaucer keeps his complex structure of ironies in mind. The first nineteen lines, usually interpreted either as 'digression' in the interests of framework portraiture,[10] or as somewhat irrelevant topical satire, a portrait of a particular archdeacon over-zealous in haling into his court offenders against ecclesiastical law, have subtle thematic purpose. This archdeacon is most implacable with 'lecchours' (1310) and with 'smale tytheres' (1312), and the most successful limb of his law, reaching out infallibly to sinners, is the summoner of our tale. Yet it is precisely the smallest tither in all Chaucer, the widow Mabely, who, falsely accused of lechery by this specialist in its detection, becomes the instrument of his downfall by indignantly consigning him to the devil.

After the archdeacon's portrait, the tale passes into a deliberate build-up of this Alazon-Summoner, this Greek comedy boaster, that he may have the highest possible fall. The archdeacon-inquisitor, the master, may be locally great, but his servant, the summoner, is of national stature: 'A slyer boye nas noon in Engelond;/For subtilly he hadde his espiaille ...' (1322–3). He is a great criminal investigator who works through undercover agents and informers; by extending protection to 'lecchours oon or two' he learns how to get his hands on 'foure and twenty mo' (1325–6). By such and other means he becomes a walking repository of secrets. The text carefully emphasizes this; the summoner had contact not only with ordinary bawds who 'tolde hym al the secree that they knewe' (1341), but also he had

> wenches at his retenue,
> That, wheither that sir Robert or sir Huwe,
> Or Jakke, or Rauf, or whoso that it were
> That lay by hem, they tolde it in his ere."   (1355–8)

His confidence, then, is based not only on his master's might and his own successes in spotting the guilty; he moves assured because he thinks he knows, in respect to local sexual scandals, everything. He has the disillusioned sophistication of a hardened vice-squad detective who assumes that everybody has something to hide. And it is precisely this self-confidence which will betray him into accusing a respectable widow of adultery, and getting his 'comeuppance' from her. Notice that he has presumably picked her before he met the devil, as part of the day's business, as someone he might be able to scare into a bribe with a false accusation. She is an untested victim, and once he becomes aware that he is in competition with nothing less than a fiend from hell, he might well have left her for another day. But he believes in his own infallibility, in that detective instinct which the tale is careful to endow him with at the start:

> For in this world nys dogge for the bowe
> That kan an hurt deer from an hool yknowe
> Bet than this somour knew a sly lecchour,
> Or an avowtier, or a paramour.   (1369–72)

If the story were only this, it would not of course be much more sophisticated than the original anecdote in its ironic effects. A zealous law-enforcement officer, out of over-confidence and exhibitionism, accuses an innocent person and is in consequence carried off to everlasting hell. What is wrong is that the punishment vastly exceeds the crime, even for such an unpopular professional, in an age when Hell was as real as it was terrible and there was no doubt that the loss of one's soul was the ultimate punishment. What is needed to raise the story is that irony we call poetic justice, and this is supplied within the first fifty lines, and with it the motivation for the summoner's zeal.

This motivation is not social dedication but private profit. The archdeacon's treasury got only half what this summoner extorted, for, as we are now told, he served fake summonses to people who could not read them but who were usually guilty enough to be 'glade for to fille his purs./And make hym grete feestes atte nale' (1348–9). At other times he merely used the information brought him by his protected prostitutes to threaten their customers with court action, and allowed himself to be bought off with bribes. Surely there is an implication too, that he is not above committing the sin he specializes in sniffing out. These informer-whores are 'alwey ... redy to his hond ... ;/For hire acqueyntance was nat come of newe' (1339–42). In short, to quote one of the many beautifully polished couplets of this tale,

> He was, if I shal yeven hym his laude,
> A theef, and eek a somnour, and a baude. (1353–4)

Chaucer now moves into the tale proper, and in the same motion, by a sleight of hand of style, casually introduces through an image a new theme of the expanding comedy:

> This false theef, this somonour ...
> Hadde alwey bawdes redy to his hond,
> As any hauk to lure in Engelond. (1338–40)

The summoner's relation to the sinner, in effect, is that of the hunter to the hunted. Twenty lines later the image is again glanced at by a single word. The summoner, we are told, would arrest with a false mandement both the lecher and the informer-bawd he lay with; then he would 'pile the man, and lete the wenche go' (1362). All editors gloss *pile* in this passage as *rob*, but the process is not so much simple robbery as blackmail, fleecing, and the word *pile*, modern dialectal *pill*, carrying the image of 'skinning,' is surely calculated to call up once more the falconry image. The summoner, who through the falcon of his mandement and the feathered lure of his bawd has brought his bird-sinner within reach, now skins the fowl and preserves the lure for use again.[12]

Seven lines later we have another hunting image, already quoted, where the summoner is likened to a 'dogge for the bowe' (1369) who can perceive at once when a deer is wounded and run it down for his master.[13] Then, plunging into the narrative, we pass imperceptibly from this image world to the real world of the hunter, itself a double and deceptive one:

> And so bifel that ones on a day
> This somnour, *evere waityng on his pray*,
> Rood for to somne an old wydwe, a ribibe,
> Feynynge a cause, for he wolde brybe.
> And happed that he saugh bifore hym ryde
> A gay yeman, under a forest syde. (1375–80)

Entering the story we have entered into the world of dramatic irony. Scene: a forest. Discovered: a mounted bowman dressed in hunter's green. To him a summoner, riding,[14] a master hunter of men on the path of his prey, a villain of devilish skill in scenting and fastening on the guilty secrets of others. But he knows not this stranger's secret. He fails to detect a greater hunter and devil then himself when clothed in Kendal green. 'Le premier tour du Diable,' as Denis de Rougemont has remarked in another context, 'est son *incognito.*'[15]

Some critics have felt the summoner should have been warned by the colour that the stranger is from the underworld, but I think, with D.W. Robertson, that Chaucer's listeners and readers, as well as the summoner, would have been insensitive to such pedantries.[16] Green cloth was habitually worn by foresters, yeomen, and hunters; for the latter especially, the colour made sense as camouflage; also it was thought to be naturally attractive to beasts. What more likely a person to find 'under this grene-wode shawe' than a man in green? If the summoner is obtuse at all here it is in assuming that the stranger is an ordinary yeoman rather than a hunter; if he had guessed the latter he might just conceivably have been able to suspect the stranger's diabolic origin, for demons often disguised themselves this way. Satan himself was sometimes described by the sermonists as the hunter of men in the wilderness of this world; there were tales of ghostly hunters on Dartmoor and elsewhere in Chaucer's England; and in France, as late as Reginald Scot's day, belief persisted in a certain Oray, 'a great marquesse' among devils, 'shewing himselfe in the likeness of a galant archer, carrieng a bowe and a quiver.'[17]

The summoner, however, had never read Grimm, nor on the other hand was he one of those holy innocents like St Dunstan who could tell a devil by his smell; consequently he greets the strange green man with instinctive comradeship: 'Hayl, and wel atake!' (1384). The yeoman's reply seems at first reading to be simply in kind: 'Welcome, and every good felawe!' But 'good felawe' is a phrase that never occurs in good faith in Chaucer.[18] The summoner of the *General Prologue*, we remember, would lend his concubine to a 'good felawe' for a year and teach any 'good felawe' to free himself, by salting the summoner's palm, from fear of the archdeacon's curse (1650 ff). Colloquially a 'good felawe' was a rascal, though it might mean only a 'boon companion.'[19] Perhaps the mysterious man in green intends only the latter but I think we are being given our first hint here that the fiend knows very well who the rider is who has so well overtaken him. And it is just possible that he is savouring his devil's prevision when he askes the summoner if he intends to ride far today, and elicits the answer: 'Nay;/Heere faste by' (1388–9). Certainly Chaucer has arranged it so that, on a second reading, we remember the summoner will be riding all the way to hell before the day is over.

The extent of the devil's foreknowledge in this tale has not, I believe, been critically considered, and yet it is basic to an understanding of its ironies. He is not, of course, The Devil, Satan himself, whom Chaucer mentions twice only in his writings and each time as 'ybounde' in Hell. This pseudo-bailiff is, in biblical terminology, only a demon or fiend, an anonymous lesser devil, in fact a hard-worked servant-hellion – somewhat like Juliana's tempter – as he himself explains later (1426–9).[20] But to Chaucer's public even the humblest fiends would be expected to have superior knowledge, if only, as Isidore of Seville had pointed out, because they had lived so long, being of angelic origin.[21] Though neither angels nor devils had full knowledge of the future they were thought to have more than mortal vision, speaking both physically and psychologically.[22] A demon visiting earth was, in particular, almost invariably portrayed as a soul-hunter of dreadful intuition, quick to detect the nearness of vulnerable prey, confident of victory.

The confidence was not always justified, however, for even the catastrophic consequences of a pact with a devil could be entirely avoided, at the last stroke of the clock, as Theophilus avoided them, and Celestin, by appeal from a repentant heart to the peculiar powers of the Virgin.[23] Indeed such escape must always be possible, since no devil, nor angel even, could share God's foreknowledge of a demonic victory over a man's soul.[24] The possibility of a happy reversal will become, as we shall see, structurally significant in the *Friar's Tale* too, but what is more important to understand at the initial stages of the story is that the yeoman-devil would have sufficient insight into the summoner's character to feel at least ninety per cent sure of carrying him off to hell.

Against this well-based confidence, manifested already through slyness and anticipatory irony, Chaucer now sets the equally strong but illusory confidence of the summoner himself, displayed through bold-faced lie and shameless boasting. It is the Eiron-Alazon conflict of Greek comedy all over again. Note how even the words the summoner picks to explain his business – 'He dorste nat, for verray filthe and shame/Seye that he was a sommonour' – reinforce his pride in himself as a man of affairs:

> Myn entente [is] ...
> To ryden, for to reysen up a rente
> That longeth to my lordes duetee.   (1389–94)

'Artow thanne a bailly?' asks the yeoman (1392), quickly cutting the summoner down to size. Receiving the answer 'Ye,' the stranger proceeds straight-faced to admit that he too is a bailiff. That the fiend is not deceived, that he knows all along his companion is a summoner, we can surely infer from the fact that eighty lines later, without further information from his victim, he calls him 'sire somonour' (1474). But though the devil is not deluded, the summoner is. Moreover he is hooked on his own lie, and the fiend slyly tightens the line to him, meanwhile savouring the ironies of the situation. 'Depardieux,' he says – swearing an unusual and fancy oath which in itself carries a verbal irony – 'Depardieux ... deere brother,/Thou art a bailly, and I am another' (1395–6). Brother-bailiffs, so why not friends, he adds. Why not, indeed, sworn brothers, like Palamon and Arcite, or Amis and Amiloun?

This is rushing matters, however, and we would lose faith in the reality of both summoner and devil if the latter had not, before the fomer could hesitate, smoothly dangled a real lure.

> I have gold and silver in my cheste;

If that thee happe to comen in oure shire,
Al shal be thyn ...   (1400–2)

The lure has been feathered by an ironist. All the devil's possessions
will indeed be the summoner's, though he will have to remain in that
dim shire to enjoy them.

And so each lays 'his trouthe' in the other's hand (1404), as they
must to pledge brotherhood, brotherhood unto death. 'Grantmercy ...
by my feith' (1403) intones the summoner – a cliché plighting perhaps,
but note how the irony of two deceivers swearing fidelity to each other,
and swearing it on their own sinister and undefined faiths, is played
upon henceforth. The summoner, now that he is a brother to the yeoman, demands to be told 'feithfully' (1420) the yeoman-bailiff's tricks,
so that he may improve his own technique. 'As my brother tel me,
how do ye?' (1423). And the disguised fiend replies, 'Now, *by my trouthe*,
brother deere ... /As I shal tellen thee a *feithful* tale' – then hands him
a carefully vague story about his having a master so niggardly he must
take anything that 'men wol me yive' (1430), or that he can get out of
them by trickery or extortion, to make ends meet. 'I kan no bettre
telle, *feithfully*, he concludes (1433).

But in this new comedy of false brotherhood we are not allowed to
forget the old one of the hunter unwittingly hunted. The very first
question the summoner asks in seeking to exploit the advantages of
brotherhood with a bailiff is the yeoman's dwelling place, in case he
wants to look him up 'another day' (1411):

This yeman hym answerde in softe speche,
'Brother,' quod he, 'fer in the north contree.'   (1412–13)

The ambiguity of this remark, with what Robinson calls its 'veiled
revelation of the Yeoman's character,' has long been enjoyed.[25] *Ab
aquilone omne malum*, including the Satan of Job and Jeremiah. On
the medieval stage Hell was sited north.[26] And the rest of the stranger's
'softe' reply is such a conscious double-dealing in words it raises him
to the company of the fox in the *Nun's Priest's Tale*:

... fer in the north contree,
Where-as I hope som tyme I shal thee see.
Er we departe, I shall thee so wel wisse
That of myn hous ne shaltow nevere mysse.   (1413–16)

What follows is even more subtle. As Mrs Dempster has put it, 'in the summoner's failure to perceive this irony, in his easy, unconcerned way of dropping the question as satisfactorily settled, there is almost as much dramatic irony as in any answer he might have given.'[27]

And now the devil's disingenuous confession that he must live by extortion leads the summoner on to a worse one. He also has to live, he assures his new brother, by conscienceless blackmailings which, moreover, he never confesses at shrift (alas for his soul). And of course he too will accept anything offered: 'I spare nat to taken, God it woot,/ But if it be to hevy or to hoot' (1435–6). The last expression, as all Chaucer editors hasten to tell us, is proverbial.[28] Perhaps, however, it is there not because Chaucer could not resist a proverb but because this one points unerringly forward to the denouement, when the summoner will extort his last gift, a curse from the widow which proves so heavy and so hot it sinks him straight to hell.

Meantime the summoner is happy and at ease. He has met a charming fellow-rogue, a generous one who promises him a share in the loot, a sophisticated one to whom he can unbutton his rogueries without being under the necessity of pretending penitence,[29] and a learned one from whom even he may hope to acquire new tricks in extortion. It was a wonderful overtaking. 'Wel be we met,' says the summoner again, 'By God and by Seint Jame!' (1443). They will ride forth to adventure, brother-hunters. Casually then, as a polite after-thought, the summoner turns to his 'leeve brother' and enquires his name (1444). 'This yeman gan a litel for to smyle' – the smile of Pandarus and of the *diabolus cachinnans*[30] about to release the dramatic irony he has created upon its victim – ' "Brother," quod he, "wiltow that I thee telle?/ I am a feend; my dwellyng is in helle" ' (1446–8). How simply he puts it! 'And heere I ryde aboute my purchasyng,/To wite wher men wol yeve me any thyng./My purchas is th'effect of al my rente' (1449–51) – just as the ferreting out of lechers is, for the summoner, 'the fruyt of al *his* rente' (1373). The yeoman, confessed devil now, proceeds to underline the parallel between them: 'Looke how thou rydest for the same entente,/To wynne good, thou rekkest nevere how' (1452–3) – a pretty ambiguity in that word *good* – 'Right so fare I, for ryde wolde I now/Unto the worldes ende for a *preye*.'

With a less skilful narrator than Chaucer there might well have been a slump in the dramatic interest at this point. The devil has revealed himself, the irony of the mistaken identity is ended. At once, however, the central idea latent in the original *facezia* takes over, the hair-raising comedy of a rogue so confident he will compete with, even advise, a declared devil. A lesser villain would have taken fright at the mere thought that he has got himself into sworn brotherhood with a fiend, into a demon-compact. This was an age when, as Coulton has remarked, the ordinary man believed utterly in the existence of devils.[31] Even a hardened criminal would have murmured 'Retro me Sathanas' out of pure prudence. But this summoner is of the stuff that Fausts are made. He is only momentarily startled:

> *Benedicite!* what sey ye?
> I wende ye were a yeman trewely.
> Ye han a mannes shap as wel as I.[32]   (1456–8)

Surprise gives place at once to coolly admiring curiosity. Here is an excellent trick; it would be valuable to learn how it is done: 'Han ye a figure thanne determinat/In helle ...?' (1459–60). The information of power, the sort of knowledge that might bring illimitable earthly position and pleasure beyond what is obtainable by natural means, this is what Gerbert and Theophilus and Faust wanted, what all who sold their souls hoped to gain. It is the quality in this summoner which makes him far more 'modern' than Benét's Daniel Webster, but it is also that fatal illimitable curiosity about the devil's secrets which is as old as Eve and as medieval as the dabblers in black magic denounced by Passavanti in Chaucer's century.[33]

The fiend, replying, continues to savour the irony of his role. He assures the summoner that in hell devils can have any shape or no shape, at will, and on earth choose that form which 'moost able is oure preyes for to take' (1472). A less confident Alazon than our summoner might have asked himself at this point why the fiend had chosen this day to utilize the form of an extortionist bailiff, the very disguise which the summoner himself had assumed. But the blissfully assured apparitor is puzzled only by something apparently impractical in the devil's conduct. What motivation could a fiend have to busy himself with various human disguises and sweaty ridings over the earth, only to make the same chancy living as himself? Where lay the profit? Particularly, perhaps he is thinking, where did it lie for someone who already has chests of gold at home? 'What maketh yow to han al this labour?' (1473). It never crosses the summoner's mind that the devil might be interested in anything as immaterial as a soul.

And now the fiend evades the revelatory answer, just as the summoner had missed the key question. He reminds his friend that time is getting on and he prefers to spend the rest of the day winning something rather than explaining all the wits and wiles of hell. His attitude to the summoner, we begin now to realize, has been subtly changing from the moment he has declared his own identity. The *leeve brothers* that larded his speech have disappeared, and will reappear only as open ironies. And he has gone on to betray a little contempt for the summoner's powers, as a mere mortal, to penetrate the disguises of devils:

> Somtyme lyk a man, or lyk an ape,
> Or lyk an angel kan I ryde or go.
> It is no wonder thyng thogh it be so;
> A lowsy jogelour kan deceyve thee,
> And pardee, yet kan I moore craft than he.   (1464–8)

A little contempt here, and, though the fiend is not claiming more than his due,[34] a little archetypal devil's pride.

The subtleties of the changing relationships between these two, first as stranger-equals, then as false-bailiff brothers, now as declared devil to undeclared summoner, are reflected even by such trivia as the wavering from polite *ye* to familiar *thee* in the summoner's speech, and back (as Norman Nathan has recently pointed out).[35] He addresses the stranger formally at meting, slips into the familiar (1396), pulls himself back when he hears the yeoman has a chest of gold at home (1410), drops to the intimate when the yeoman complains that his income is nevertheless small (1444), nips back to the polite when he discovers the yeoman is a fiend (1456), and does not return to the familiar till the devil assures him they are still sworn brothers and will share their loot (1526). The devil, on the other hand, starts to *tutoyer* the summoner from the moment they meet.

Meanwhile, in the slyest possible manner, the irony of the disguises comes to an end. The stranger from hell had already taken off his double masks of yeoman and bailiff. But what of the summoner and his bailiff-mask? We have seen that the fiend has all along subtly shown his awareness of the summoner's identity, and his intention in respect to him, but he has revealed this only to the audience, so that they may enjoy with him the divine *eironeia* of omniscience looking down on the summoner's proud human ignorance. It is only when the pseudo-bailiff at last asks the declared devil what his real purpose is that the latter, in an evasive answer, casually and politely lifts the summoner's own false-face:

> What maketh yow to han al this labour?
> Ful many a cause, leeve sire *somonour*. (1473–4)

Even now the summoner gives no sign, makes no protest, his villainous imperturbability equal even to this demonstration of the supernatural insight possessed by the creature with whom he is playing a game of brotherhood. He simply listens, tacitly acknowledging his identity, while the devil, enjoying his first little triumph, drives home the point of his superior intelligence. He will not, he says, take valuable time from the day's hunt to explain everything about his profession, 'For, brother myn, thy wit is al to bare ...' (1480). The demon proceeds nevertheless, as by a condescending after-thought, to read the summoner a lecture on the diabolic function, while the summoner rides in silence – the only weapon he has left in this 'daliance' he was so eager to begin.

Most critics treat the devil's disquisition here as an author's digression, a piece of interesting but non-functional, even disharmonious pedantry by Chaucer. One solemn analyser is quite sure the passage constitutes the most open satiric attack to be found in the whole *Canterbury Tales* upon theology in general.[36] Yet the lecture is surely entirely functional and in harmony with the spirit of comic irony that pervades this whole tale. In the first place, it is not only the summoner who has grown curious about the motivations and intentions of the devil. So has the reader, and the story would be less understandable and less satisfying if the reader were not supplied with good reasons for diabolic visitations to earth. In the second place, the narrator turns this expositional necessity into an opportunity for further ironies. The devil is only mock-humble in his sceptical asides and his vaguenesses, for he is being diabolically careful not to disclose which of the various purposes are activating him – with the result that the summoner is left just sufficiently in the dark to preserve his own *hubris*. The climax is still to come and it is not to be anticipated. Devils, we learn, are sometimes sent to deal with men at the command of God Himself, and so operate, despite themselves, for man's salvation. Is this why he has appeared to the summoner? No, since the methods used in such cases are apparently all painful, involving torment of the body, as with Job, or of the spirit, or of both. But so far this fiend has troubled neither the proud flesh nor the avaricious soul of the summoner. Is there another permutation? Yes, and the fiend carefully ends the first half of his commentary on this climax:

> And somtyme be we servant unto man,
> As to the erchebisshop Seint Dunstan,
> And to the apostles servant eek was I. (1501–3)

A servant unto man! What a glowing prospect for this summoner. True he is neither apostle, saint, nor even archbishop, but has not the very devil who was once assigned to serve the apostles themselves been sent today to him?[37] Some such comforting thoughts, and not fearsome ones, must certainly be the summoner's at this moment for he does not ask if the demon is after his body or soul or both, but only for professional information: exactly how do fiends make up complete 'newe bodies' for themselves (1504–6)? It is not only a nice scientific problem, it is a technical secret that might, who knows, prove of value to a man whose profession, as we have seen, puts him in need of disguise, and whose last mask has been found quite inadequate. This *soigné* summoner-Faust, so far from being frightened, is seizing the moment to study how to be a complete devil himself.

The demon is amused enough to give him a sort of answer. Sometimes we create the illusion of new bodies, but often we simply make use of old ones, as when we raised Samuel to speak to the Witch of Endor. It is a dubious example, since the theologians held it was Samuel's true ghost, with no witchcraft or hellcraft involved, and our devil quickly leaves the subject, ending his sermon with the scornful shrug of a man of Satan speaking to a mere man of the Church: 'I do no fors of youre dyvynytee' (1512). He cannot, however, resist an extra touch of foreshadowing:

> But o thyng warne I thee, I wol nat jape,
> Thou wolt algates wit how we been shape;
> Thou shalt hereafterward, my brother deere,
> Come there thee nedeth nat of me to leere. (1513–6)

Below the obvious implication that the summoner is ultimately hell-bound there lies, on second reading, the nice ambiguity of 'hereafter-ward,' since the summoner is to learn it all firsthand before this day is over.

What a worthy forerunner this learned tricky *diabolus* is of the Mephistopheles of the Elizabethans! Like Faust's betrayer he has the stamp of the Apocryphal Asmodeus on him, that devil whom the Middle Ages pictures as a most handsome and likable sophisticate, gambler, authority on the occult, author and patron of the arts (he was supposed to have helped Boccaccio write the *Decameron*) and a scholarly Master of Arts himself from the great College of Hell.[38] Chaucer's devil indeed thinks of Hell in academic terms:

> For thou shalt, by thyn owne experience,
> Konne in a chayer rede of this sentence
> Bet than Virgile, while he was on lyve,
> Or Dant also.[39] (1517–20)

Yet, beneath the comedy of this conception of the summoner mounting the hard way to a flaming professor's chair of Infernal Economy and expounding from it with more authority than any mere imagining poet lies the curious comi-tragedy which is the hallmark of Chaucer. If the summoner protested at this moment, or even gave heed, there would only be comedy. It is his silence, his heedlessness, his terrible preoccupation with what he can get out of the devil, not what the devil may get out of him, that carries the poem into the realm of the ironies of fate. So far as his soul goes, this summoner is what we might call today a 'murderee'; his deafness to all warnings, his assumption of his own invulnerability, his very indifference to the subject of souls, of his own soul above all, predetermines his loss of it. What Nevill Coghill has said of the Pardoner is perhaps even more apropos of this summoner:

He has taken the root of all evil to be his good; as the Maiorcan proverb has it, he is seeing black white. But Chaucerian irony has a quality ... beyond the power of this root principle of opposition between what is said and meant or what is done and intended. It is the quality of doom ... What is more ironical than a will supposed free, freely struggling to attain a preordained doom, the opposite of its intention?[40]

For see now how the summoner forces his fate upon himself. The devil has ended his sermon and its monitory peroration, and he seeks to restore the conversation to simple 'daliance,' and even to give the summoner a way out by letting him feel free to end their companionship. The fiend's phrasing, of course, may also contain another sinister foreboding:

' ... Now lat us ryde blyve,
For I wole holde compaignye with thee
Til it be so that thou forsake me.'
'Nay,' quod this sumonour, 'that shal nat bityde!
I am a yeman, known is full wyde;
My trouthe wol I holde, as in this cas.'   (1520–5)

The devil had already unmasked the summoner's pretence to be a yeoman bailiff, but the summoner, with his usual effrontery and reckless avarice, claps the mask back on. He has caught a devil by the tail for a partner, and he is not going to let go; let the devil understand he is dealing with a respectable citizen who keeps, and demands, businesslike fidelity to a troth:

'As I am sworn, and ech of us til oother,
For to be trewe brother in this cas;
And bothe we goon abouten oure purchas.
Taak thou thy part, what that men wol thee yive,
And I shal myn; thus may we bothe lyve.
And if that any of us have moore than oother,
Lat hym be trewe, and parte it with his brother.'
'I graunte,' quod the devel, 'by my fey.'
And with that word they ryden forth hir wey.   (1528–36)

There follows the incident of the carter and his mired horses, the first possible bit of business for the partnership. When the infuriated driver consigns his animals, cart, load, and all to the devil the summoner is fascinated. How easy it's going to be. 'Heere shal we have a pley' (1548), but not the pley he thinks. Characteristically it is the summoner who proposes that the devil take possession of property which has been, so to speak, only orally delivered to him. For the former it is 'the more taken the more shared.' Here of course Chaucer is following the ancient story, by making the devil more ethical, judging men by their intentions not their words.[41] But it is very much Chaucer's devil who takes time, when the horses free the cart and the carter calls on Christ to bless them, to underline the lesson with a couplet which in itself is almost a definition of one kind of irony:

> 'Heere may ye se, myn owene deere brother,
> The carl spak oo thing, but he thoghte another.' (1567–8)

The manifold implications of that remark are lost on the summoner. What is in his thought, as they pass through the town (his last earthly town) and out its farther end, is simply that the fiend has muffed a chance, and that he is now in a position to score over him. Cowling has remarked that 'the Summoner is so hardened and determined in his trickery that, compared with him, the devil is a country bumpkin.'[42] This, however, is only what the devil wants the summoner to think.

Now they stop at the gate of a widow, presumably the victim the summoner originally set out for. She constitutes, he is careful to inform his brother, a real test of a summoner's skill, for she is notoriously stingy on the one hand, and without a vice on the other – at least so far as the summoner knows. Nevertheless, he boasts, he will have twelvepence or summon her to court. In the flush of his anticipation he even rises to irony himself, at the devil's expense:

> 'But for thou kanst nat, as *in this contree,*
> Wynne thy cost, taak heer ensample of me.' (1579–80)

I do not know if it has been observed that this is the last thing he ever gets to say to the devil. From now on till the fiend wins him and whisks him to hell the summoner is fully engaged in coping with his intended victim.

His method is instant aggression. He bangs on the gate and roars the sort of insult that will winkle the old woman out at once: 'I trowe thou hast som frere or preest with theee' (1583). If she hasn't why doesn't she show herself? She emerges; he immediately declares he has a summons, and orders her, on pain of excommunication, to appear the next morning and 'answere to the court of certeyn thynges' (1589) carefully unspecified.

At once she calls upon the heavens in protest. Yet it should be observed that it is not her innocence she asserts but her inability to appear in court. She has been sick, she cannot walk or ride any distance, she has a pain in her side. Can't he leave a copy of the charge and have her attorney answer for her? This lady doth protest too much, it seems, and not about the right things, and the effect upon the reader is a certain suspense: has the summoner, with his infallibly lucky nose, scented out a stricken deer after all, a victim too guilty to curse him?

Certainly the summoner thinks so, and it is our awareness of this which gives the climax its dramatic power. He does not stop to remind himself that the threat of his master's court could strike terror even into the innocent – for who could be sure they had not involuntarily exposed themselves to some charge in a century when mere association with certain excommunicated persons might lead to the same penalty for the associate, and when inability to pay the accompanying fine could lead to indefinite imprisonment?[43] He does not pause to consider that she has called on the Lord in witness, on 'Crist Jhesu, kyng of kynges' (1590), and finally on 'Seinte Marie' – the only Power, in the tradition of devil-pacts, whom the summoner could have called upon effectively at this juncture to save himself.[44] Such adjurations, to a summoner, are only expletives, signs of her guilty agitation, and they spur him on to his own fate. Even her request for delay he takes as a readiness to bribe. All right, he says, in effect, pay me five dollars and I'll let you off. I won't make much out of it, believe me, 'My maister hath the profit, and nat I' (1601).

The various ironies of the tale have so come together at this point that this line can be read on at least three levels. First we accept it as a piece of the summoner's technique. Then we remember that it must be a briber's lie, since he has no summons against her and will pocket anything he gets. Third, we perceive that the statement is an unconscious prophecy, for his 'maister' is no longer the archdeacon but the fiend who will shortly take the 'profit', that is, both the widow's pan (the only object the summoner apparently succeeds in depriving her of) and the summoner himself, as his just and agreed-on 'rente.'

The widow continues to protest, in exactly the terms which lure the summoner on. It is her poverty now, still not her innocence, she pleads – what good to plead innocence to a summoner? Have mercy, she cries, let me off this time. He is sure he has hooked her! And now in his delusion of triumph he bellows a denial of mercy, and by the very wording of his denial puts into his victim's mind the formula which will in a few moments remove him forever from access to the seat of Mercy:

'Nay thanne,' quod he, 'the foule feend me fecche

If I th'excuse, though thou shul be spilt!'   (1610–1).

Then, and only then, does the forlorn old woman say: 'Allas! ... God woot, I have no gilt' (1612).

It is too late. He takes note but he cannot retreat, driven by his inner nemesis of avarice and pride. He must get something today, and he must outdo the fiend, nay instruct him in the fine art of extortion. He reduces the demand to her new pan. Also, in reckless desperation, he makes precise at last his accusation. It is a double one, so scabrous he must have hoped she would pay him, however innocent, to get rid of him rather than to suffer the sheer scandal of the charges. She has defaulted, he says, on a debt she owes him, a bribe he paid to protect her from the consequences of her secret adultery.

He has gone too far. The quarry turns on the hunter, the slandered widow falls on her knees, not before the archdeacon, as the summoner had threatened, but before heaven, and blasts her tormentor.[45] He lies, she is utterly innocent, 'Ne nevere I nas but of my body trewe!' (1621). As for *his* body,

> Unto the devel blak and rough of hewe
> Yeve I thy body and my panne also!   (1622–3)

Upon the dreadful agent of Christ's curse the most dreadful of all curses has fallen.[46] Yet still there is a moment of suspense. She has uttered the fatal formula – but does she mean it? The witnessing fiend has, we have seen, his principles and his punctilio in these matters, and he intervenes now, with the utmost respect, not to say affection, to make sure that it is time to whisk the summoner off to his master, the black and shaggy Satan himself:

> Now, Mabely, myn owene mooder deere,
> Is this youre wyl in ernest that ye seye?   (1626–7)

It is, and she repeats it – or does she? Is there still a chance for the summoner?

> 'The devel,' quod she, 'so fecche hym er he deye,
> And panne and al, *but he wol hym repente!*'   (1628–9)

Unless he will repent! The summoner still balances on the pit's edge.
And now, in the last words he speaks on earth, he topples himself over:

> 'Nay, olde stot, that is nat myn entente,'
> Quod this somonour, 'for to repente me ...
> I wolde I hadde thy smok and every clooth!' (1630–3)

It only remains now for the fiend smoothly, with brotherly firmness,
to bring down the curtain – and with a final jest at the summoner's
lifelong passion to imitate and outdo the devil himself:

> 'Now, brother,' quod the devel, 'be nat wrooth;
> Thy body and this panne been myne by right.
> Thou shalt with me to helle yet to-nyght,
> Where thou shalt knowen of oure privetee
> Moore than a maister of dyvynytee.' (1634–8)

The last ambiguities have been uttered. In a single line we pass to
the ultimate irony of the deed: 'And with that word this foule feend
hym hente' (1639). Two lines more and we are at the moral:

> And, God, *that maked after his ymage*
> *Mankynde*, save and gyde us, all and some,
> And leve thise somonours goode men bicome! (1642–4)

Conventional, an insincerely pious hope of the narrating Friar,[47]
since he has just told us that hell is the 'heritage' of all summoners
(1641), these three lines are nevertheless most delicately calculated by
Chaucer to do most important things. The phrase 'after his ymage'
reminds us of all that has gone before. What was the summoner's sin
that cast him into eternal hell if it was not his insensitivity, in his
avaricious pride, to the idea that he was modelled by God, and his
determination to make over his image into that of the devil? The theme
of human faces and the masks they wear, the realities beneath disguises, a theme which we have seen to be constant in this tale, is
sounded once more in the first two lines of this moral.

The third leads us back from the tale told, which alone I have been
concerned with, the tale complete in itself and as labyrinthine in its
ironies as any Chaucer wrote, to the outer and almost equally intricate

maze that surrounds it – to the tale's teller and to the Canterbury pilgrimage, the scene of the telling.[48]

NOTES

1 Norman Brett-James *Introducing Chaucer* (London, Harrap 1949) 98. Even H.S. Bennett refers to it as a 'lewd tale' though 'the brilliance of the telling makes us condone the coarse nature ... ' etc.; *Chaucer and the Fifteenth Century* (Oxford, Oxford University Press 1947) 73.
2 H.D. Sedgwick *Dan Chaucer* (New York, Bobbs-Merrill 1934) 293. Cp. the condescending attitude of Raymond Preston to both tales in his *Chaucer* (London; Sheed & Ward 1952) 246: 'The tellers have little or nothing to say.' Cp. also G.K. Anderson *Old and Middle English Literature* (Oxford, Oxford University Press 1950) 159, who dismisses the *Friar's Tale* as a weak fabliau and Edward Hutton *The Franciscans in England* (London, Constable 1926) 192.
3 Even Germaine Dempster's usually valuable *Dramatic Irony in Chaucer* (Stanford, Stanford University Press 1932) treats the tale from the assumption, which will not bear analysis, that 'a rather un-Chaucerian' anxiety to fit the tale to the framework has involved 'a sacrifice of realism to the requirements of satire' (42). More appreciative, though sketchy, is R.K. Root's commentary in his *Poetry of Chaucer* rev. ed. (Boston, Houghton-Mifflin, 1934) 245–9. The most satisfying analysis of the ironies within and around the tale became accessible only after the present article was committed for publication; *vide* A.C. Cawley 'Chaucer's Summoner, the Friar's Summoner and the Friar's Tale' *Proceedings of the Leeds Philosophical and Literary Society (Literary and Historical Section)* 8 (1957) 173–80.
4 Noted by B.H. Bronson as a rare departure from Chaucer's normal practice of sacrificing suspense to make clear his aim, in oral delivery; 'Chaucer's Art in Relation to His Audience' *Five Studies in Literature, University of California Publications, in English* 8 (1940) 11 n7. Bronson says that W.M. Hart called this peculiarity of the *Friar's Tale* to his attention, but neither critic seems to have pursued the point.
5 See R.D. French *A Chaucer Handbook* 2nd ed. (New York, Crofts 1947) 287; and Archer Taylor 'The Friar's Tale' *Sources and Analogues of Chaucer's Canterbury Tales*, ed. W.F. Bryan and G.Dempster (Chicago, University of Chicago 1941) 269–74. See also F.N. Robinson's headnote to the tale in the second edition of his *Works of Geoffrey Chaucer* (Bos-

ton, Houghton-Mifflin 1957). Textual references in this article are to this edition.

6 Introduction to *Facetiae of Poggio* (London, Routledge 1928) 4. See also Archer Taylor 'The Devil and the Advocate' *PMLA* 36 (1921) 35–59; Dempster *Dramatic Irony* 44n; Stith Thompson *Motif-Index of Folk Literature*, rev. ed. (Copenhagen, Rosenkilde 1955–8) IV 249–50, V 40–1

7 Archer Taylor prints this version, ibid. 38–9.

8 'O karissime, ista maledictio et donacio non procedit ex corde et ideo non possum eam tollere,' says Demon to Rusticus in Taylor's exemplum, ibid.

9 Nevill Coghill *The Poet Chaucer* (London, Oxford University Press, 1949) 162

10 E.g., A.C. Baugh 'The Original Teller of the Merchant's Tale' *MP* 35 (1937) 24

11 Priests are presumably referred to in line 1356, excellent sources of information if one accepts the tale-teller's bias. See Robinson's note, *Works* 705, and B.L. Manning *The People's Faith in the Time of Wyclif* (Cambridge: Cambridge University Press 1919) 35.

12 See *English Dialect Dictionary*, *pill*, v. 1: 'to ... strip off the outer skin.' Cp. also lines 1407–8, where the summoner is compared to a butcherbird, which, as Speght long ago noted, is 'very rauenous, preying vpon others.' See T.P. Harrison 'Chaucer's "Wariangles" ' *N&Q* 199 (1954) 189; Thomas Speght, ed. *Workes of ... Chaucer* (London: Bishop 1598), annotation to Fo°. 39 p. 1.

13 In the *Memoriale presbiterorum* of 1344 corrupt archdeacons and their apparitors are described as *canes infernales*; see W.A. Pantin *The English Church in the Fourteenth Century* (Cambridge, Cambridge University Press 1955) 207, 271.

14 Not walking, though archdeacon's apparitors such as he were not allowed horses; see L.A. Haselmayer 'The Apparitor and Chaucer's Summoner' *Spec* 12 (1937) 56. It may be assumed he uses a horse the better to round up his victims.

15 *La part du diable* (Paris, Gallimard 1946) 15

16 'Why the Devil Wears Green' *MLN* 69 (1954) 470–2. In point of fact, though devils could be green, red, yellow, or blue, the popular notion was that of Widow Mabely, that they were ragged and 'blak and rough of hewe' (1622), so that if anything could have warned the summoner it would have been the unusual black fringes on the devil's green courtepy. Devils with black mantles are frequent in Germanic legends; it seems to be only in Spanish tales that green devils are frequent, but the Spanish

proverb 'as green as the devil' is supposed to have arisen because green was a sacred colour of the enemy Moor: see M.J. Rudwin *The Devil in Legend and Literature* (Chicago, Open Court 1931) 45f.; A. Warkentin *The Devil in the German Traditional Story* (Chicago, University of Chicago 1937) 23.

17 Scot *The Discouerie of Witchcraft* 1584 facs. ed. (London Rodker 1930) 218). For an example from the sermons, see *Blickling Homilies* II 209 (on Psalm CXIX) cited by L.W. Cushman *The Devil and the Vice in the English Dramatic Literature before Shakespeare* Studien zur englischen Philologie 6 (1900) 9. For ghostly hunters in general see M.D. Conway *Demonology and Devil Lore* (New York, Holt 1879) II 353–61, and Edward Langton *Satan, a Portrait* ... (London, Skeffington 1945) 73.

18 The use is pejorative in all six of the instances listed in J.S.P. Tatlock and A.G. Kennedy *A Concordance to ... Chaucer* (Washington, Carnegie 1927); see entry for 'fellow.'

19 See Robinson's note, *Works* 667 (to I 650).

20 See Montagu Summers *The History of Witchcraft and Demonology* (London, Kegan Paul 1926) 51f. For the conception of Satan bound see *CT* II 361, 634, and T. Spencer 'Chaucer's Hell ... ' *Spec* 2 (1927) 187. In the Harley manuscript of the *Harrowing of Hell* Christ tells Satan that he will bind him so fast that only 'þe smale fendes þat bueþ nout stronge,/ he shulen among men yonge'; ed. W.H. Hulme *EETS* 100 (London 1907) 13, lines 125, 133–4.

21 See Langton, *Satan* 64.

22 Ibid 65. The concept of a disguised fiend using superhuman knowledge to trap souls is, of course, common to many literatures, including Old English (see *Juliana*) and Scandinavian (Loki); see R.E. Woolf 'The Devil in Old English Poetry' *RES* n.s. 4 (1953) 1–12.

23 The Theophilus story was widely known in western Europe from the sixth century; among those who treated it were Paulus Diaconus, Hrotswitha, and Rutebeuf. See E.A. Grillot de Givry *Le Musée des sorciers, mages et alchimistes* (Paris, Libraire de France 1929) 112f; and Rudwin *The Devil* 179. For the Celestin legend see G.H. Gerould *Saints' Legends* (Boston Houghton-Mifflin 1916) 228.

24 Aquinas held that devils experience frustration and sorrow when souls which they had wished to be damned are saved; see *Summa Theologia* 1. qu. lxiv art. 3.

25 *Works* 705. The irony was first noted by Thomas Wright in his edition of the *Canterbury Tales*, Percy Soc. Pubs., nos. 24–6 (1847–51) II 7n.

26 See Rudwin *The Devil* 63. There may also be lingering here, in the suggestion of the vagueness and bleakness of the devil's home, a touch of

the OE conception of the fiend as a wanderer without meadhall or kin, *fah and freondleas*; see Woolf 'The Devil' 8.

27 *Dramatic Irony* 43

28 See Robinson *Works* 705.

29 It is surely a failure to recognize the peculiarly sophisticated villainy of this summoner and the conditions of 'brotherhood,' which has led even such a perceptive critic as D.S. Brewer to find in the summoner's self-revelation only a 'non-realistic ... satiric convention' of the times; see his review of G.H. Gerould's *Chaucerian Essays* in RES n.s. 5 (1954) 404.

30 The detail is paralleled in one of the analogues, Bryan and Dempster *Sources and Analogues* 269f. Cp. T&C II 505.

31 G.G. Coulton *Five Centuries of Religion* (Cambridge, Cambridge University Press 1923) I 95

32 Note the strong contrast, extending even to the verbal, with the reaction of the prototypal character in the exemplum printed by Taylor 'The Devil and the Advocate': 'DEMON: Ego sum demon. RUSTICUS: O maledicte ... '

33 See Fra Jacopo Passavanti *Lo specchio di vera penitenzia* ed. M. Lenardon (Florence, 1925) 350, 376f; and Arpad Steiner 'The Faust Legend and the Christian Tradition' PMLA 54 (1939) 400–1.

34 Demonic disguises included even the clerical; there is a report of a devil appearing as a grey friar in Banbury, Essex, in 1402. For angelic cloakings there is the authority of St Paul (2 Cor. 11:14). 'Lyk an ape' has reference rather to the conception of Satan as one who sought to rival, and so to mimic, to ape God. Rudwin ascribes the tendency to carve devils in monkey form to this conceit and notes that in the early patristic writings Satan is frequently called *simia Dei; The Devil* 43f.

35 'Pronouns of Address in the *Friar's Tale*' MLQ 17 (1956) 39–42

36 Wilhelm Ewald *Der Humor in Chaucers Canterbury Tales* Studien zur englischen Philologie 45 (Halle, Niemeyer (1911) 73–4. Ewald cites 1506–12, 1517–20, 1636–8.

37 Ironically, too, it does not cross the summoner's mind that devils become men's servants only through the power of men's holiness, as with St Dunstan. See Sister Mary Immaculate 'Fiends as "Servant unto Man" in *The Friar's Tale*' PQ 21 (1942) 240–4.

38 See Rudwin *The Devil* 91; Conway *Demonology* 263–5; and H. Engel *Structure and Plot in Chaucer's Canterbury Tales* (doct. diss., Rhein. Fried. Wilh. Univ., Bonn 1931) 75.

39 Cp. the *diabolus* in the 'Death of Herod' scene, *Ludus Coventriae*, who promises to bring Herod 'on to my celle. / I xal hem teche pleys fyn / and showe such myrthe as is in helle'; ed. K.S. Block EETS e.s. 120 (1922)

176, lines 234–6. In the 'Last Supper' scene from the same cycle a demon addresses 'Judas Derlyng Myn': 'Anon þou xalt come where þou xalt wonne / In fyre and stynk þou xalt sytt me by'; 258, lines 787f.

40 *The Poet Chaucer* 161

41 In Taylor's *exemplum*, 'The Devil and the Advocate' 38, the farmer points out to the devil a sheep being cursed by its drover, then a child by its mother. The devil says he will accept only 'quicquit michi spontanee offertur.' See also Rudwin *The Devil* 177, for evidence that in all demon-compacts the fiend never cheats though the man often attempts to, occasionally even successfully.

42 G.H. Cowling *Introduction to Chaucer* (New York, Dutton 1927) 169–70

43 See Muriel Bowden *A Commentary on the General Prologue to the Canterbury Tales* (New York, MacMillan 1949) 267; and H.M. Gwatkin *Church and State in England ... (London, Longmans 1917) 99.

44 See Rudwin *The Devil* 179.

45 Shifting, as she does so, scornfully to the familiar 'thou'; *vide* Nathan 'Pronouns of Address' 40f.

46 F.J. Tupper had noted this 'poetic' irony in his 'Chaucer and Seven Deadly Sins' *PMLA* 29 (1914) 112.

47 Though not of Chaucer, whose characteristic Augustinian *charitas* towards all sinners makes itself heard even here, as Sister Mary Makarewicz has remarked: *The Patristic Influence on Chaucer* (Washington, DC, Catholic University of America Press 1953) 208.

48 My thanks are due to Professor Beatrice White, Westfield College, University of London, for helpful counsel in the final preparation of this paper.

Structural Irony within
the *Summoner's Tale*

Ⲧ HOUGH THERE HAS BEEN a great deal of admiring commentary on the craftsmanship with which Chaucer fitted the *Summoner's Tale* into the Canterbury framework – suiting tale to teller, and the teller's friar to the friar of the *General Prologue* – there continues to be a tendency to regard the tale itself as a somewhat negligible example of Chaucer's narrative art. Adverse remarks range from criticism of its form ('rather disorganized,'[1] 'lacks solidity ... does not add up to much ... remains an extended anecdote'[2]) to general disapproval of the story ('highly unsavory' and not calling for 'further comment,'[3] 'the humour of stableboys and swineherds,'[4] 'worthless'[5]). Undoubtedly the more exaggerated disprizals are made by prudish readers unable to project themselves into an earlier world where physically gross acts in literature were entirely acceptable at all levels of society so long as they contributed either 'sentence' or 'solaas.'[6] Nevertheless the notion that the tale, in itself, lacks art is still so persistent that even a critic as knowledgeable as Professor Nevill Coghill is driven to theorizing that it was 'deliberately ill-constructed' by Chaucer to fit a supposedly inferior intelligence in the Summoner who tells it.[7]

Such desperate conclusions are quite unjustified, and it may be that sufficient has been written by more appreciative critics on the complex characterizations and evocative scenes of this tale to make an overall defence of it unnecessary.[8] What has not been recognized, however, except in most general terms, is the subtlety and variety of the ironies, particularly of the 'dramatic' order, which Chaucer has woven into its very structure.[9] Indeed, Mrs G. Dempster, who alone has approached specifically this aspect of the tale, believes that Chaucer was so much less interested in the story than in developing a satiric portrait of a friar that he suppressed ironies already latent in the basic plot and added others only as it were by chance, when they happened to serve this external purpose.[10] It is the intention of this paper to show that, on the contrary, Chaucer has woven a rich texture of ironic foreshadowings, ambiguities, and reversals into the tale itself, which give it a subtle and satisfying unity, greater perhaps than that achieved by its function as a passing riposte of the Summoner's.

In Chaucer's version, as in its closest analogue, *Li dis de le versie a prestre*, an avaricious and hypocritical begging-friar calls on an ailing man to wheedle an offering out of him for his friary. The pestered invalid, in revenge, promises a rich gift, involves the friars in elaborate preparations to receive it, and presents them, in the French fabliau, with his bladder, in Chaucer's, with a *peditum*.[11] Essentially, then, it is a story based upon dramatic irony, upon expectation monstrously and comically frustrated. Throughout, Chaucer keeps this denouement in mind, and most of his apparent digressions in the interests of framework satire will be seen, on a second reading, to be contributions to this central irony.

At the outset Chaucer creates a friar who is not only a paragon of beggars but a highly successful popular preacher. At the beginning of his fatal day he has been singularly effective in exciting the congregation of the local parish church to divert their offerings to the support, not of the parish, but of 'hooly houses,' and specifically not monastic houses but those of the friars, and more precisely still to pay for the singing of 'trentals' in a peculiarly streamlined manner which his own friary was ingenious and cynical enough to provide. 'Trentals' were masses for souls in purgatory, said daily over a period of thirty days – if the parish priest were employed. This friar, however, offers the services of thirty friars at once, to get the process over with in a single day, and the souls of relatives freed from being clawed 'with flesshhook or with oules' twenty-nine days (and fees) sooner.[12] Having succeeded, by his eloquent tongue, in ingeniously diverting so much business away from the parish priest, in the latter's own church, he sets out upon the day's begging, a confident and successful master-salesman. All this is not mere incidental satire of friars; it is ironic preparation. For this Friar John's downfall will come about through over-confident practice of his pulpit skills; and it may even be that his first mis-step has already been taken when, in his zeal to establish masses on an assembly basis, he has been too preoccupied to discover that there is a single soul for whom he should be most particularly saying masses, if he wishes to speed in this day's begging.

We see him moving now in a panoply of his own efficiency and success; his skirts are tucked high, perhaps for greater speed,[13] but nevertheless he is officially impressive. With him is another friar acting as amanuensis and carrying a horn-tipped staff and writing tables 'al of yvory'; and they are trailed by a servant with a sack to perform the secular chore of transporting the gifts.[14] That he has chosen a 'sturdy harlot' suggests his confidence in his powers to wheedle a heavy sackful that morning. From house to house they go until, presumably, the bag is full and the friar sends the other two ahead to arrange for the night's lodgings. He himself seeks rest and refreshment which, however, he will combine with business, by visiting an easy mark, Thomas, a bed-ridden burgher and lay-brother,[15] and his gullible wife. In their home he is 'wont to be / Refresshed moore than in an hundred placis' – but will not be again.

He enters into the sick man's room with the easy pieties and humilities of a begging-friar on his lips, but with all the assurance and directness in his manner of a 'doctour of phisik' come to extract yet another fat fee from a trusting and permanent patient. Driving away the cat, he takes his seat at once on the bench on which, as he tells Thomas, he has so often 'faren ful weell.' It is the friar's favourite seat not because it is necessarily the 'snuggest' – Lowell and others have thought so because the cat was on it – but because it is the most strategic, the nearest vantage point both to the table beside it (1774) and to Thomas's low couch, where the friar can be so close he can dominate the helpless ear of his victim, so handy he will later be fatally able to slip to his knees and reach under the bedclothes for the sick man's malicious gift.[16]

And now we hear the voice of the comedy's real protagonist, the instrument of humiliation for this confident master-beggar, the *Eiron* to his *Alazon*. It is, properly, a voice even more convincingly humble and friendly than the friar's, and charged with a false naïvety that quite deceives Brother John. It should not deceive us, however. The bedridden Thomas will prove to be, if a churl in deeds, a cunning one; he is no 'lewed' serf but a townsman who has, or had, money, still keeps good fare, and can summon servants to his aid when he needs them (2156). He is, in part, a literary development of the 'riche sik usurer' whom Fals-Semblant prefers to visit when begging,[17] but not even that hypocrite could deceive Thomas now; he is that dangerous man, a gull whose gullibility has run out. His opening expressions of flattering interest in how his 'deere maister' has been faring are, in fact, so phrased as to set a secret test for the friar. As we learn later from Thomas's wife, their son has died 'withinne thise wykes two.' If the friar is keeping as close an eye on the souls of this parish as he pretends, if in particular he is watchful of the welfare of this favourite family, whose head is a lay brother of the friary, should he not have heard of the child's death the day it occurred, and have offered his spiritual aid even before the burial? All this may well lie behind the sick man's apparently artless opening:

> How han ye fare sith that March bigan?
> I saugh yow noght this fourtenyght or moore.   (1782–3)

The friar is quick with an answer, but it is one that fails him the test. He pretends that he has been occupied in praying for Thomas's salvation, 'And for oure othere freendes'; he does not mention the child. Then he adds minuses to his score by humbly assuring Thomas that he had indeed been preaching in Thomas's church that very morning – 'after my symple wit.' This is the church in whose yard there must now lie the fresh grave of Thomas's son. The father listens, and waits. He has surely no illusions left now about this friar, but he is perhaps still only apathetic, lacking passion or plan to rid himself of this useless visitor. But the friar, in his blind persistence, will eventually supply him with both. Insensitive to the sick man's glum silence, he talks glibly on, betraying, among other things, his swollen pride in his own clerkish skill in 'glosynge,' that ability to turn a plain text into self-advantage, that dialectical artfulness which Thomas will be goaded into testing when the invalid presents his monstrous conundrum.[18]

The wife of Thomas enters the scene, and the confident visitor boldly takes advantage of his right to a fraternal kiss of peace, by hugging her close and 'chirking' like Venus's lecherous bird, the sparrow.[19] His belief that he can, as usual, charm her into preparing him the richest meal at her command may not be misplaced. For she gives him welcome words, and aids and abets his intent to play the wheedling confessor to her sick husband by reciting Thomas's sins in advance and inviting the friar to stay and admonish him while she goes off to procure the various dainties he orders for his dinner. But is she simply 'a perennial type – the woman who dotes on the dominie,'[20] as has been generally assumed? Or is Chaucer suggesting that she, like her husband, is already disillusioned with the friar? It is interesting that after the friar's shameless display of gluttony, under a cloak of mock-humble abstinence so thin a child would see through it, after his ordering of a gourmet's dinner of capon's liver and roast pig's head – 'but a pitifull man! he would have no creature killed for him, not he'[21] – the goodwife neither protests at his expensive requests nor promises to fulfil them. She is not looking happy about it, it would seem, for the friar ends his dinner-order with the plea that she 'be nat anoyed.' All she says in reply, and they are the last words we hear from her, is an immediately irrelevant and abrupt disclosure:

> 'Now, sire,' quod she, 'but o word er I go.
> My child is deed withinne thise wykes two,
> Soone after that ye wente out of this toun.'   (1851–3)

It is a revelation which, as we have seen, at once recalls for us her husband's opening words and charges them with searching irony. If the death of her child were not in any case uppermost in her mind, the memory would be bitterly reawakened by the tardy appearance of this neglectful friend and self-appointed spiritual brother whose prayers were wanting when most needed. What is perhaps most significant for apprehending Chaucer's intention in this scene is that, sometime in the course of the friar's specious reply to her flat announcement of the child's death, she leaves the room, and the story.[22] Was it only the difficulty of fulfilling the greedy mendicant's order that delayed her return? Or was she in connivance with her husband to stay away until Thomas had somehow contrived to get rid of him, if possible permanently? We are not told, but it is highly unlikely that the friar's hasty attempt to pretend that he knew of their bereavement all along would pacify her, even if she were still gullible enough to believe it.

Certainly it is not to be thought that the cunning Thomas believes, as he lies prone and silent, that his son's death was revealed to the friar and his convent in a heavenly vision a half-hour after the event, and that the friar himself saw the child's soul entering heaven, so that there was no need of prayers but only of a *Te Deum*. The lie could be effective, of course, it is produced so promptly and developed so circumstantially, and contains the assurance the parents most want to have: that their child's soul is safe. But the friar's convent is in their very parish – how did it happen they did not hear the friary bells which should have tolled for the death of a member of a lay-brother's family? It is a thought which rather belatedly crosses the friar's mind, and he tries quickly to transform the sin of omission into a seeming virtue;[23] they avoided, he says, 'noyse or claterynge of belles,' and then dexterously turns his monologue into a sales talk on the superior efficacy of the prayers of friars. He and his brethren are so blessed with vision because they 'lyve in poverte and in abstinence.' The hypocrisy of this, delivered while he is waiting for the roast hog's head he has ordered, is self-evident;[24] it would merely add fuel to the smouldering fires of Thomas, whose hog it is, and whose gold, we are later to learn, has already all been wheedled away from him by 'diverse manere freres.'

If this Friar John were merely a conscious hypocrite he might, in turn, be sensitive enough of disingenuousness in others to have perceived Thomas's state of mind, and drawn back in time. But, like so many of Chaucer's clerical rogues, like the Pardoner, and like the summoner of the *Friar's Tale*, he deceives partly by compulsion and on such a huge scale that eventually he deceives himself in the process of undeceiving others.[25] Success leads to the pride that goes before a fall; it is Chaucer's favourite situation for dramatic irony. This friar is in love with himself, with his own preaching and his glorious glosing, with his own words and the jingling of them.[26] He pours them out now, in seemingly endless inflation of his order and himself. And if the ninety-odd lines he delivers before Thomas can get a word in, and the even longer sermon on wrath he later slides into the ear of his helpless patient, served only as satiric illustrations by the tale-telling Summoner of the canting hypocrisy of friars, these passages would indeed justify criticisms of the story as anecdotal and disorganized. But they are, on the contrary, most subtly functional.

We must keep the scene in mind, and its denouement. Here is a sick man ambushed; he has been ill long, and tried many remedies. Now all his money is gone, he is not a whit better, and leaning over him, stuffing him endlessly with learned assurances of the efficacy of his prayers, is one of the oiliest and most pompous of all the friars who have ever haunted his bedside and carted off his substance with false promises of curing him. The friar does not bore *us*, he is too fascinating a rogue, and our ox is not gored, our capon's throat is not cut, but he is unwittingly yet inexorably producing in Thomas, through the protracted stuffing quality of his monologue, an indigestion of words, a swelling of unreleased wrath, to add to the tabour-tight swell of the sick man's belly. The insult Thomas will visit upon this friar will be, for all its physical grossness, a piece of poetic justice, a return of flatulence for flatulence.

These ironies are deepened by Chaucer's care to have the friar, in his pratings, put peculiar emphasis on the virtues of non-flatulence, on the lean belly, the slim clean body. 'Clennesse' he talks of as a physical as well as a spiritual purity;[27] the abstinence of friars ensures the greater success of their prayers. Even Moses had to achieve an 'empty wombe' before he gained the tablets. Monks, on the other hand, are useless as supplicants, being gross, boozy, whale-fat fellows, swollen with pomp and gluttony. Blind to his own intellectual flatulence he turns ironist in his attack on these competitors in the business of prayer-selling, and even puns upon their belching:

> Hir preyere is of ful greet reverence,
> Whan they for soules seye the psalm of Davit;
> Lo, 'buf!' they seye, '*cor meum eructavit!*'[28]   (1932–4)

On he talks, shamelessly boasting to Thomas that where he cannot supply a Biblical text for his doctrine he can invent 'a manner glose.' Thomas endures in ominous silence, perhaps only half listening, since the friar has twice to arouse his attention (1918, 1942), and certainly unconvinced. For when Brother John at last feels he can clinch his exhortation with the point it is all designed to make, that Thomas cannot recover without the prayers of his friary, the invalid bursts out that he does not 'thryve' at all; the friars of England have all his gold and he is as sick as ever. John counter-attacks with the reproach that Thomas should have given it all to his own friary, not scattered it among the 'diverse manere freres' of the country; yet in the very phrasing of his argument the mendicant sets stirring in Thomas's mind the scabrous outline of his revenge:

> Nay, nay, Thomas, it may no thyng be so!
> What is a ferthyng worth parted in twelve?
> Lo, ech thyng that is oned in himselve
> Is moore strong than whan it is toscatered.[29]   (1966–9)

And as Thomas's thoughts stir, so does his anger. The latter the friar perceives, though without any loss of confidence. He simply shifts his attack, bending all his self-prized pulpit eloquence to the task of cooling his victim down again to the temperature necessary for alms-giving. If he had been less in love with himself as a sermonist, the friar would have realized that there are surer ways of soothing a wrathful man than by berating him for his wrathfulness. Perhaps he is deceived by the sick man's relapse into silence now; after all, Thomas did not protest earlier, when his wife gave the friar *carte blanche* to rebuke him for his ire. At any rate this preacher has a sermon in his head, full of elegant turns, maxims, and exempla, and he gives it.

Far from being a dislocated fragment of satire, 'a deviation or retardation' in the story,[30] this preachment, like the earlier one, is full of ironic relation to the scene and its outcome. For the friar, as befits his worldly character, puts his main emphasis not upon the spiritual harm of anger but on its physical dangerousness, and not upon the sin of being angry but on the imprudence of provoking men of wrathful natures. Two of his three exempla, and the more developed ones, are solely on this tack. Do not go demanding justice from quick-tempered judges, or reproach an 'irous' one for his vices – unless, of course, he is 'a povre man,' the friar adds hastily. And from his third example the preacher draws simply the moral that one should 'be no felawe to an irous man.' This is the sermon he offers to a man he senses is seething with anger, who has the reputation for getting 'angry as a pissemyre,' who he is presuming is so far from being poor that he may be persuaded to give forty pounds to pay off the convent's debt for stone, and whose 'felawe' he insists on being. Yet, far from anticipating that the wrath of Thomas will be diverted upon him, he expresses concern that Thomas may, by his continued bad temper, call down upon himself what the friar assumes would be the far more deadly anger of a woman, his wife.

> Be war from hire that in the bosom slepeth;
> War fro the serpent that so slily crepeth
> Under the gras, and styngeth subtilly ...   (1993–5)

Do not tread on this tail. But it is the dormant Thomas who will subtly sting, whose resentment will very soon now become the 'executour of pryde' (2010) in this friar whose confidence in the power of his specious preaching has destroyed his grasp of immediate reality.[31] His very peroration now, urging Thomas to turn from wrath and confess, for 'Thou shalt me fynde as just as is a squyre' (2090), adds to that anger whose outlet will evoke a rough justice to be elaborately sustained by none other than a squire.

At once Thomas bluntly refuses confession; he has already been shriven by his curate. And Friar John, learned Master of Divinity, having failed in his sermon, for all his 'diligence ... in prechyng,' must now return to his less glorious *métier*, the craft of wheedling. Help us, Thomas, he says; if we don't have money, we must sell our books –

and then, for lack of our glosing, you and all the world will be destroyed. Perhaps it is the sheer effrontery of this, the 'false dissymulacioun' of a well-appointed beggar from a convent of beggars prosperous enough to hoard expensive manuscripts (while they beg from bankrupt sick 'brothers' money to build yet another chapel), which finally channels the ire of the householder into action.[32] Yes, he will give

> Swich thyng as is in my possessioun ...
> Ye sey me thus, how that I am youre brother?   (2124–6)

How valuable, in the sardonic structure of the tale, is this device of the lay brother! It is obviously a distinction Thomas did not desire to achieve but had, probably through the combined efforts of his wife and the friar, thrust upon him. On the friar's part it is only a stratagem to make it easier to pry money out of this household. Now the friar's insistence on the reality of the fraternal tie is what entangles him; for his 'brother,' by alluding directly to the relationship as he prepares to lure the friar's greedy hand under the bedclothes, easily tricks Brother John into thinking that an especially valuable gift, and therefore one which Thomas might naturally demand to be shared by the whole friary, is about to be his for the grasping. The friar's willingness to swear the oath Thomas so smoothly requires,

> That thou departe it so, my deere brother,
> That every frere have also muche as oother,   (2133–4)

is by this device of fraternity superbly and ironically motivated.

So, with a hand fresh from the fraternal grip, Brother John begins to 'grope wel bihynde,'[33] and straight into his eternally grasping palm, the bound, protesting body of Thomas hurls the hire worthy of this self-styled Christian workman (1937, 1973). For this 'chaste, bisy frere,' who boasts that his prayer 'Up springeth into th'eir' skyward like a hawk, for this windy pedant and glosing hypocrite, a final brief gloss of air fouler and grosser than a cart-horse's.

On the instant, Master John, that most eloquent preacher against wrath, starts up wrathful as 'a wood leoun,' swearing revenge.[34] But the sinner, as Augustine held, sometimes punishes himself with his own sin.[35] The friar, 'chaced out' of this erstwhile Paradise (2157), as Adam was 'out chaced for his glotonye,' to recall the friar's own words (1916), rushes off in unthinking fury to demand vengeance from the lord of the manor himself. He arrives, this 'Raby' of persuasion, still too upset to speak, and his first utterances are scarcely comprehensible. There has been blasphemy against his convent, 'an odious meschief' – not to say an odorous one. Tell me what it is, says the manor lord, 'ye be my confessour; / Ye been the salt of the erthe and the savour.' No one feels less savorous than this worthy confessor at this moment, but he manages to make his own confession. He has been foolish-enough, he admits, to swear on the word of his profession that he will divide with his convent a gift he had not seen and which turns out to be both invisible and indivisible.

From now to the story's end the comedy is more on the surface, but it does not cease to have its ironic undertones. The friar's false voice insinuates no more, he has lost control of the situation, but we hear the gentles, who take over. Though they dare not, for gentility's sake, laugh openly at this 'cherles dede,' their suppressed amusement is audible in their silences – 'The lady of the hous ay stille sat ... The lord sat stille as he were in a traunce' – as well as by the somewhat convulsed mildness of their comments in the face of the friar's sput-tering rage. They urge him to dismiss it all as the 'frenesye' of a sick churl, a 'demonyak,' but the lord betrays his inner lack of sympathy with Brother John by his bemused dwelling on the impossibility of this problem in geometry, in 'ars-metrike,' which the friar has talked him-self into the position of having to solve.[36]

It is the squire, however, who is the final ironist, taking over the situation by a combination of smoothness and bargaining sharpness worthy of the friar himself. And, when he has been assured of the good gown-cloth he wants for a reward, he proceeds to outline his diaboli-cally plausible solution to the problem with an impassivity of coun-tenance and yet with a mockery of utterance which are wholly what the bedridden Thomas would have wanted. Moreover, his scheme forges the last necessary link in the tale's chain of ironies. It rounds out the poetic justice by involving the whole grasping convent and so com-pleting the friar's humiliation; what status will he ever again have with his brethren if they must submit to sharing in this obscene public ordeal? It is also an 'intellectual' solution, so ingeniously founded on the laws of physics and mathematics that every man

> save the frere,
> Seyde that Jankyn spak, in this matere,
> As wel as Euclide dide or Ptholomee.   (2289)

In other words, it is the sort of solution the friar himself, the ingenious master-divine, who could predicate the most awkward of set texts to his own advantage, should have thought of. Here indeed is a squire's justice. And there is even an implication that the squire's motive for this last fiendish blow, which must level Brother John forever, is not merely desire to gain a 'gowne-clooth' or seize the manorial limelight. Jankyn, too, has had to listen to the friar's monstrously hypocritical and longwinded sermons, had listened, in fact, that very morning to his appeal 'to yeve, for Goddes sake, / Wherwith men myghte hooly houses make.' He has some idea how Thomas felt and he is careful, in his scheme, to ensure that it is Thomas's persecutor whose nose shall be nearest to the wheel-hub and to Thomas. After all, is not Brother John the worthiest?

> ... this worthy man, youre confessour,
> By cause he is a man of greet honour,
> Shal have the firste fruyt, as resoun is.
> ... And certeinly he hath it weel disserved.
> He hath to-day taught us so muche good
> With prechying in the pulpit ther he stood,
> That I may vouche sauf, I sey for me,
> He hadde the firste smel of fartes thre;
> And so wolde al his covent hardily,
> He bereth hym so faire and hoolily.   (2275–86)

Whatever was needed to verbalize the ironic justice of Thomas's deed is now supplied. The squire's plan for the 'ferthyng ... parted in twelve' had already paid proper respect to Brother John's alleged devotion to fraternal sharing and his efficient rationalization of industry in conventual services. The squire's peroration now acknowledges his claim to a bad eminence among his peers. The tale ends, but not before a last twist of the knife of irony. All present in the scene, as the curtain falls, all 'save the frere,' are heard giving praise to the 'subtiltee and heigh wit,' not of the subtle and learned Friar John, but of Thomas the churl, now seen to have been neither fool not maniac to have 'speken as he spak.'

NOTES

1 Sister Mary Makarewicz *The Patristic Influence on Chaucer* (Washington, DC, Catholic University of America Press 1953) 223. Cf. Margaret Schlauch: 'a loosely organized diatribe,' *English Medieval Literature* ... (Warsaw, Panstwöwe Wydawnictwe Naukowe 1956), 266; and G.H. Cowling *Chaucer* (London, Methuen, 1927) 170: 'in construction this is Chaucer's weakest tale.'

2 J.A. Burrow 'Irony in the *Merchant's Tale*' Anglia 75 (1957) 207. Cf. R. Preston *Chaucer* (New York, Sheed and Ward 1952), 246.

3 G.K. Anderson *Old and Middle English Literature* (New York: Oxford University Press, 1950), 159

4 J.S. Kennard *The Friar in Fiction* (New York, Bretano, 1923), 16

5 Marchette Chute *Geoffrey Chaucer of England* (New York, Dutton 1946) 254. Cf. H.D. Sedgwick *Dan Chaucer* (New York, Bobbs-Merrill 1934), 293: 'another of those stable-boy stories'; and Theodore Roosevelt, letter to C.A.S. Rice, 3 May 1892, quoted by T.A. Kirby, 'Theodore Roosevelt on Chaucer ... 'MLN 68 (1953) 36.

6 See *Works of Geoffrey Chaucer* ed. F.N. Robinson, 2nd ed. (Boston, Houghton-Mifflin 1957), *Canterbury Tales* I 798. Textual references in this article are to this edition. Cf. F.W. Cornish *Chivalry* (London, Swan Sonnenschein 1901), 301; and W.A. Madden 'Chaucer's Retraction and the Medieval Canons of Seemliness MS 17 (1955) 178: 'Even in sermons the sex act, genital and excremental organs and processes, physical blemishes, and so forth were discussed quite bluntly in public.'

7 *The Poet Chaucer* (London: Oxford University Press, 1949), 164. In contrast, Kemp Malone classes this tale among those where the self-characterizing function is 'a mere by-product of the tale-telling'; *Chapters on Chaucer* (Baltimore, Johns Hopkins Press 1951) 230.

8 E.g., see R.K. Root *The Poetry of Chaucer* (Boston, 1906, rev. ed. Houghton-Mifflin 1922) 249–52; and P.V.D. Shelly *The Living Chaucer* (Philadelphia, University of Pennsylvania Press 1940) 251–4.

9 Since the few known analogues do not parallel the *Tale* except in the bare bones of the central anecdote, there is no reason for denying to Chaucer the subtleties, characteristically Chaucerian, to be found in it. See W.M. Hart 'The Summoner's Tale' *Sources and Analogues of Chaucer's Canterbury Tales* ed. W.F. Bryan and G. Dempster (Chicago, University of Chicago Press 1941) 275–87; also R.D. French *A Chaucer Handbook* 2nd ed. (New York, Appleton-Century-Crofts 1947) 288.

10 *Dramatic Irony in Chaucer* (Stanford, Stanford University Press 1932) 45–6
11 See Hart 'The Summoner's Tale,' who supplies text of *Li dis de le vescie a prestre.*
12 III 1711–32. For 'trentals' see Robinson's note, *Works* 707. Cf. Wilhelm Ewald *Der Humor in Chaucers Canterbury Tales* (Halle, Studien zur englischen Philologie 45 Niemeyer 1911) 80; and E.L. Cutts *Parish Priests ... in the Middle Ages ... (London, Christian Knowledge Society, 1898) 375f.*
13 As Chute suggests, *Geoffrey Chaucer* 274.
14 This attendant may be a banal survival of the secular *bursarius,* 'who received goods, and especially money, which the Franciscans were forbidden to touch,' according to Arnold Williams; 'Chaucer and the Friars' *Spec* 28 (1953) 506.
15 See line 1944 and Robinson's note to it. That Thomas lives in a house of his own in the suburbs of a town may be inferred from lines 1765–8, 1778–80, 1853, 2180; that he is a man of means is clear from 1949–53, 2099. He was a 'brother' presumably because his wife or he had bought a 'letter of fraternity' from the friary in return for sharing in the spiritual credit for the friars' good deeds; see H.B. Workman *John Wyclif ...* (Oxford, Clarendon Press 1926) II 107.
16 It was, in fact, William Godwin who, long before Lowell, called attention to Thomas's cat, *Life of Geoffrey Chaucer* (London, T. Davison for R. Phillips 1803) II 575; cf. J.R. Lowell *Study Windows* 2nd ed. (London, Ward 1871) 208. A. Abram thought the friar drove the cat away to be 'humbly servisable' to Thomas because the cat should not be in the bedroom; see her *English Life and Manners in the Later Middle Ages* (London, Routledge 1913), 277. But it was only at night that medieval people did not tolerate pets in bedrooms – and the friar's humility is confined to words. From the cat's viewpoint, the snuggest, warmest place is on Thomas's bed, where it is presumably not allowed; the bench is a strategic way-station and equally close to the source of impending food, the table. For much the same reasons the friar displaces the cat.
17 Robinson *Works, Romance of the Rose* 6507–10
18 See III 1781f., esp. 1791–3, 1919–20, 2109–10. If *glosynge (*1793) had, because it was so often used by clerical hypocrites, developed 'a second meaning ... to dissemble, to deceive,' as C.E. Shain believes, the irony here is deepened, since the friar would not be such a fool as to be unaware of the *double entendre,* but he would presume that Thomas was

too simple to perceive it. See 'Pulpit Rhetoric in Three Canterbury Tales' MLN 70 (1955) 242; cf. CT IV 2351, V 166, IX 34.

19 III 1800–5. See A.L. Kellogg 'The Fraternal Kiss in Chaucer's *Summoner's Tale Scriptorium* 7 (1953) 115; and T.P. Harrison *They Tell of Birds* (Austin, Texas, University of Texas Press, 1956) 43.

20 Shelly *The Living Chaucer* 253. See Robinson *Works* III 1810–37.

21 See 1838–47. The paraphrase is for an anonymous Roundhead pamphlet, *Powers to be Resisted* (1643), quoted by Caroline F.E. Spurgeon *Five Hundred Years of Chaucer Criticism and Allusion* 1337–1900 (Cambridge, Cambridge University Press 1925) III iv 72.

22 See 1848f. She is included in the friar's address, 1869, and perhaps at 1911, but by 1918 he is speaking solely to Thomas.

23 1854–65. J.S.P. Tatlock first pointed this out, 'Notes on Chaucer: The Canterbury Tales MLN 29 (1914) 144.

24 See 1869f., and Sister M.E. Whitmore, *Medieval English Domestic Life ... in ... Chaucer* (Washington, DC, Catholic University of America Press 1937) 107–8.

25 I have discussed this aspect of the *Friar's Tale* in ' "After His Ymage" ...' MS 21 (1959) [pp. 85–108 above].

26 He seems to pun out of sheer rhetorical habit. For the play on 'chaced' and 'chaast,' 1916–17, see Tatlock 'Puns in Chaucer' *Flügel Memorial Volume* (Stanford, Stanford University Press 1916) 232. There is surely another jingle, 'Dives ... divers,' in 1877–8; cf. 'irous Cirus,' 2079.

27 1879–84; cf. 1910, 1936.

28 1932–4. For the double meaning in the last line ('My heart has spoken out ... My stomach has belched') see P.E. Beichner 'Non Alleluia Ructare' MS 18 (1956) 136 n. 4. For the jest at the monk's expense in 1933, see M.P. Hamilton 'The Summoner's "Psalm of Davit" ' MLN 57 (1942) 655–7.

29 1966–9. J.E. Whitesell suggests that use of the word *ferthyng* by a friar who might normally lisp – i.e., if the summoner is modelling him on Huberd of the *General Prologue* – may have suggested to Thomas his choice of gift; see 'Chaucer's Lisping Friar' MLN 71 (1956) 160–1. Whether or not a pun lurks in 'ferthyng,' the whole passage is plainly anticipatory.

30 As Hildegard Engel thinks, *Structure and Plot in Chaucer's Canterbury Tales* (Bonn diss. 1931) 69.

31 For a somewhat different analysis of the friar's 'inability to cope with objective reality,' see R.O. Bowen, 'The Flatus Symbol in Chaucer' *Inland* (Salt Lake City) 2 (1959) 21.

32 See 2108f. The hoarding of manuscripts bought from the profits of begging forms an item in the long list of complaints made against the friars by the anti-mendicant archbishop, Fitzralph of Armagh. See Kennard *The Friar in Fiction* 14, who quotes from a sermon (which Chaucer, when young, may actually have heard) delivered by the visiting archbishop, at St Paul's Cross, complaining that Oxford students could, as a result of the friar's bibliomanic greediness, no longer obtain 'a profytable boke of the faculte of art, of dyvynyte, of law canoun, of physic, ether of law civile.'

33 See 2137f. Even this action had perhaps been sardonically signalled in the friar's insistence to Thomas on the need 'to grope tendrely a conscience / In shrift; ... and fisshe Cristen mennes soules' (1817–20); cf. also 2148.

34 This neat, if obvious, irony is the only one which Mrs Dempster, *Dramatic Irony* 46, observes to be a Chaucerian addition! No one seems to have remarked that Chaucer has foreshadowed the image at line 1989. The friar, urging Thomas to abjure wrath, quotes 'what the wise seith: / "Withinne thyn hous ne be thou no leon." '

35 See the comment of Makarewicz on this passage, *The Patristic Influence* 223–5.

36 Line 2222. 'The context,' says Baum, 'leaves no doubt of the pun'; 'Chaucer's Puns' PMLA 71 (1956) 231.

Chaucer's 'Gentil' Manciple
and his 'Gentil' Tale

*T*O WHAT EXTENT, if at all, Chaucer kept the character of the Manciple in his *General Prologue* in mind when he wrote the *Manciple's Tale* continues to be an unsettled question. Lawrence, Malone, and others think there is no special appropriateness of tale to teller, and Hulbert, while granting some general suitability of theme, feels that 'the Greek setting, the rather learned rhetorical development, and the moral disquisition are completely incongruous with the dishonest Manciple.'[1] No evidence has been advanced, however, to suggest that Chaucer had any other character in mind when he wrote it, and there is no doubt at all that Chaucer assigned it to the Manciple. Those who deny its suitability cannot therefore explain its curious pedantries and homiletic displays otherwise than by supposing, with F.N. Robinson, that Chaucer wrote it early in his career and later inserted it without readjustment into the Canterbury frame.[2] Such a conclusion is not only a dubious tribute to Chaucer's earlier art, as we know it, but one that does scant justice to the tale itself. Indeed, a re-examination of the latter, in relation to the clues Chaucer has supplied for the understanding of the Manciple's character, both in the prologue to the tale and in the *General Prologue* may render such a conclusion unnecessary.

Certainly there are obvious links between the character of this pilgrim as he appears in the *Manciple's Prologue* and the nature of the tale he tells, of which some commentators have been aware. The Manciple, having indiscreetly ridiculed Roger the Cook's drunkenness, is reminded by the Host that the wrathful Cook may take revenge by exposing the Manciple's dishonesties in 'rekenynges.' The Manciple apologizes and then tells a story in which a talking crow is punished for indiscreetly revealing to a husband the infidelity of his wife. Whether such an exemplum is to be understood as directed by the Manciple against himself, an extension of his amends to the Cook and an earnest of his intention to avoid 'to much speche' in the future,[3] or as a warning to Roger and to Harry Bailly not to meddle in his own affairs,[4] it is equally pat in its ironical-logical resolution of the situation the Manciple has created for himself in the tale's prologue. Moreover, the intrusive moralizings and the long, didactic conclusion of the tale, with what has been called its 'smug unctuousness,' may well be taken as an unconscious reflection, by this 'gabby little meddler,' of his inability to shake off the very faults he has revealed in his attack on the Cook and which he is attempting to repudiate.[5]

The consistency of the Manciple's character is, however, more extensive than this and reaches back to the *General Prologue* itself. William Wordsworth long ago argued, in defence of the literary merit of the *Manciple's Tale*, that 'the formal prosing at the end and the selfishness that pervades it flows from the genius of Chaucer, mainly as characteristic of the narrator whom he describes in the Prologue as eminent for shrewdness and clever wordly Prudence.'[6] Though his prudence may have been more fitful than Wordsworth suggests, there is no question of the Manciple's shrewdness, a curious mixture of shyness and boldness which, in a sense, helps him to triumph over his moments of imprudence. The pilgrim who insults a drunken cook and then has the adroitness to win his immediate gratitude by blatantly forcing more drink upon him is the same resourceful, impudent trickster as the London purveyor (professional watchdog of cooks) who has the ability and the audacity to line his pockets, undetected, at the expense of more than thirty members of a learned profession, all of whom were skilled in the unmasking of cheats, and a dozen specially trained in the intricacies of accounting, 'Worthy to been stywardes of rente and lond.'[7] And it is this same defrauding, cynical rascal who elects to tell a tale about cheating in love[8] and to repeat solemnly the moral that silence pays off much more often than truth-telling.

Surely, however, the thematic relationship goes even deeper than this. We should not forget that our first report of the Manciple is, like so many in the *General Prologue*, an essay in ironic praise. The Pilgrim Chaucer, the naive 'mixer,' the perfect listener and confidant, relays to us, with his usual uncritical enthusiasm, the substance of a self-portrait presented to him by yet another paragon whose 'felaweshipe' he had made in the Tabard Inn. The irony begins with the opening phrase: 'A gentil Maunciple.' No one in his fourteenth-century audience would imagine that Chaucer the Poet intended this adjective seriously, for no manciple was 'gentil' by position, and it is quickly clear that this specimen could not conceivably be philosophically elevated into the ranks of 'gentilesse' by any nobility of word or deed. Manciples were servants; this one, we are told, buys food, and keeps account of it, for a college attached to one of the Inns of Temple. Presumably he would be required, among other things, 'to stock the buttery; to attend the cook; to examine and keep an account of the meat bought, and to see that there was no waste of it; to collect money from the lawyers and students who ate in Commons.'[9] And he juggles the accounts to his own advantage. He is a 'gentil Maunciple' only as the Summoner is a 'gentil harlot' and his compeer 'a gentil Pardoner,' in that topsy-turvy world of gullible Pilgrim Chaucer.[10] His is the 'gentility,' the self-appointed elevation above the workaday world, of the successful rascal. As Ralph Baldwin has remarked, he is 'the menial in position who is master by craft' or, better, craftiness.[11] In everything that follows in the portrait we hear the slyly boasting voice of this self-confessed 'lewed' man whose satisfactions are derived from outsmarting 'an heep of lerned men,' many of whom would also be true 'gentils,' sons of the landed gentry.[12]

There is irony within irony here, for Chaucer is not only highlighting the Manciple's rascality by pretending, through his Pilgrim double, to admire it; he is also presenting a figure who fancies himself to be an ironist, albeit a crude and mocking one. For who other than the Manciple could have revealed his dishonesty, since he remains undetected by his victims? It is *his* voice and *his* sardonic phrasing we hear in the *General Prologue*, echoed by Pilgrim Chaucer's. The canniness of 'ay biforn and in good staat,' sober accountant's phrases, to be accompanied by an eye-wink perhaps; the mock-pomposity of the long involved sentence describing so specifically the number and quality of his duped 'maistres'; the final banal colloquialism which, after so much cautious *double entendre*, spills the whole situation – in all of these we can hear, behind the amused pretence of wonder and approval by Chaucer, the irrepressible savouring of his own slyness by the talkative Manciple.

For talkative he undoubtedly is, and least able to control his tongue about the secret most necessary for him to keep. It is not only the Chaucer of the Tabard he has blabbed to; both the Cook and the Host, by the time the pilgrimage has reached Bobbe-up-and-doun, know that the Manciple's bookkeepings would be found 'nat honest, if it cam to preef' (IX 69–75). And if the disreputable Roger and the indiscreet Harry

Bailly have his secret, it is probable that the Manciple has been silly enough to boast of his duplicities to the entire company. There is a conflict of needs within this Manciple: to triumph over others by trickery, and to secure social approval by revealing his tricks. It is a contradiction which has brought more than one modern criminal to grief, and appears also to have given Chaucer's Pardoner trouble. Here it is basic to Chaucer's first conception of the Manciple's character, and it becomes the central theme of the *Manciple's Prologue*. It is when the Manciple sees the Host's success in making a fool of the helplessly besotted Cook that he is unable to restrain himself from breaking in and displaying his own more heartless abilities in the same game of ragging. He begins with elaborate pretences of courtesy and friendship for the dazed Roger, addresses him as 'Sire Cook,' arrogates to himself the privilege of excusing him from the necessity of telling a tale 'as now,' and then shifts with treacherous suddenness to the crudest ridicule of his victim. Where the Host's rallying had the technical justification that it was his duty to make sure all the pilgrims discharged their agreement for tale-telling, the Manciple has no other purpose than to demonstrate to the company his own cleverness at the expense of a fellow-pilgrim to whom he was presumably already professionally hostile:

> A! taketh heede, sires, of this lusty man.
> Now sweete sire, wol ye justen atte fan?
> Thereto me thynketh ye been wel yshape! (41–3)

The voice carries the same smug tone, the same jeering of the betrayer at his dupe, we have heard behind the lines of the Manciple's portrait.

And there is, as we have seen, the same indiscretion. Carried away by this passion to show his proficiency in gulling, he has to be reminded by the Host that, by a previous display, he has given the Cook a weapon for revenge. He is shocked, for the moment, back into the caution of the peculator, effusively apologizes to Harry Bailly (whose rebuke is also a reminder of his own power over the Manciple) and passes the incident off as a joke. But at once his exhibitionism reasserts itself in a piece of baldly sardonic yet this time successful foolery. To the semiconscious angry drunk, whom they have just been at pains to heave back on his horse from the ditch, the Manciple offers, as apology, another drink, a pull from the rare old wine in the Manciple's own flagon. Out of his long experience in setting other people's caps and getting away with it, the Manciple has chosen exactly the right gambit. The Cook is immediately pacified, gulps and, instead of passing out completely, is revived enough to thank his persecutor 'in swich wise as he koude.' Moreover, the Host of the Tabard is thereby handed the opportunity, which he makes the most of, to draw appropriate conclusions on the pre-eminent virtues of wine-drinking for keeping the common peace. The Manciple has, momentarily at least, repaired the breaches his own folly has made; and he has at the same time, unobtrusively and without argument, not only manoeuvred himself into the narrator's bastion but managed to convince the Host that, unlike the Cook, he will not 'lewedely ... telle his tale.'[13]

In view of all this, the fact that the Manciple does indeed offer a story which is, superficially at least, not at all 'lewed' either in theme or treatment is just what we should expect. Yet it is this fact which alone has supplied any serious argument against the suitability of the *Manciple's Tale* to its teller. It is, of course, not impossible to presume, as Plessow and others do, that Chaucer wrote the piece early, at a time when he was markedly under the influence of the moral-rhetorical-digressive style of the *Roman de la Rose*,[14] but even if this speculation is adopted there is still no reason to suppose that Chaucer failed to construct the Manciple's portrait, and his development of it in the *Manciple's Prologue*, with due regard for *their* suitability to the already written tale. And there is much evidence in the story itself that, whenever it was written, it is our Manciple's tale.

It has, in fact, all the earmarks of an unsuccessful attempt at a 'gentil' tale by a fundamentally 'lewed' man. It is 'Greek' only in the name of its god-hero; the setting is anywhere, or nowhere, 'in this erthe' when Phoebus lived upon it. There is no attempt to sketch in a classical background, as there is, for example, in the *Knight's Tale*. Nor, on the other hand, is there any real understanding of the world of the medieval noble. Though the Manciple assures us that his hero is 'fulfild of gentillesse' and a 'flour of bachilrie' (123, 125), yet, to the extent that he is medievalized, he is a plebeian figure, whose prowess is all with the bow and arrow (108–12); twice later the teller's puffings of this 'semelieste man' that ever lived (119–20) end in a curiously anticlimactic emphasis on his archery.[15] Sometimes indeed the narrator seems to be brought up short by his own lapses, as when he refers to the lover of Phoebus's wife as her 'lemman.' 'Hir lemman? Certes, this is a knavyssh speche! / Foryeveth it me ... ' (204–6), and he is off on an involved apology which betrays his fear that he cannot handle the genre he has chosen. 'I am a boystous man,' he says, 'I am a man noght textueel,' and rushes on into the story's climax, lapsing as he does into a repetition of the very word he has just stigmatized (211–38). The faithful crow witnesses his master's cuckolding, and tells Phoebus everything, in a speech which, though commencing with the courtly language of flattery – 'Phoebus ... for al thy worthynesse, / For al thy beautee and thy gentilesse' – sinks abruptly into phrases of such crude 'vilenye' that it is difficult to imagine the crow could have learned them from his teacher, that seemliest man 'that is or was, sith that the world began' (119–20):

> For al thy waityng, blered is thyn ye ...!
> For on thy bed thy wyf I saugh hym swyve.   (252, 256)

In the crow's accents at this moment it is difficult to hear the white bird of Phoebus Apollo that outsang the nightingale, but it is easy to catch the sardonic tone of that un-gentle pilgrim who could not restrain himself from jeering at anyone who has been made a fool of, whether it be a drunken cook or a college of lawyers.

The story is also, as we have seen, not only apt in its preoccupation with both decit and indiscretion; the morals extracted from it are oily with the sort of worldly wisdom and utterly selfish expediency we find in the Manciple. Phoebus had a wife whom he guarded jealously, but no amount of watchfulness, says the narrator, can ever prevent deceit and defection (139–54). Who could speak with more authority on this truth than an embezzling provisioner for a full college of attorneys? Keep an animal in a cage (the tale-teller continues), however luxuriously, and he will act, when he has the chance, according to his 'vileyns kynde' (183, 163f.). The narrative application is to Phoebus's wife, but the speaker assures us he is thinking of men, in whom 'appetit fleemeth discrecioun' (182, 187–95). He might, with most justice, have been thinking of himself. And in that same self-justifying apology for the use of the word 'lemman' the narrator reveals just the right amount of cynical awareness of the disparities of justice in a feudal society we would expect in a servant who listened to the talk in a law-students' hall. A 'gentile' paramour, he says, is called a lady; a poor one a wench or lemman; what they do is no different. 'Men leyn that oon as lowe as lith that oother.'[16] Just so, 'a titlelees tiraunt / And an outlawe, or a theef erraunt' (223–4) – again the phrasing smacks of legal jargon – play the same game; but where the latter two are accorded no alternate euphemisms, are given no quarter, the tyrant, because he steals enough to gain the nobility of power, is 'cleped a capitayn' (230), becomes a Jonathan Wild.[17] The tone and the thinking remain in keeping with the character of an insecure 'vileyn' thief who longs for the security and the prestige of a powerful 'gentil' one.

It is highly significant that these pretentious moralizings and digressions, and their anticlimaxes of tone and monotony of diction, are not to be found in the known analogues to the story.[18] Chaucer seems to have added them and, at the same time, to have made some curious changes in the cloth of the story itself. It is only in the *Manciple's Tale* that the wife of Phoebus and her lover are portrayed with complete lack of sympathy, and only here that the actual murder of the wife is passed over in a single casual line. It is only Chaucer's crow who acts not out of a natural desire to be rewarded for loyalty to his master, but out of a reckless and almost gleeful desire to cry 'Cokkow!' Chaucer, the most alert of all poets to the values of irony, has in fact, in this last particular, gone to the length of suppressing a dramatic irony existing in the analogues.[19]

Considered apart from the Manciple's character as revealed in the *General Prologue* and the *Manciple's Prologue*, all these changes of structure and tone and style are far too extensive and too meaningful to be dismissed as the pedantic fumblings of an apprentice craftsman. Considered in relation to the narrator and the pilgrimage, they are, moreover, entirely harmonious with the intricate, ironic comedy which Chaucer created in the maturest sections of his *Canterbury Tales*.

NOTES

1 W.R. Hulbert 'The Canterbury Tales and their Narrators' *SP* 45 (1948) 576. Cp. W.W. Lawrence *Chaucer and the Canterbury Tales* (New York, Columbia University Press, 1950) 147; Kemp Malone *Chapters on Chaucer* (Baltimore, Johns Hopkins University Press, 1951) 232. For a summary of varying critical opinion up to 1952, see J.B. Severs 'Is the *Manciple's Tale* a Success?' *JEGP* 51 (1952) 1–16.

2 *Works of Geoffrey Chaucer* 2nd ed. (Boston, Houghton-Mifflin 1957) 15, 762–3. Textual line references in this article are to this edition. An assumption that the tale lacks relationship with its framework underlies much of the popular disprizing or ignoral of it, as by Nevill Coghill, *The Poet Chaucer* (London, Oxford University Press 1949) 127–8; cf. R. Pres-

ton *Chaucer* (New York: Sheed and Ward 1952) 282: 'a left-over from the marriage-feast'; and N.H. Wallis *Canterbury Colloquies* (London, Brodie 1957) 98.

3 As M. Donner suggests, 'The Unity of Chaucer's Manciple Fragment' *MLN* 70 (1955) 249. Cf. E.T. Donaldson, ed. *Chaucer's Poetry* (New York, Ronald Press 1958) 947; and W. Shumaker 'Chaucer's *Manciple's Tale* as Part of a Canterbury Group' *UTQ* 22 (1953) 151.

4 This is J.D. Elliott's opinion, 'The Moral of the *Manciple's Tale' N&Q* 199 (1954) 512. Either interpretation seems far more plausible than R.D. Spector's attempt to treat the moralizings as 'a rebuttal of the *Canon's Yeoman's Tale*,' 'Chaucer's The Manciple's Tale' *N&Q* 202 (1957) 26. An ironical relevance, noted by D.S. Brewer, exists between the threat of the Cook's wrath, in the Manciple's Prologue, and the digressive sermon against 'ire' in the *Manciple's Tale* itself; see his *Chaucer* (London, Longmans 1953) 164.

5 Marchette Chute *Geoffrey Chaucer of England* (New York, Dutton 1951) 308. Cf. B.H. Bronson: 'there seems to be a roughness about the Manciple's intrusive comments which Chaucer would not have employed in his own person': 'Chaucer's Art in Relation to his Audience' *Five Studies in Literature* University of California Publications in English VIII (1940) 45.

6 Letter to Dora W. *Poetical Works of William Wordsworth* ed. E. de Selincourt IV (Oxford, Clarendon Press, 1947) app. B 471. Wordsworth had prepared a modernization for Powell's *Chaucer Modernized* but ultimately withdrew it under pressure from his friend Quillinan and others, who thought the tale not worth inclusion.

7 I 579. As J.M. Manly noted, many law students of the time were preparing themselves for the direct management of estates; see his edition of *Canterbury Tales* (New York, 1929) 530; also M. Bowden *A Commentary on the General Prologue to the Canterbury Tales* (New York, MacMillan 1949) 257; and H. Cohen *A History of the English Bar and Attornatus to 1450* (London, Sweet and Maxwell 1929) 495–6.

8 This relation of tale to teller has been noted by H.R. Patch, *On Rereading Chaucer* (Cambridge, Mass., Harvard University Press, 1939) 159, and more fully discussed by Severs, 'Is the Manciple's Tale a Success?' 11–12. Cf. Donaldson *Chaucer's Poetry* 947.

9 Bowden *Commentary* 257

10 See I 567, 647, 669 and cp. 'gentil Roger' (I 4353); also IV 1995 VII 195, 2865, 3455. W. Ewald has noted the frequency with which this word is ironically used by Chaucer; *Der Humor in Chaucers Canterbury Tales* Studien zur englischen Philologie 45 (Halle, Niemeyer 1911) 110.

11 *The Unity of the Canterbury Tales* (Copenhagen 1955) 46

12 See Cohen *History of the English Bar* 496.

13 See IX 57–103. R.M. Lumiansky, in an article on 'Chaucer's Cook-Host Relationship' MS 17 (1955) 208–9, assumes that it is the Host who, belatedly deciding that he himself might be the victim if the Cook now tells a tale, 'is pleased to have the Manciple perform instead.' But the Manciple needed no encouragement and makes the initial proposal of excusing the Cook (29). The phrasing of this line suggests that the Manciple is proposing himself as a substitute, and certainly the Host so assumes when he says, 'Telle on thy tale' (68).

14 See G. Plessow, ed. *Des Haushalters Erzählung* (Berlin, de Gruyter 1929) 160–2; E. Hammond *Chaucer: A Bibliographical Manual* (New York, MacMillan 1908) 257f.; and Robinson, *Works* 762–3.

15 Lines 129, 269. In having Phoebus kill his wife with an arrow, Chaucer departs from the medieval tradition in the telling of this story, to which he otherwise holds. In Gower, Phoebus slays with a sword. See J.A. Work 'The Manciple's Tale' in W.F. Bryan and G. Dempster, eds. *Sources and Analogues of Chaucer's Canterbury Tales* (Chicago, University of Chicago Press 1941) 709.

16 As P.F. Baum has pointed out, this line (222) puns on the sexual as well as on the social meanings of lay and lie; 'Chaucer's Puns: A Supplementary List' PMLA 73 (1958) 169. As such, it is a further example of the narrator's tendency to lapse into jeering and uncourtly asides. Severs, 'Is the *Manciple's Tale* a Success?' 5, observes that 'the coarseness – and justice – of the Manciple's rude speech' is dramatically fitting to him, and that the whole passage is a departure of Chaucer's from the known sources. So also is the section on the keeping of animals in cages.

17 J.J. Jusserand praises the humours here as being 'si vraiment anglais qu'ils font songer à Swift et à Fielding,' *Histoire Littéraire de Peuple Anglais* I (Paris, Mesnil 1894) 341. It is of course possible that, in addition, Chaucer's own 'democratic sentiments are cleverly referred to an ignorant man' here, as Mrs H.R. Haweis long ago believed; see her *Tales from Chaucer* (London, n.p. 1887) 97.

18 Severs, 'Is the Manciple's Tale a Success?'

19 Noted by G. Dempster, *Dramatic Irony in Chaucer* (Stanford, Stanford University Press 1932) 86. Mrs Dempster, however, thought that the *Manciple's Tale* 'was probably written before Chaucer's appreciation of dramatic irony was fully developed.' In fact, Chaucer has added structural ironies where it suited his purpose, e.g., the early emphasis on Phoebus's pleasure in the crow's beautiful song, ironic preparation for the single note of 'Cokkow!'

BIBLIOGRAPHIES

Bibliographies

1 BIBLIOGRAPHY TO 'SEVEN KINDS OF IRONY'

Batts, M.S. 'Hartmann's Humanitas: A New Look at Iwein' in *Germanic Studies in Honour of Edward Henry Sehrt* ed. F.A. Raven, W.K. Legner, and J.C. King, 37–51. Coral Gables, Fla., University of Miami Press 1968

Bede 'De schematibus et tropis' in *Rhetores Latini minores* ed. C. Halm. Leipzig, Teubner 1863

Birney, Earle 'Chaucer's Irony' (vols. I and II). Dissertation, University of Toronto 1936

– 'English Irony before Chaucer' *UTQ* 6 (1937) 538–57

– 'The Beginnings of Chaucer's Irony' *PMLA* 54 (1939) 637–55

– 'Is Chaucer's Irony a Modern Discovery?' *JEGP* 41 (1942) 303–19

Booth, Wayne C. *The Rhetoric of Fiction* Chicago, University of Chicago Press 1967

Now Don't Try to Reason with Me: Essays and Ironies for a Credulous Age Chicago, University of Chicago Press 1970

– *A Rhetoric of Irony* Chicago, University of Chicago Press, 1974

– 'The Pleasures and Pitfalls of Irony: or Why Don't You Say What You Mean?' in *Rhetoric, Philosophy and Literature* ed. D. Burks, 1–13. Lafayette, Purdue University Press 1978

Brooks, Cleanth 'Irony and Ironic Poetry' *CE* 9 (1947–8) 231–37

– 'Irony as a Principle of Structure' (1949) rpt in *Literary Opinion in America* ed. Morton Dauwen Zable, 3rd rev. ed., 729–41. New York, Harper and Row 1962

Burke, Kenneth *A Grammar of Motives* and *A Rhetoric of Motives* Cleveland, World Publishing 1962 (first printed individually in 1945 and 1950 respectively)

Cicero *De officiis* trans. Walter Miller. Cambridge, Harvard University Press
(The Loeb Classical Library) 1913
– *De oratore* (vols I and II). trans. H. Rackham. Cambridge, Harvard
University Press (The Loeb Classical Library) 1942
– *Rhetorica ad Herennium* trans. H. Caplan. Cambridge, Harvard
University Press (The Loeb Classical Library) 1954
De Mott, Benjamin 'The New Irony: Sickniks and Others' *American Scholar*
31 (1962) 108–19
Dempster, Germaine *Dramatic Irony in Chaucer* (1932) rpt New York, The
Humanities Press 1959
Donaldson, E. Talbot *Speaking of Chaucer* London, Athlone Press 1970
Elbow, Peter *Oppositions in Chaucer* Middleton, Wesleyan University Press
1973
Empson, William *Seven Types of Ambiguity* London, Chatto and Windus
1963
Faral, Edmond (ed.) *Les Arts Poétiques du XIIe et du XIIIe siècle* Paris,
Librairie Honoré Champion 1962
Frye Northrop *The Anatomy of Criticism* Princeton, Princeton University
Press 1957
Graff, Gerald *Literature Against Itself* Chicago, University of Chicago Press
1979
Green, D.H. 'Irony and Medieval Romance' in *Arthurian Romance: Seven
Essays* ed. D.D.R. Owen, 49–64. Edinburgh, Scottish Academic Press 1970
– 'Alieniloquium: Zur Begriffsbestimmung der mittelalterlichen Ironie' in
Verbum et Signum: Festschrift for F. Ohly ed. Hans Fromm, Wolfgang Harms,
and Uwe Ruberg. Munich, Fink 1975
– *Irony in the Medieval Romance* Cambridge, Cambridge University Press
1979
Haury Auguste *L'Ironie et l'Humour chez Ciceron* Leiden, Brill 1955
Howard, Donald 'Chaucer the Man' PMLA 80 (1965) 223–32
Hunt, T. 'The Rhetorical Background to the Arthurian Prologue' *Forum for
Modern Language Studies* 6 (1970) 1–23
– 'Irony and Ambiguity in *Sir Gawain and the Green Knight*' FMLS 12
(1976) 1–16
Hutchens, Eleanor N. 'The Identification of Irony' ELH 27 (1960) 352–63
Isidore of Seville *Etymologiarum sive originum: Libri XX* ed. W. M. Lindsay
(1911) rpt. Oxford, Oxford University Press 1957
Jameson, Fredric *The Prison House of Language* Princeton, Princeton
University Press 1972

Julian of Toledo *Devitiis et Figuris* trans W.M. Lindsay. Oxford, Oxford University Press 1922

Keil, H. (ed.) *Grammatici Latini* (7 vols 1857) rpt Hildesheim, Georg Olms 1961

Knox, Norman *The Word Irony and its Context, 1500–1755* Durham, NC, Duke University Press 1961

– 'On the Classification of Ironies' *MP* 70, no. 1 (August 1972) 53–62

Lentricchia, Frank *After the New Criticism* Chicago, University of Chicago Press 1980

Muecke, D.C. *The Compass of Irony* London, Methuen 1969

– 'The Communication of Verbal Irony' *JLS* 2 (1973) 35–42

– 'Irony Markers' *Poetics: International Review for the Theory of Literature* 7 (1978) 363–75

Muscatine, Charles *Chaucer and the French Tradition: A Study in Style and Meaning* Berkeley, University of California Press 1957

Payne, R.O. 'Chaucer and the Art of Rhetoric' in *Companion to Chaucer Studies* ed. B. Rowland, 2nd ed., 42–64. New York, Oxford University Press 1979

Quintilian *Institutio oratoria* (vol. III) trans. H.E. Butler. Cambridge: Harvard University Press (The Loeb Classical Library) 1921

Ramsey, Vance 'Modes of Irony in the *Canterbury Tales*' in *Companion to Chaucer Studies* ed. B. Rowland, 2nd ed., 352–79. New York, Oxford University Press 1979

Richards, I.A. *Practical Criticism: A Study of Literary Judgement* New York, Harcourt, Brace 1929

– *Theory of Literature* New Haven, Yale University Press 1969

Ruggiers, Paul *The Art of the Canterbury Tales* Madison, University of Wisconsin Press, 1965

Sedgewick,G.G. *Of Irony, Especially in Drama* Toronto, University of Toronto Press 1935

Tanakce, Ronald 'The Concept of Irony: Theory and Practice' *JLS* 2 (1973) 43–56

Wells, D.A. 'Medieval Literature' *Year's Work in Modern Language Studies* 34 (1973) 508–51

Worcester, David *The Art of Satire* (1940) rpt New York, Russell and Russell 1960

Wright, Edmond L. 'Transparency and Opacity and Their Relation to Intentional Meaning' *JLS* 3 (1974) 81–90

2 GENERAL BIBLIOGRAPHY ON CHAUCER'S IRONY

Abraham, David H. 'Cosyn and Cosynage: Pun and Structure in the *Shipman's Tale' ChauR* 11 (1977) 319–27

Adams, John F. 'The Structure of Irony in *The Summoner's Tale' EIC* 12 (1962) 126–32

Allen, Judson B. 'The Ironic Fruyt: Chauntecleer as Figura' *SP* 66 (1969) 25–35

– 'The Old Way and the Parson's Way: An Ironic Reading of the Parson's Tale' *JMRS* 3 (1973) 255–71

Allen, Judson B. and Patrick Gallacher 'Alisoun Through the Looking Glass: Or Every Man His Own Midas' *ChauR* 4 (1970) 99–105

Baldwin, Ralph *The Unity of the 'Canterbury Tales'* Anglistica 5. Copenhagen, Rosenkilde og Bagger 1955

Baum, Paull F. 'The Man of Law's Tale' *MLN* 64 (1949) 12–14

– 'Chaucer's Puns' *PMLA* 71 (1956) 225–46

– *Chaucer: A Critical Appreciation* Durham, NC, Duke University Press 1958

– 'Chaucer's Puns: A Supplementary List' *PMLA* 73 (1958) 167–70

Besserman, Lawrence L. 'Chaucerian Wordplay: The Nun's Priest and his *Womman Divyne' ChauR* 12 (1979) 68–73

Blanch, Robert J. 'Irony in Chaucer's *Merchant's Tale' LHR* 8 (1966) 8–15

Bloomfield, Morton W. 'The Gloomy Chaucer' in *Veins of Humor* ed. H. Levin, 57–68. Cambridge, Mass, Harvard University Press 1972

Brewer, D.S. *Chaucer* (1953) 3rd rev. ed. London, Longmans 1973

– 'Towards a Chaucerian Poetic' *PBA* 60 (1974) 219–54

– 'The Fabliaux' in *Companion to Chaucer Studies* ed. B. Rowland, rev. ed. (New York, Oxford University Press 1979) 296–325

Bronson, Bertrand H. *In Search of Chaucer* Toronto, University of Toronto Press 1960

– 'Afterthoughts on *The Merchant's Tale' SP* 58 (1961) 583–96

Burger, Douglas A. 'Deluding Words in the *Merchant's Tale' ChauR* 12 (1977) 103–10

Burlin, Robert B. *Chaucerian Fiction* 165–7. Princeton, NJ, Princeton University Press 1977

Burrow, J.A. 'Irony in the *Merchant's Tale' Anglia* 75 (1957) 199–208

Caldwell, Robert A. 'Chaucer's *taillynge ynough, Canterbury Tales B²* 1624' *MLN* 55 (1940) 262–5

Cooke, Thomas D. *The Old French and Chaucerian Fabliaux: A Study of Their Comic Climax* Columbia: University of Missouri Press 1978

Copland, Murray 'The Reeve's Tale: Harlotrie or Sermonyng?' MAE 31 (1962) 14–32

– 'The Shipman's Tale: Chaucer and Boccaccio' MAE 35 (1966) 11–28

David, Alfred The Strumpet Muse: Art and Morals in Chaucer's Poetry Bloomington, Indiana University Press 1970

Delany, Sheila 'Clerks and Quiting in the Reeve's Tale' MS 29 (1967) 351–56

Delasanta, Rodney 'Alisoun and the Saved Harlots: A Cozening of Our Expectations' ChauR 12 (1978) 218–35

Dempster, Germaine Dramatic Irony in Chaucer (1932) rpt New York, Humanities Press 1959

– 'A Period in the Development of the Canterbury Tales Marriage Group and of Blocks B² and C' PMLA 68 (1953) 1142–59

De Neef, A. Leigh 'Chaucer's Pardoner's Tale and the Irony of Misinterpretation' JNT 3 (1973) 85–96

Donaldson, E. Talbot 'Chaucer the Pilgrim' PMLA 69 (1954) 928–36

– 'Idiom of Popular Poetry in the Miller's Tale' in Speaking of Chaucer 13–29. London, Athlone Press; New York, Norton 1970

– 'Chaucer and the Elusion of Clarity' E&S 25 (1972) 23–44

– ed. Chaucer's Poetry: An Anthology for the Modern Reader (1958) 2nd ed. New York, Ronald Press 1975

Duffey, B.I. 'The Intention and Art of The Man of Law's Tale' ELH 14 (1947) 181–93

Duncan, Edgar H. 'Narrator's Point of View in the Portrait-sketches, Prologue to the Canterbury Tales' in Essays in Honor of Walter Clyde Curry 77–101. Foreword by Hardin Craig. Nashville, Tenn., Vanderbilt University Press 1955

Eliason, Norman E. 'Some Word-Play in Chaucer's Reeve's Tale' MLN 71 (1956) 162–4

Elliott, Ralph W.V. 'Our Host's "Triacle": Some Observations on Chaucer's "Pardoner's Tale"' REL 7 (1966) 61–73

– Chaucer's English London, André Deutsch 1974

Ethel, Garland 'Chaucer's Worste Shrewe: The Pardoner' MLQ 20 (1959) 211–27

Evanoff, Alexander 'The Pardoner as Huckster: A Dissent from Kittredge' BYUS 4 (1962) 209–17

Finlayson, John 'The Satiric Mode and the Parson's Tale' ChauR 6 (1971) 94–116

Fisher, John H. The Complete Poetry and Prose of Geoffrey Chaucer (New York, Holt Rinehart and Winston 1977)

Forehand, Brooks 'Old Age and Chaucer's Reeve' PMLA 69 (1954) 984–9

Frank, Grace 'Chaucer's Monk' *MLN* 55 (1940) 780–1
Frost, William 'An Interpretation of Chaucer's Knight's Tale' *RES* 25 (1949)
    289–304
Garbaty, Thomas J. 'Satire and Regionalism: The Reeve and His Tale'
    ChauR 8 (1973) 1–8
– 'The Degradation of Chaucer's "Geffrey" ' *PMLA* 89 (1974) 97–104
Gaylord, Alan T. 'The Promises in *The Franklin's Tale* *ELH* 31 (1964) 331–65
Gerould, G.H. *Chaucerian Essays* Princeton, Princeton University Press
    1952
Gordon, James D. 'Chaucer's Retraction: A Review of Opinion' in *Studies in*
    Medieval Literature in Honor of Professor Albert Croll Baugh ed.
    MacEdward Leach, 81–96. Philadelphia, University of Pennsylvania Press
    1961
Griffith, Dudley D. 'On Word Studies in Chaucer' in *Philologica: The*
    Malone Anniversary Studies ed. Thomas A. Kirby and Henry Bosley
    Woolf, 195–9. Baltimore, Johns Hopkins University Press 1949
Halverson, John 'Chaucer's Pardoner and the Progress of Criticism' *ChauR* 4
    (1970) 184–202
Hamilton, Alice 'Helowys and the Burning of Jankyn's Book' *MS* 34 (1972)
    196–207
Harrington, David V. 'Dramatic Irony in the *Canon's Yeoman's Tale*' *NM* 66
    (1965) 160–6
Heninger, S.K. 'The Concept of Order in Chaucer's *Clerk's Tale*' *JEGP* 56
    (1957) 382–95
Hoffman, Arthur W. 'Chaucer's Prologue to Pilgrimage: The Two Voices'
    ELH 21 (1954) 1–16
Holman, C. Hugh 'Courtly Love in the Merchant's and the Franklin's Tales'
    ELH 18 (1951) 241–52
Howard, Donald R. 'The Conclusion of the Marriage Group: Chaucer and
    the Human Condition' *MP* 57 (1960) 223–32
– 'Chaucer the Man' *PMLA* 80 (1965) 337–43
– *The Idea of the Canterbury Tales*. Berkeley, University of California Press
    1976
Jennings, Margaret, CSJ 'Chaucer's Beards.' *Archiv* 215 (1978) 362–8
Jones, C. 'Chaucer's *Taillynge Ynough*' *MLN* 52 (1937) 570
Jordan, Robert M. 'Chaucer's Sense of Illusion: Roadside Drama
    Reconsidered' *ELH* 29 (1962) 19–33
Kaske, R.E. 'An Aube in the "Reeve's Tale" ' *ELH* 26 (1959) 295–310
– 'January's "Aube" ' *MLN* 75 (1960) 1–4

Kauffman, Corinne E. 'Dame Pertelote's Parlous Parle' *ChauR* 4 (1970) 41–8
Kimpel, Ben 'The Narrator of the *Canterbury Tales*' *ELH* 20 (1953) 77–86
Knapp, Robert S. 'Penance, Irony and Chaucer's Retraction' *Assays* 2 (1982) 45–67
Knoepflmacher, U.C. 'Irony Through Scriptural Allusion: A Note on Chaucer's Prioresse' *ChauR* 4 (1970) 180–3
Knox, Norman *The Word Irony and Its Context, 1500–1755* Durham, NC, Duke University Press 1961
Kökeritz, Helge 'Rhetorical Word-play in Chaucer' *PMLA* 69 (1954) 937–52
Kolve, V.A. *Chaucer and the Imagery of Narrative: The First Five Canterbury Tales* Stanford, Stanford University Press 1984
Lawrence, William Witherle *Chaucer and the Canterbury Tales* New York, Columbia University Press 1950
– 'Chaucer's *Shipman's Tale*' *Spec* 33 (1958) 56–68
Lenaghan, R.T. 'The Nun's Priest's Fable' *PMLA* 78 (1963) 300–7
– 'The Irony of the *Friar's Tale*' *ChauR* 7 (1973) 281–94
McPeek, James A.S. 'Chaucer and the Goliards' *Spec* 26 (1951) 332–6
Major, John M. 'The Personality of Chaucer the Pilgrim' *PMLA* 75 (1960) 160–2
Mann, Jill *Chaucer and Medieval Estates Satire: The Literature of Social Classes and the General Prologue to the Canterbury Tales*, 194–8 *et passim.* New York and London, Cambridge University Press 1973
– '*Speculum Stultorum* and the *Nun's Priest's Tale*' *ChauR* 9 (1975) 262–82
Manning, Stephen 'The Nun's Priest's Morality and the Medieval Attitude Toward Fables' *JEGP* 59 (1960) 403–16
Meech, Sanford B. *Design in Chaucer's Troilus* Syracuse, NY, Syracuse University Press 1959
Mehl, Dieter 'The Audience of Chaucer's *Troilus and Criseyde*' in *Chaucer and Middle English Studies in Honour of Rossell Hope Robbins* ed. Beryl Rowland 173–89. London, Allen & Unwin 1974; Kent, Ohio, Kent State University Press 1974
Miller, Robert P. 'Chaucer's Pardoner, the Scriptural Eunuch, and the Pardoner's Tale' *Spec* 30 (1955) 180–99
Millns, T. 'Chaucer's Suspended Judgments' *EIC* 27 (1977) 1–19
Miskimin, Alice S. *The Renaissance Chaucer* New Haven, Yale University Press 1975
Mitchell, Charles 'The Worthiness of Chaucer's Knight' *MLQ* 25 (1964) 66–75
Mroczkowski, Przemyslaw 'Medieval Art and Aesthetics in *The Canterbury Tales*' *Spec* 33 (1958) 204–21

Muscatine, Charles *Chaucer and the French Tradition: A Study in Style and Meaning* Berkeley, University of California Press 1957
– 'The Canterbury Tales: Style of the Man and Style of the Work' in *Chaucer and Chaucerians: Critical Studies in Middle English Literature* ed. D.S. Brewer 88–113. London, Nelson 1966
– *Poetry and Crisis in the Age of Chaucer* 111–45. Notre Dame, Ind., University of Notre Dame Press 1972
Nevo, Ruth 'Chaucer: Motive and Mask in the *General Prologue*' MLR 58 (1963) 1–9
Olson, Paul A. 'The *Reeve's Tale:* Chaucer's *Measure for Measure*' SP 59 (1962) 1–17
O'Reilly, William M., Jr 'Irony in the *Canon's Yeoman's Tale*' Greyfriar 10 (1968) 23–39
Owen, Charles A., Jr 'The Crucial Passages in Five of the *Canterbury Tales:* A Study in Irony and Symbol' JEGP 52 (1953) 294–311
– 'Chaucer's *Canterbury Tales*: Aesthetic Design in Stories of the First Day' ES 35 (1954) 49–56
– 'Morality as a Comic Motif in the *Canterbury Tales*' CE 16 (1955) 226–32
Page, Barbara 'Concerning the Host' ChauR 4 (1970) 1–13
Park, B.A. 'The Character of Chaucer's Merchant' ELN 1 (1964) 167–75
Parker, David 'Can We Trust the Wife of Bath?' ChauR 4 (1970) 90–8
Payne, Anne *Chaucer and Menippean Satire* Madison Wisconsin, University of Wisconsin Press 1981
Payne, Robert O. *The Key of Remembrance* Newhaven, Yale University Press 1963
Pearsall Derek, ed. *The Nun's Priest's Tale: A Variorum Edition of the Works of Geoffrey Chaucer* II, pt 9 Norman, University of Oklahoma Press 1983
Preston, Raymond *Chaucer* (1952) rpt Westport, Conn, Greenwood Press 1969
Reid, David S. 'Crocodilian Humor: A Discussion of Chaucer's Wife of Bath' ChauR 4 (1970) 73–89
Reiman, Donald 'The Real *Clerk's Tale*: or, Patient Griselda Exposed' TSLL 5 (1963) 356–73
Reiss, Edmund 'The Final Irony of the *Pardoner's Tale*' CE 25 (1964) 260–6
Richardson, Cynthia C. 'The Function of the Host in the *Canterbury Tales*' TSLL 12 (1970) 325–44
Richardson, Janette 'Friar and Summoner, the Art of Balance' ChauR 9 (1975) 227–36
Ridley, Florence H. *The Prioress and the Critics.* UCPES 30. Berkeley, University of California Press 1965

Robertson, D.W., Jr *A Preface to Chaucer: Studies in Medieval Perspectives* Princeton, Princeton University Press 1962

Ross, Thomas W. *Chaucer's Bawdy* New York, Dutton 1972

Rothman, Irving N. 'Humility and Obedience in the *Clerk's Tale*, with the Envoy Considered as an Ironic Affirmation' PLL 9 (1973) 115–27

Rowland, Beryl 'The Chess Problem in Chaucer's *Book of the Duchess*' Ang 81 (1962) 384–9

- 'Pandarus and the Fate of Tantalus' OL 24 (1969) 3–15
- 'Chaucer's Dame Alys: Critics in Blunderland?' NM 73 (1972) 381–95
- 'The Wife of Bath's "Unlawfull Philtrum" ' *Neophil* 51 (1972) 200–6
- 'On the Timely Death of the Wife of Bath's Fourth Husband' *Archiv* 209 (1972) 273–92
- 'The Physician's "Historical Thyng Notable" and the Man of Law' ELH 40 (1973) 165–78
- 'New Light on the *Physician's Tale*' ELH 40 (1973) 165–78
- 'Chaucer's Idea of the Pardoner as Hermaphrodite' ChauR 14 (1979) 140–54

Ruggiers, Paul G. 'The Form of *The Canterbury Tales: Respice Fines*' CE 17 (1956) 439–44

- 'Some Philosophical Aspects of *The Knight's Tale*' CE 19 (1958) 296–302
- *The Art of the Canterbury Tales* Madison, University of Wisconsin Press 1965

Schoeck, R.J. 'Chaucer's Prioress: Mercy and Tender Heart' in *The Bridge, A Yearbook of Judaeo-Christian Studies* II. New York, Pantheon 1956 pp. 239–55

Sedgewick, G.G. 'The Structure of *The Merchant's Tale*' UTQ 17 (1948) 337–45

- 'The Progress of Chaucer's Pardoner' TSE 1 (1949) 1–29

Severs, J. Burke, 'Chaucer's Originality in the *Nun's Priest's Tale*' SP 43 (1946) 22–41

Shallers, A. Paul 'The *Nun's Priest's Tale*: An Ironic Exemplum' ELN 42 (1975) 319–37

Shumaker, Wayne 'Chaucer's Manciple's Tale as Part of a Canterbury Group' UTQ 22 (1953) 147–56

Siegel, Paul N. 'Comic Irony in *The Miller's Tale* BUSE 4 (1960) 114–20

Silverman, Albert H. 'Sex and Money in Chaucer's *Shipman's Tale*' PQ 32 (1953) 329–36

Slade, Tony 'Irony in the *Wife of Bath's Tale*' MLR 64 (1969) 241–7

Sledd, James 'The *Clerk's Tale:* The Monsters and the Critics' MP 51 (1953) 73–82

Speirs, John *Chaucer the Maker* (1951) 2nd rev ed. London, Faber 1960

Steadman, John M. 'Old Age and *Contemptus Mundi* in *The Pardoner's Tale*
   MAE 33 (1964) 121–30
Stillwell, Gardiner 'Chaucer's "Sad Merchant" ' *RES* 20 (1944) 1–18
Stockton, Eric W. 'The Deadliest Sin in *The Pardoner's Tale*' *TSL* 6 (1961)
   47–59
Stokoe, William C., Jr 'Structures and Intention in the First Fragment of the
   Canterbury Tales' *UTQ* 21 (1952) 120–7
Swart, J. 'Chaucer's Pardoner' *Neophil* 36 (1952) 45–50
Tatlock, J.S.P. 'Chaucer's *Merchant's Tale*' *MP* 33 (1936) 367–81
– 'Chaucer's Monk' *MLN* 55 (1940) 350–4
Taylor, Willene P. 'Chaucer's Technique in Handling Anti-Feminist
   Material in "The Merchant's Tale": An Ironic Portrayal of the *Senex-
   Amans* and Jealous Husband' *CLAJ* 13 (1969) 153–62
Toole, William B., III 'Chaucer's Christian Irony: The Relationship of
   Character and Action in the *Pardoner's Tale*' *ChauR* 3 (1968) 37–43
Utley, Francis L. 'Stylistic Ambivalence in Chaucer, Yeats and Lucretius –
   The Cresting Wave and Its Undertow' *UR* 37 (1971) 174–88
Winstanley, Lilian, ed. *The Prioress's Tale, The Tale of Sir Thopas*
   Cambridge, Cambridge University Press 1922
Wood, Chauncey 'Chaucer and *Sir Thopas*: Irony and Concupiscence' *TSLL*
   14 (1972) 389–403
Woolf, Rosemary 'Chaucer as Satirist in the General Prologue to the
   Canterbury Tales' *CritQ* 1 (1959) 150–7
Wurtele, Douglas 'Ironical Resonance in the *Merchant's Tale*' *ChauR* 13
   (1978) 66–79
– 'The Predicament of Chaucer's Wife of Bath: St. Jerome on Virginity'
   Florilegium 5 (1983) 208–36

3 BIBLIOGRAPHY ON THE *MILLER'S PROLOGUE* AND *TALE*

Ames, Ruth M. 'Prototype and Parody in Chaucer's Exegesis' in *The
   Fourteenth Century* ed. P.E. Szarmach and B.S. Levy, 87–105.
   Binghampton, State University of New York 1977
Beichner, Paul E. 'Absolon's Hair' *MS* 12 (1950) 222–33
– 'Chaucer's "Hende Nicholas" ' *MS* 14 (1952) 151–3
– 'Non Alleluia Ructare' *MS* 18 (1956) 135–44
– 'Characterization in *The Miller's Tale*' in *Chaucer Criticism* 1: *The
   Canterbury Tales* ed. R.J. Schoeck and J. Taylor, 117–29. Notre Dame,
   Ind., University of Notre Dame Press 1960

– 'Chaucer's Pardoner as Entertainer' *MS* 25 (1963) 160–72
Beidler, Peter G. 'Art and Scatology in *The Miller's Tale*' *ChauR* 12 (1977) 90–102
Bentley, Joseph 'Chaucer's Fatalistic Miller' *SAQ* 64 (1965) 247–53
Blechner, Michael Harry 'Chaucer's Nicholas and Saint Nicholas' *NM* 79 (1978) 367–71
Bloomfield, Morton W. 'The Miller's Tale – An UnBoethian Interpretation' in *Medieval Literature and Folklore Studies: Essays in Honor of Francis Lee Utley* ed. Jerome Mandel and Bruce A. Rosenberg, 205–11. New Brunswick, Rutgers University Press 1970
Bolton, W.F. 'The Miller's Tale: An Interpretation' *MS* 24 (1962) 83–94
Boothman, Janet ' "Who Hath No Wyf, He Is No Cokewold": A Study of John and January in Chaucer's Miller's and Merchant's Tales' *Thoth* 4 (1963) 3–14
Bowker, Alvin W. 'Comic Illusion and Dark Reality in *The Miller's Tale*' *MLS* 4 (1974) 27–34
Bratcher, James T., and Nicolai von Kreisler 'The Popularity of the *Miller's Tale*' *SFQ* 35 (1971) 325–35
Brown, William J. 'Chaucer's Double Apology for the Miller's Tale,' *UCSLL* 10 (1966) 15–22
Burkhart, Robert E. 'Chaucer's Absolon: A Sinful Parody of the Miller' *Cithara* 8 ii (1969) 47–54
Clark, Roy Peter 'Squeamishness and Exorcism in Chaucer's *Miller's Tale*' *Thoth* 14 (1973) 37–43
– 'Christmas Games in Chaucer's *The Miller's Tale*' *SSF* 13 (1976) 277–87
Coffman, George R. 'The Miller's Tale: 3187–215: Chaucer and the Seven Liberal Arts in Burlesque Vein' *MLN* 67 (1952) 329–31
Cooper, Geoffrey ' "Sely John" in the "Legende" of the *Miller's Tale*' *JEGP* 79 (1980) 1–12
Dane, Joseph 'The Mechanics of Comedy in Chaucer's *Miller's Tale*' *ChauR* 14 (1980) 215–24
Delasanta, Rodney 'Alisoun and the Saved Harlots: A Cozening of Our Expectations' *ChauR* 12 (1978) 218–34
Donaldson, E.T. 'Idiom of Popular Poetry in the *Miller's Tale*' *EIE* 1950 116–40
– 'Medieval Poetry and Medieval Sin' in *Speaking of Chaucer*. New York, Norton 1970
Gallacher, Patrick 'Perception and Reality in the *Miller's Tale*' *ChauR* 18 (1983) 38–48
Gellrich, Jesse M. 'Nicholas' Kynges Note and Melodye' *ELN* 8 (1971) 249–52
– 'The Parody of Medieval Music in the *Miller's Tale*' *JEGP* 73 (1974) 176–88

Goodall, Peter 'The Figure of Absolon in the *Miller's Tale*' *Parergon* 29 (1981) 33–6

Hamilton, Alice 'Helowys and the Burning of Jankyn's Book' *MS* 34 (1972) 196–207

Hanson, Thomas B. 'Physiognomy and Characterization in the *Miller's Tale*' *NM* 72 (1971) 477–82

Harder, Kelsie B. 'Chaucer's Use of the Mystery Plays in the *Miller's Tale*' *MLQ* 17 (1956) 193–8

Harrington, David V. 'Dramatic Irony in the Canon's Yeoman's Tale' *NM* 66 (1965) 160–6

Harwood, Britton J. 'The "Nether Ye" and Its Antithesis: A Structuralist Reading of "The Miller's Tale"' *AnM* 21 (1981) 5–30

Hatton, Thomas J. 'Absolon, Taste, and Odor in the *Miller's Tale*' *PLL* 7 (1971) 72–5

Herzman, Ronald B. 'Millstones: An Approach to the *Miller's Tale* and the Reeve's Tale' *EngR* 27 ii (1977) 18–21, 26

Hieatt, Constance B., ed. *The Miller's Tale*, introduction. New York: Odyssey Press 1970

Hill, Betty 'Chaucer: *The Miller's* and *Reeve's Tales*' *NM* 74 (1973) 665–75

Hirsch, John C. "Why does the *Miller's Tale* Take Place on Monday?' *ELN* 13 (1975) 86–90

Hoffman, Richard L. 'Ovid's *Ictibus agrestis* and *The Miller's Tale*' *N&Q* 211 (1964) 49–50

Jennings, Margaret CSJ 'Ironic Dancing Absolom in the *Miller's Tale*' *Florilegium* 5 (1983) 178–88

Kaske, Robert E. 'The *Canticum Canticorum* in the *Miller's Tale*' *SP* 59 (1962) 479–500

Kiernan, Kevin S. 'The Art of the Descending Catalogue and a Fresh Look at Alysoun' *ChauR* 10 (1975) 1–16

Lewis, Robert E. 'Alisoun's "Coler": Chaucer's *Miller's Tale* ll 3239, 3242, 3265' *MS* 32 (1970) 337–9

– 'The English Fabliau Tradition and Chaucer's *Miller's Tale*' *MP* 79 (1982) 241–55

Leyland, A. 'Miller's Tale I(A) 3449' *N&Q* 219 (1974) 126–7

McCracken, Samuel 'Miller's Tale I(A)3484' *N&Q* 218 (1973) 283

MacDonald, Angus 'Absolon and St Neot' *Neophil* 48 (1964) 235–7

Martin B.K. 'The Miller's Tale as a Critical Problem and Dirty Joke' *SAC* 5 (1983) 86–120

Miller, Robert P. 'The *Miller's Tale* as Complaint' *ChauR* (1970) 147–60

Mogan, Joseph J., Jr 'The Mutability Motif in *The Miller's Tale*' *AN&Q* 8 (1969) 19

Mullany, Peter F. *'Chaucer's Miller and Pilates Voys'* AN&Q 3 (1964) 54–5
Neuss, Paula *'Double entendre in The Miller's Tale'* EIC 24 (1974) 325–40
Nicholson, Lewis E. 'Chaucer's "Com pa me": A Famous Crux Reexamined'
ELN 19 (1981) 98–102
Nitzsche, Jane Chance "As swete as is the roote of lycorys, or any
cetewale": Herbal Imagery in Chaucer's *Miller's Tale'* Chaucer Newsletter
2 i (1980) 6–8
Plummer, John F. 'The Woman's Song in Middle English and Its European
Backgrounds' in *Vox Feminae: Studies in Medieval Woman's Songs* ed.
John F. Plummer, 134–54. Kalamazoo, Western Michigan University 1981
Poteet, Daniel P II 'Avoiding Women in Times of Affliction: An Analogue
for the *Miller's Tale* A 3589–91' N&Q 217 (1972) 89–90
Reed, Mary B. 'Chaucer's Sely Carpenter' PQ 41 (1962) 768–9
Reiss, Edmund 'Daun Gerveys in the Miller's Tale' PLL 6 (1970) 115–24
Revard, Carter 'The Tow on Absalom's Distaff and the Punishment of
Lechers in Medieval London' ELN 17 (1980) 168–70
Richards, Mary P. 'The Miller's Tale' "By seinte Note" ' ChauR 9 (1975)
212–15
Ross, Thomas W., ed. *The Miller's Tale: A Variorum Edition of the Works
of Geoffrey Chaucer* II, pt 3. Norman, University of Oklahoma 1983
– 'Astronomye in the Miller's Tale Again' N&Q 28 (1981) 202
Rowland, Beryl 'Alison Identified' AN&Q 3 (1964) 3–4, 20–21, 39
– 'The Play of the *Miller's Tale*: A Game within a Game' ChauR 5 (1970)
140–6
– 'Chaucer's Blasphemous Churl: A New Interpretation of the *Miller's Tale'*
in *Chaucer and Middle English Studies in Honour of Rossell Hope Robbins*
ed. B. Rowland, 43–55. London, Allen & Unwin 1974
– 'Distance and Authentication in Chaucer's Comic Tales' *Epopée
animale, fable et fabliau* ed. Nico van den Boogaard and Jean de Caluwé
Marche Romane 28 (1978) 199–206
– 'What Chaucer Did to the Fabliau' SN 51 (1979) 205–13
Rudat, Wolfgang H. 'The Misdirected Kisses in the *Miller's Tale'* JEGP 3
(1982) 103–8
Simmonds, James D. ' "Hende Nicholas" and the Clerk' N&Q 207 (1962) 446
Stevens, John 'Angelus and virginem: The History of a Medieval Song' in
Medieval Studies for J.A.W. Bennett ed. P.L. Heyworth, 297–328. Oxford,
Clarendon Press 1981
Stillwell, Gardiner 'The Language of Love in Chaucer's Miller and Reeve's
Tales and in the Old French Fabliaux' JEGP 54 (1955) 693–9
Thro, A. Booker 'Chaucer's Creative Comedy: A Study of *Miller's Tale* and
the *Shipman's Tale'* ChauR 5 (1970) 97–111

Vaughan, M.F. 'Chaucer's Imaginative One-Day Flood' *PQ* 60 (1981) 117–23
Williams, David 'Radical Therapy in the *Miller's Tale' ChauR* 15 (1981) 227–35

4 BIBLIOGRAPHY ON THE *FRIAR'S PROLOGUE* AND *TALE*

Baird, Joseph L. 'The Devil in Green' *NM* 69 (1968) 575–8
– 'The Devil's *Privetee' NM* 70 (1969) 104–6
Baker, Donald C. 'Exemplary Figures as Characterizing Devices in the *Friar's Tale* and the *Summoner's Tale' UMSE* 3 (1962) 35–41
– 'Witchcraft in the Dispute between Chaucer's Friar and Summoner' *South-Central Bulletin* 21, No. 4 (1961) 33–6
Beichner, Paul E. 'Baiting the Summoner' *MLQ* 22 (1961) 367–76
Bonjour, Adrien 'Aspects of Chaucer's Irony in *The Friar's Tale' EIC* 11 (1961) 121–7
Carruthers, Mary 'Letter and Gloss in the Friar's and Summoner's Tales' *JNT* 2 (1972) 208–14
Cline, Ruth H. 'St Anne' *ELN* 2 (1964) 87–9
Correale, Robert M. 'St. Jerome and the Conclusion of the *Friar's Tale' ELN* 2 (1965) 171–4
Echardt, Caroline D. ' "Canterbury Tales" D 1554 "Caples Thre" ' *N&Q* 20 (1973) 283–4
Hahn, Thomas, and Richard W. Kaeuper 'Text and Context: Chaucer's *Friar's Tale' SAC* 5 (1983) 67–101
Hassan-Yusuff. Z. Dolly ' "Wynne thy cost": Commercial and Feudal Imagery in the *Friar's Tale' Chaucer Newsletter* 1 ii (1979) 15–18
Hatton, Tom 'Chaucer's Friar's "Old Rebekke" ' *JEGP* 67 (1968) 266–71
Hennedy, Hugh L. 'The Friar's Summoner's Dilemma' *ChauR* 5 (1971) 213–17
Hieatt, Constance 'Oaths in the *Friar's Tale' N&Q* 205 (1960) 5–6
Jeffrey, David L. 'The Friar's Rent' *JEGP* 70 (1971) 600–6
Leicester, H. Marshall, Jr ' "No Vileyns Word": Social Context and Performance in Chaucer's *Friar's Tale' ChauR* 17 (1982) 21–39
Lenaghan, R.T. 'The Irony of the *Friar's Tale' ChauR* 7 (1973) 281–94
Mroczkowski, P. 'The *Friar's Tale* and Its Pulpit Background' *English Studies Today* (Berne), 2nd ser. (1961) 107–20
Murtaugh, Daniel M. 'Riming Justice in *The Friar's Tale' NM* 74 (1973) 107–12

Passon, Richard H. ' "Entente" in Chaucer's *Friar's Tale*' *ChauR* 2 (1968) 166–71

Richardson, Janette 'An Ambiguous Reference in Chaucer's *Friar's Tale*' *Archiv* 198 (1962) 388–90

– 'Hunter and Prey: Functional Imagery in Chaucer's *Friar's Tale*' *EM* 12 (1961) 9–20. Rpt. in *Chaucer's Mind and Art* ed. A.C. Cawley, Edinburgh, Oliver & Boyd 1969

– 'Friar and Summoner, the Art of Balance' *ChauR* 9 (1975) 227–36

Rowland, Beryl ' "Wood ... as an Hare" (*The Friar's Tale*, 1327)' *N&Q* 208 (1963) 168–9

Stroud, T.A. 'Chaucer's Friar as Narrator' *ChauR* 8 (1973) 65–9

Szittya, Penn R. 'The Green Yeoman as Loathly Lady: The Friar's Parody of the *Wife of Bath's Tale*' *PMLA* 90 (1975) 386–94

5 BIBLIOGRAPHY ON THE *SUMMONER'S PROLOGUE* AND *TALE*

Adams, John F. 'The Structure of Irony in *The Summoner's Tale*' *EIC* 12 (1962) 126–32

Baker, Donald C. 'Witchcraft in the Dispute between Chaucer's Friar and Summoner' *South-Central Bulletin* 21, No. 4 (1961) 33–6

– 'Exemplary Figures as Characterizing Devices in the *Friar's Tale* and the *Summoner's Tale*' *UMSE* 3 (1962) 35–41

Clark, Roy Peter 'Doubting Thomas in Chaucer's *Summoner's Tale*' *ChauR* 11 (1976) 164–78

– 'Wit and Witsunday in Chaucer's Summoner's Tale' *AnM* 17 (1976) 48–57

Crowther, J.D.W. 'The Summoner's Tale: 1955–69' *Chaucer Newsletter* 2 i (1980) 12–13

Fleming, John V. 'The Antifraternalism of the *Summoner's Tale*' *JEGP* 45 (1966) 688–700

– 'Chaucer's "Syngeth Placebo" and the *Roman de Fauvel*' *N&Q* 210 (1965) 17–18

– 'The Summoner's Prologue: An Iconographic Adjustment' *ChauR* 2 (1967) 95–107

Garbáty, Thomas 'The Summoner's Occupational Disease' *Medical History* 7 (1963) 348–58

Hartung, Albert E. 'Two Notes in the Summoner's Tale: Hosts and Swans' *ELN* 4 (1967) 175–80

Haskell, Ann S. 'St. Simon in the *Summoner's Tale*' *ChauR* 5 (1971) 218–24

Kaske, R.E. 'Horn and Ivory in the *Summoner's Tale*' in *Studies Presented to Tauno F. Mustanoja on ... His Sixtieth Birthday*. Helsinki 1972. *NM* 73, No. 1–2, 122–6

Lancashire, Ian 'Moses, Elijah and the Back Parts of God: Satiric Scatology in Chaucer's *Summoner's Tale*' *Mosaic* 14 (1980) 17–30

Levitan, Alan 'The Parody of Pentecost in Chaucer's *Summoner's Tale*' *UTQ* 40 (1971) 236–46

Levy, Bernard S. 'Biblical Parody in the *Summoner's Tale*' *TSL* 11 (1966) 45–60

Merrill, Thomas F. 'Wrath and Rhetoric in *The Summoner's Tale*' *TSLL* 4 (1962) 341–50

Pearcy, Roy J. 'Chaucer's "An Impossible" (*Summoner's Tale*, III.2231)' *N&Q* 212 (1967) 322–5

– 'Structural Models for the Fabliaux and the *Summoner's Tale* Analogues' *Fabula* 15 (1974) 103–13

Pratt, Robert A. 'Albertus Magnus and the Problem of Sound and Odor in the *Summoner's Tale*' *PQ* 57 (1978) 267–8

Severs, J. Burke 'Chaucer's *The Summoner's Tale*, D 2184–2188' *Expl* 23 (1964) item 20

Silvia, Daniel S., Jr 'Chaucer's Friars: Swans or Swains? *Summoner's Tale* D 1930' *ELN* 1 (1964) 248–50

Wentersdorf, Karl P. 'The Motif of Exorcism in the *Summoner's Tale*' *SSF* 17 (1980) 249–54

Zietlow, Paul N. 'In Defense of the Summoner' *ChauR* 1 (1966) 4–19

6 BIBLIOGRAPHY ON THE *MANCIPLE'S PROLOGUE* AND *TALE*

Brodie, Alexander H. 'Hodge of Ware and Geber's Cook: Wordplay in the "Manciple's Prologue" ' *NM* 72 (1971) 62–8

Brown, Emerson, Jr 'Word Play in the Prologue to the *Manciple's Tale*, 98' *Chaucer Newsletter* 2 ii (1980) 11–12

Cadbury, William 'Manipulation of Sources and the Meaning of the *Manciple's Tale*' *PQ* 43 (1964) 538–48

Campbell, Jackson J. 'Polonius among the Pilgrims' *ChauR* 7 (1972) 140–46

Davison, Arnold B. 'The Logic of Confusion in the *Manciple's Tale*' *AnM* 19 (1979) 5–13

Dean, James 'The Ending of the *Canterbury Tales*, 1952–76' *TSLL* 21 (1979) 17–33

Fulk, R.D. 'Reinterpreting the *Manciple's Tale*' *JEGP* 78 (1979) 485–93

Gruber, Loren C. 'The *Manciple's Tale*: One Key to Chaucer's Language' in *New Views on Chaucer: Essays in Generative Criticism* ed. William C. Johnson, Jr, and Loren C. Gruber, 43–50. Denver Society for New Language Study 1973

Harwood, Britton J. 'Language and the Real: Chaucer's Manciple' *ChauR* 6 (1972) 268–79; 7 (1972) 84

Hazelton, Richard 'The *Manciple's Tale*: Parody and Critique' *JEGP* 62 (1963) 1–31

Jeffrey, David L. 'The *Manciple's Tale*: The Form of Conclusion' *ESC* 2 (1976) 249–61

Kearney, Martin 'Much Ado in a "Litel Toun"' *Inisfree* (1978) 30–41

Marshall, David F. 'A Note on Chaucer's *Manciple's Tale*' *Chaucer Newsletter* 1 i (1979) 17–18

Mustanoja, Tauno F. 'Chaucer's *Manciple's Tale*, lines 311–13' in *Franciplegius: Medieval and Linguistic Studies in Honor of Francis Peabody Magoun, Jr.* 250–4. New York, New York University Press 1965

Pearcy, Roy J. 'Does the Manciple's Prologue Contain a Reference to Hell's Mouth?' *ELN* 11 (1974) 167–75

Scattergood, V.J. 'The Manciple's Manner of Speaking' *EIC* 24 (1974) 124–46

Trask, Richard M. 'The Manciple's Problem' *SSF* 14 (1977) 109–16

Traversi, Derek 'The *Manciple's Tale*' in *The Literary Imagination: Studies in Dante, Chaucer and Shakespeare* 120–44. Newark, University of Delaware Press 1982

Westervelt, L.A. 'The Medieval Notion of Chaucer's *Manciple's Tale*' *Southern Review: An Australian Journal of Literary Studies* 14 (1981) 107–15

Wood, Chauncey 'Speech, the Principle of Contraries, and Chaucer's Tales of the Manciple and the Parson' *Mediaevalia* 6 (1980) 209–29

Index